PoseMuse
PO Box 2105
Edwards, CO 81632 USA
www.PoseMuse.com
justin@posemuse.com

Ordering Information:
Available on Amazon.com in paperback or Kindle formats, and Gumroad.com in pdf format via PoseMuse.com. All ebook formats available on SmashWords.com. Special discounts are available on quantity purchases by businesses, corporations, associations, and others. For details, contact PoseMuse above.

Publisher's Cataloging-in-Publication Data:
Martin, Justin R.
Poses for Artists Volume 10: An essential reference for figure drawing and the human form. Inspiring Art and Artists
Series/ Justin R. Martin
1. Nonfiction - Art - Techniques - Drawing
2. Nonfiction - Art - Reference
3. Nonfiction - Art - Illustration

First Edition, First Printing 2024
ISBN: 978-1-7377937-4-8
Imprint: POSEmuse
14 13 12 11 10 9 8 7 6 5 4 3 2 1

Poses For Artists
Volume 10
Comic & Anime
Feminine & Masculine

Part One
Feminine

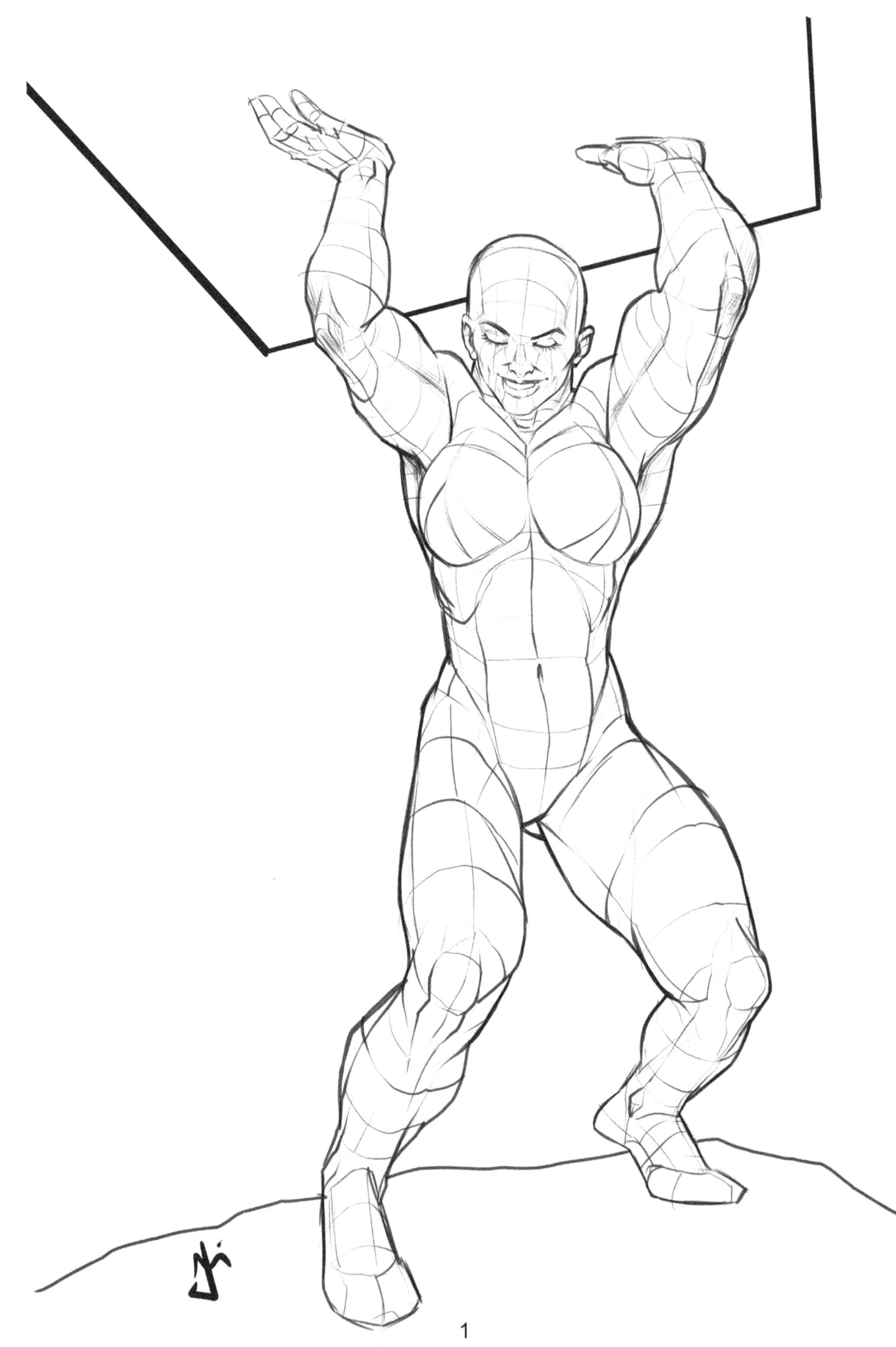

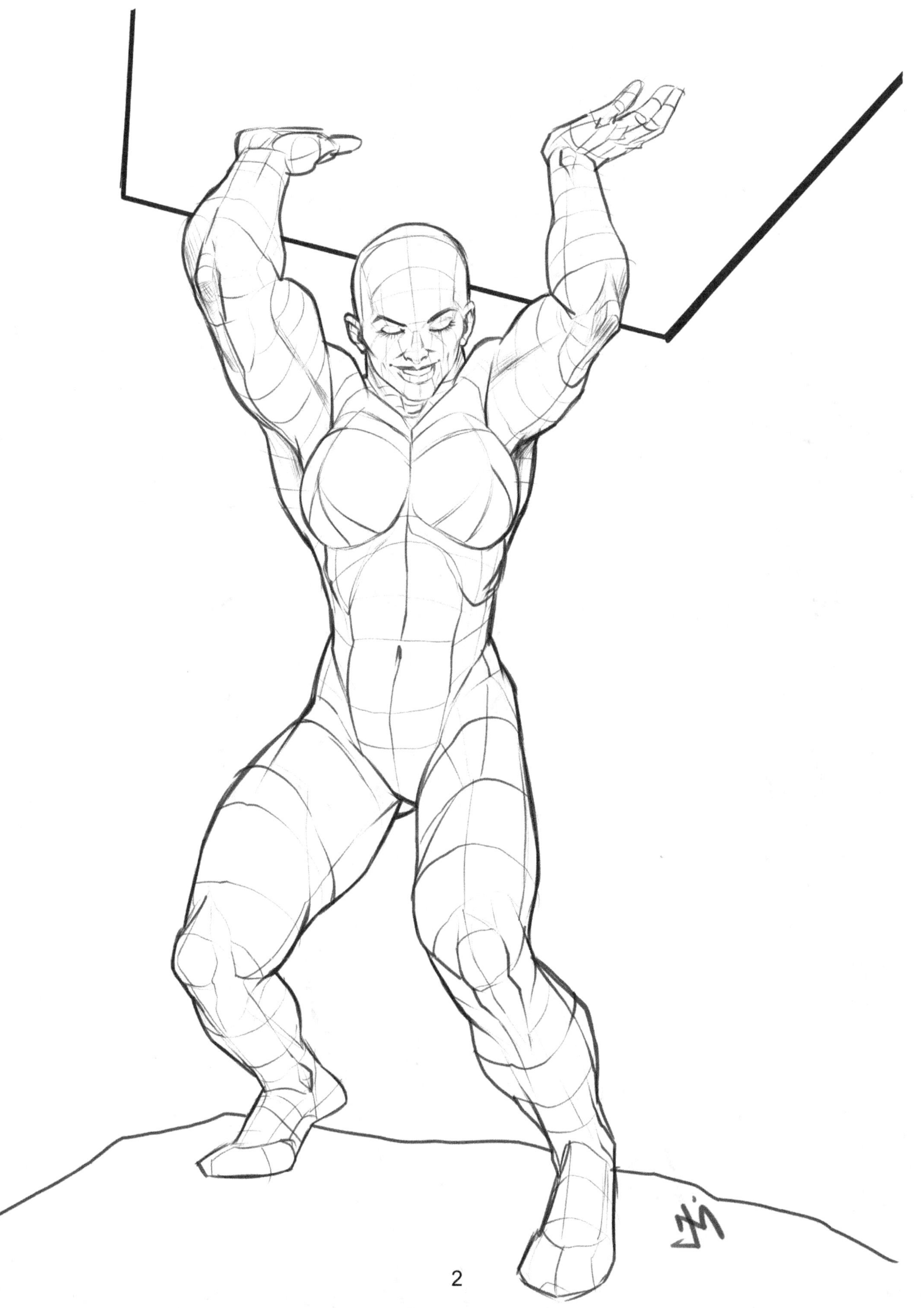

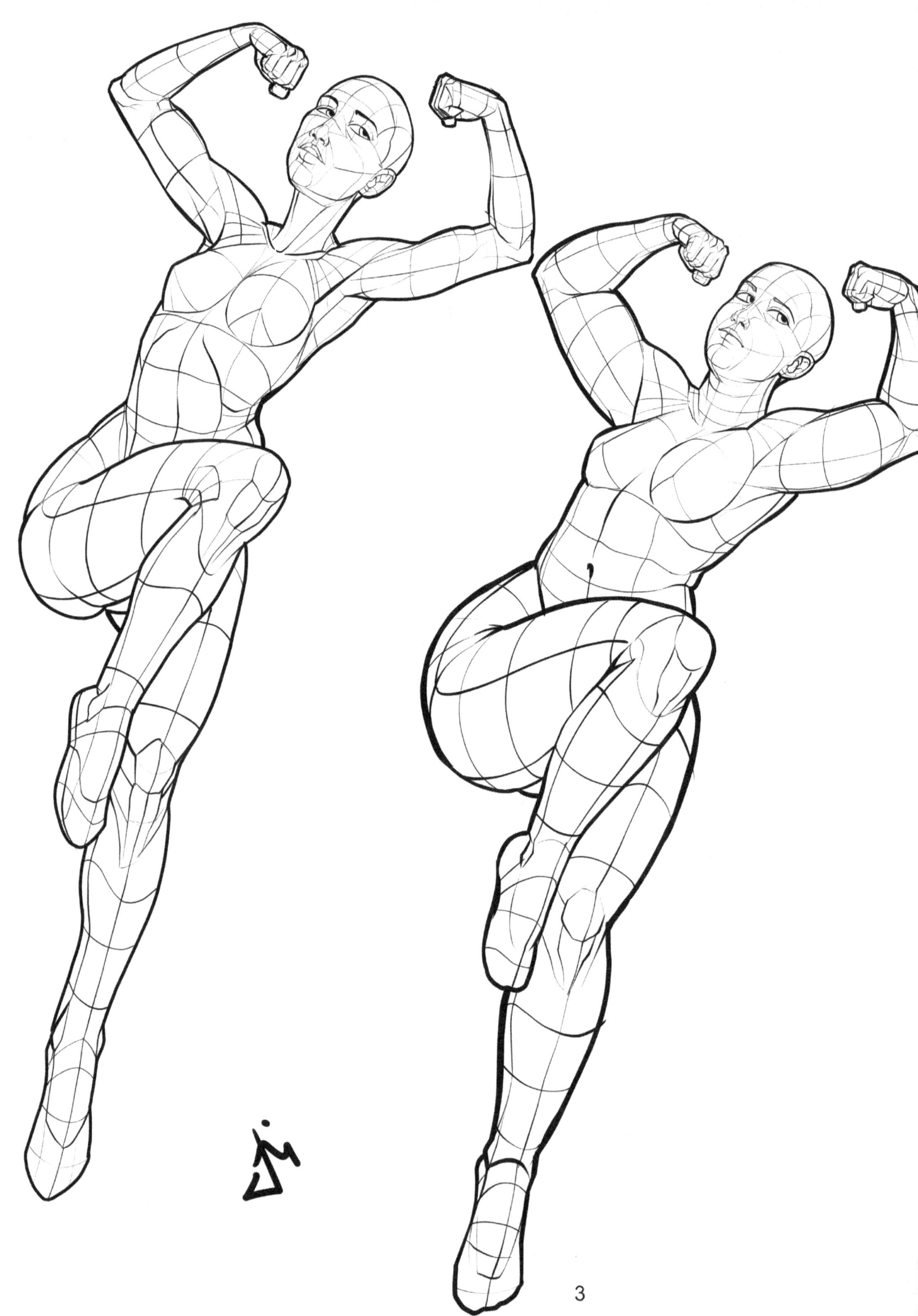

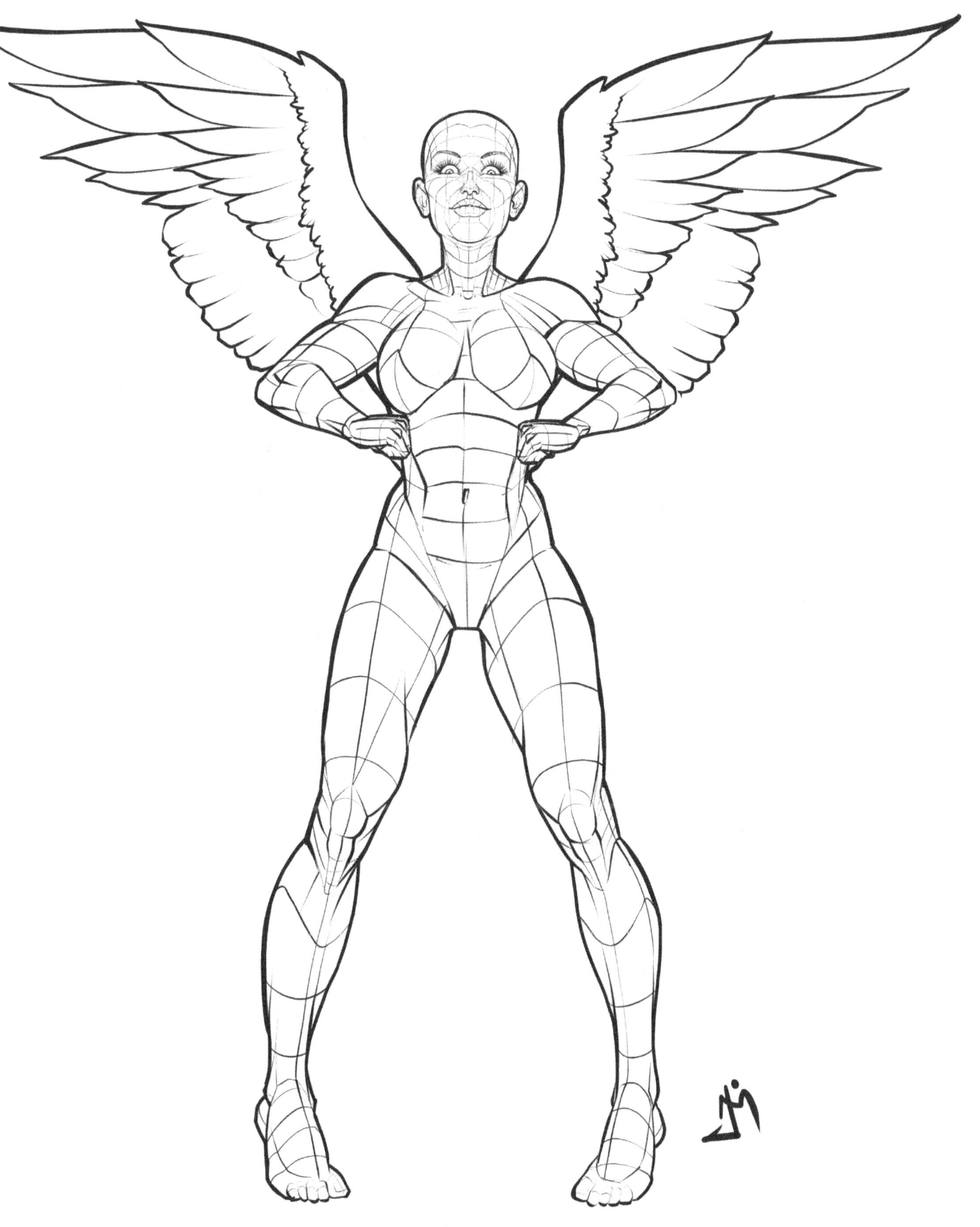

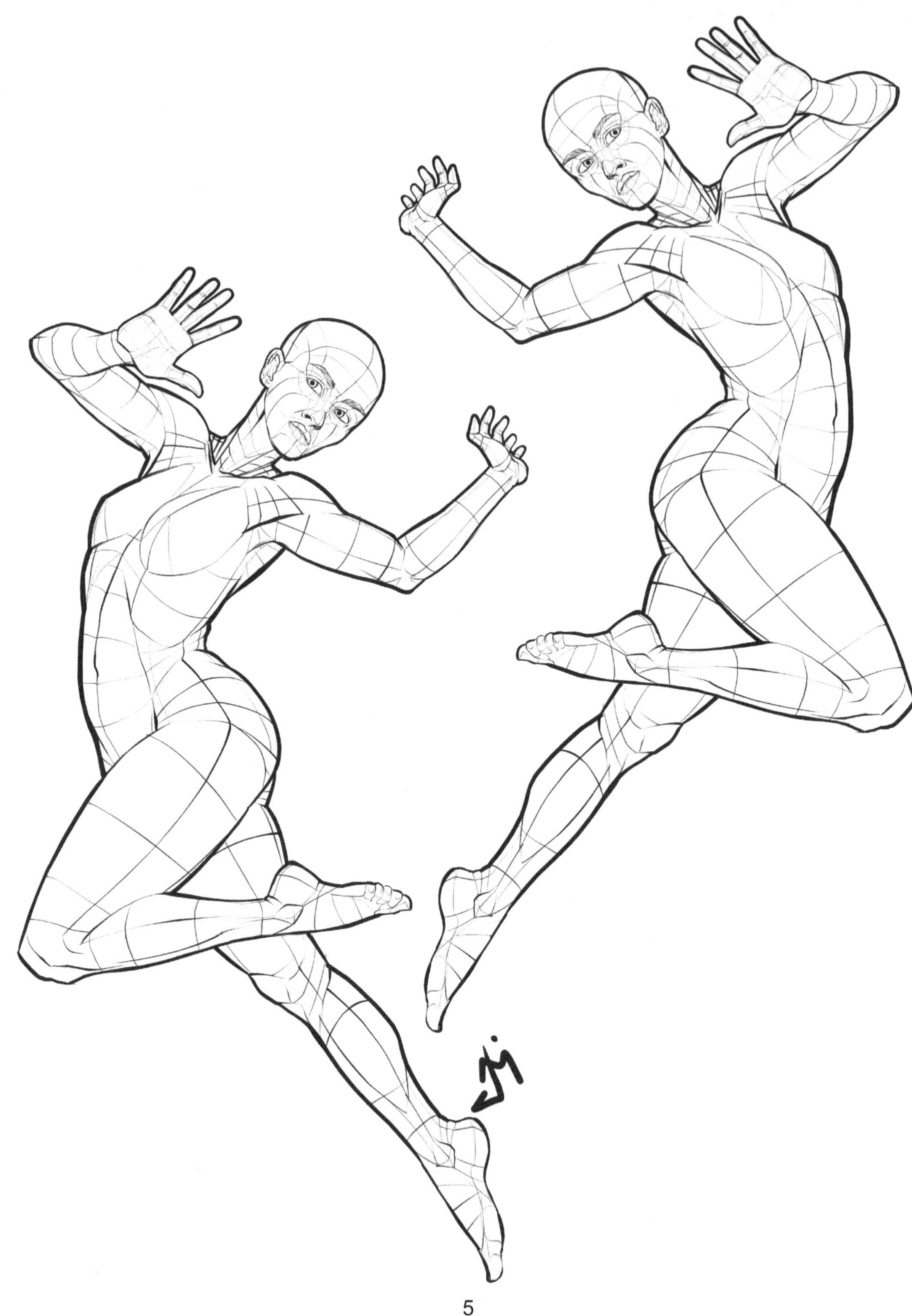

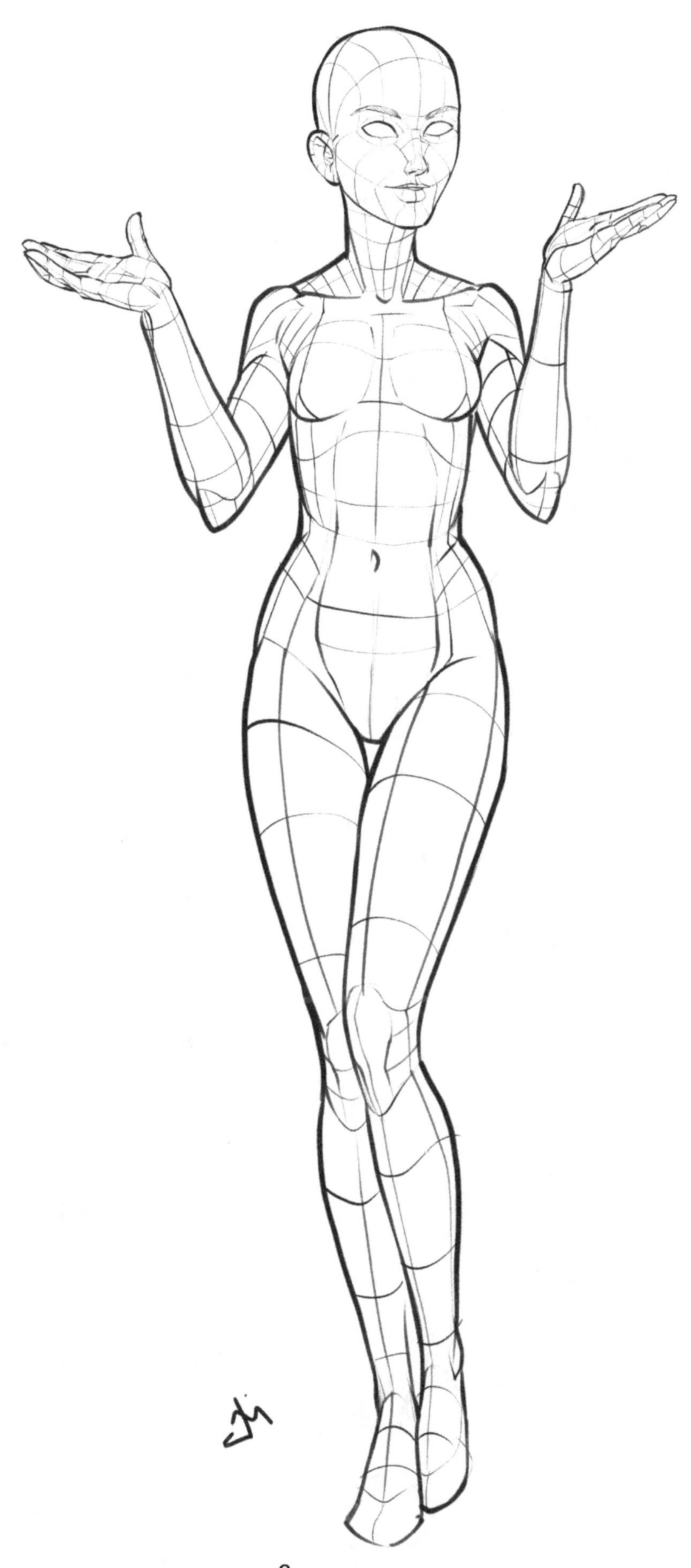

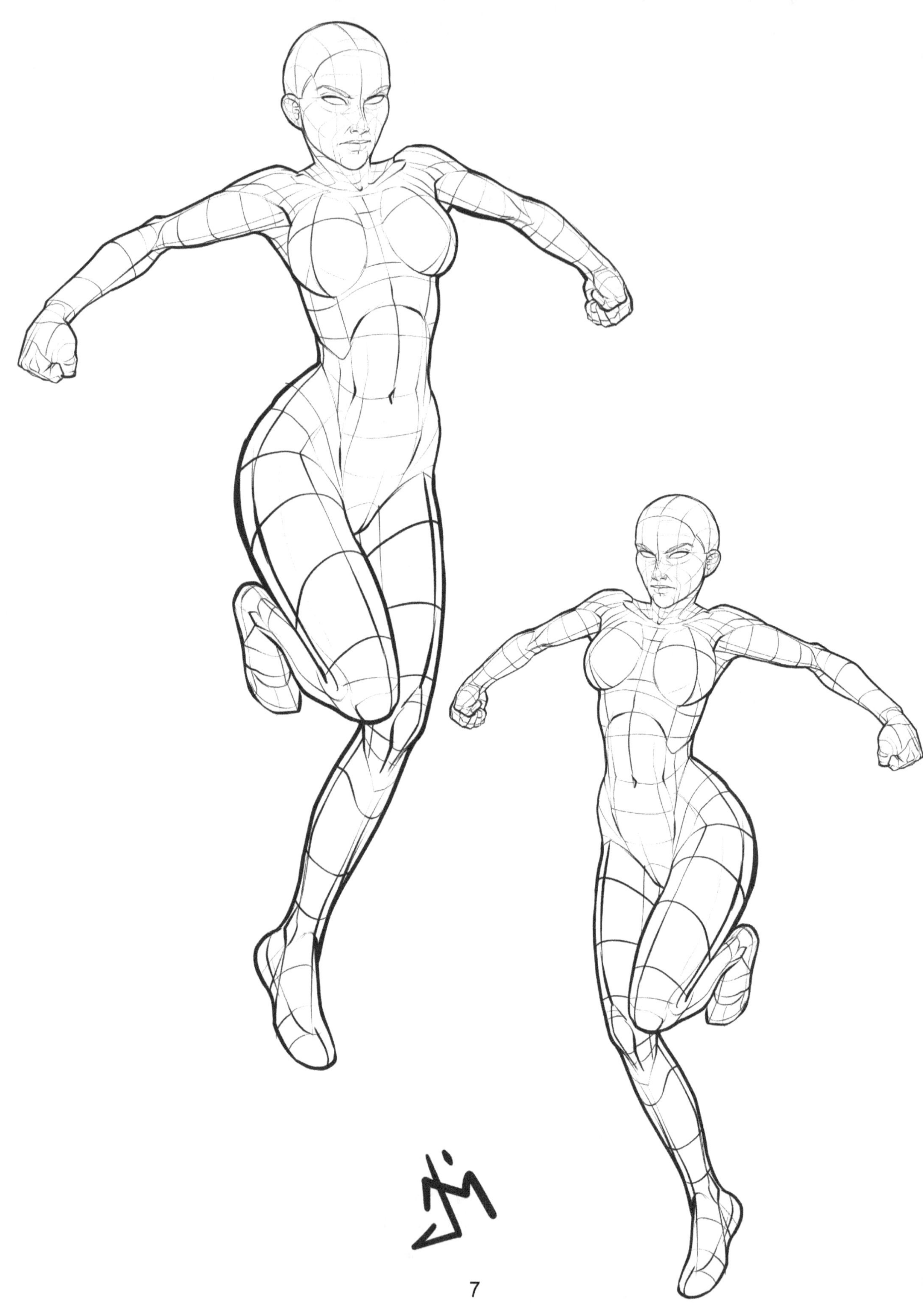

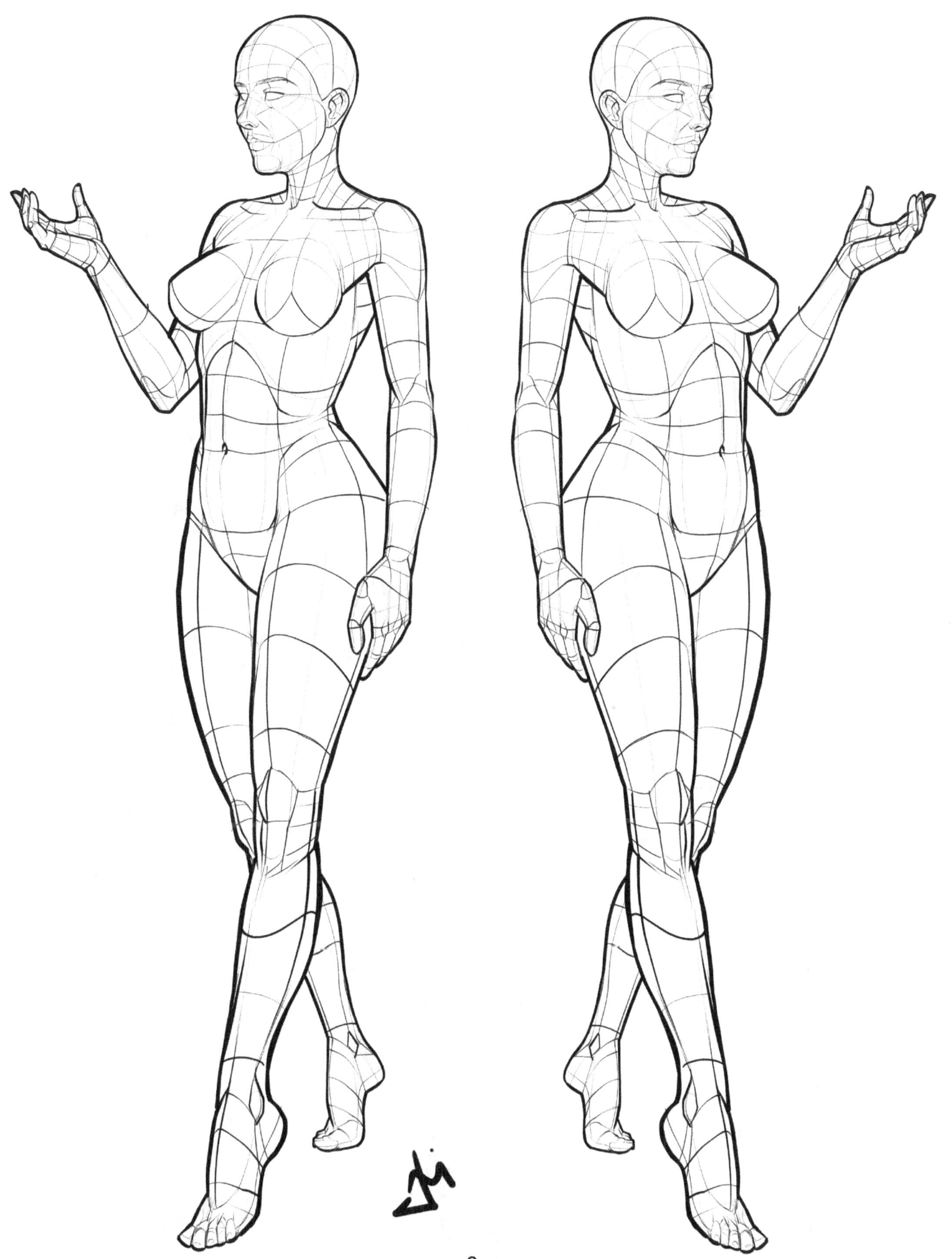

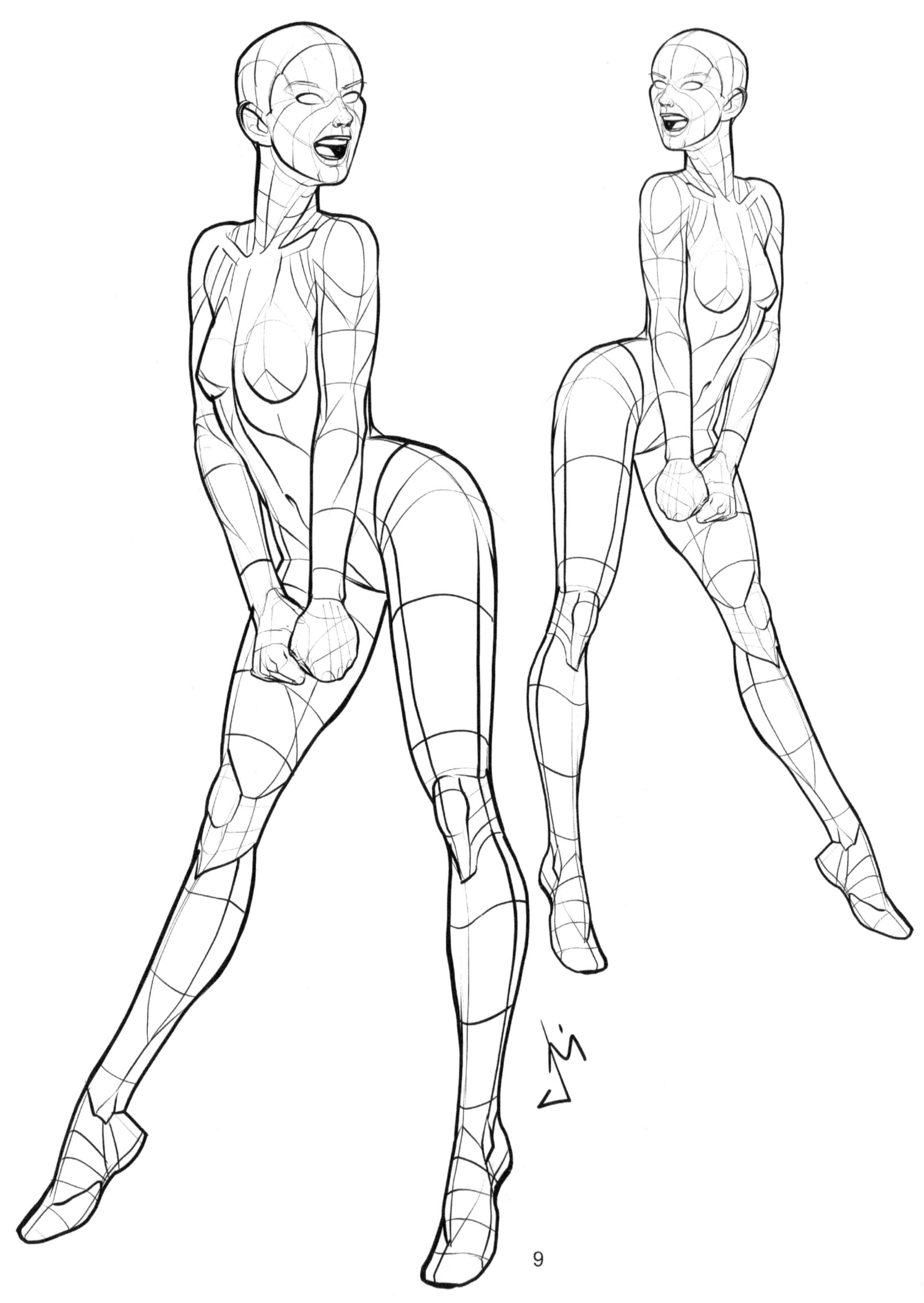

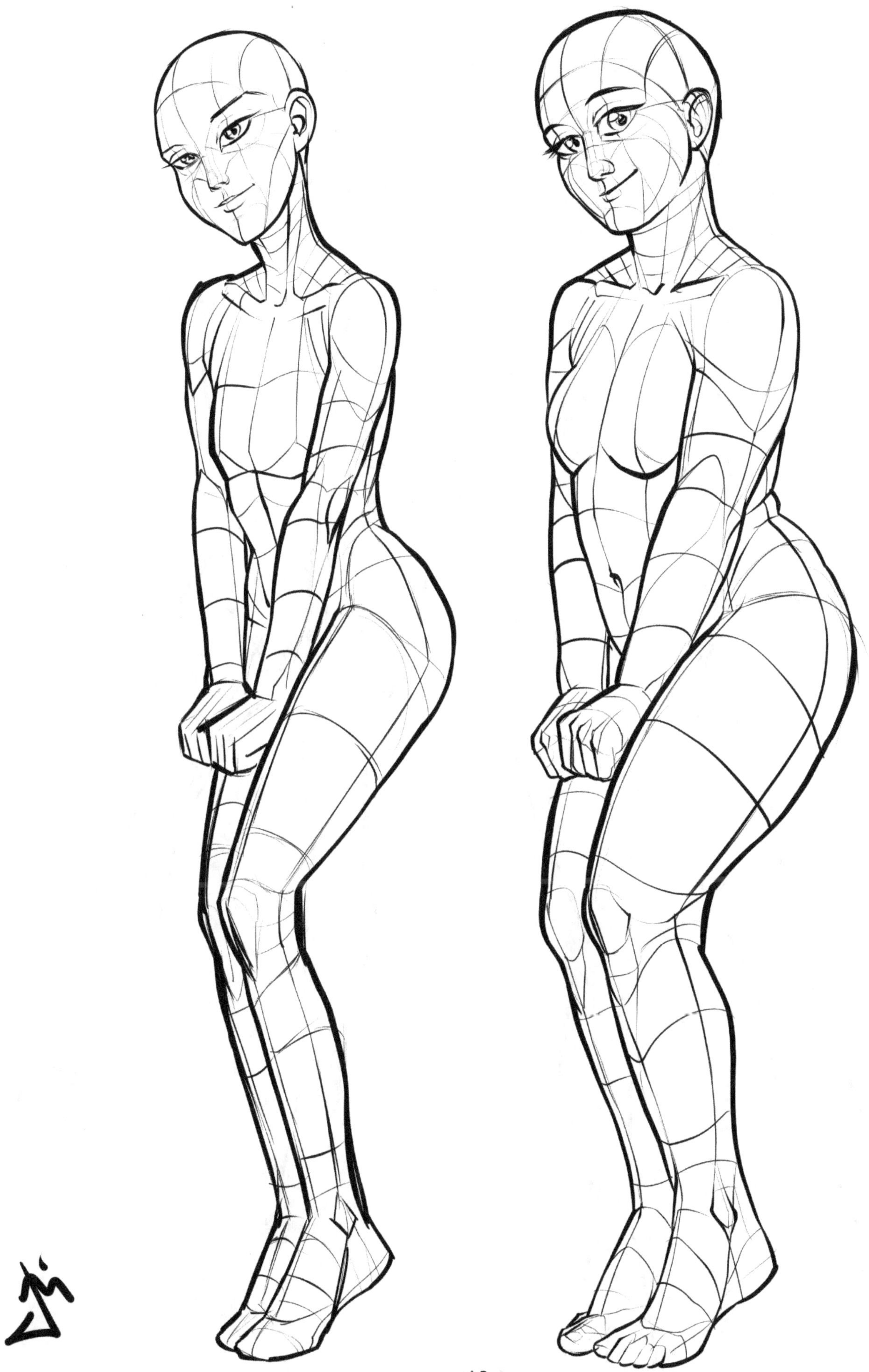

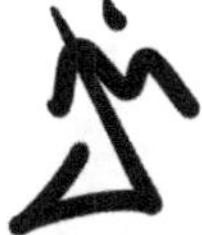

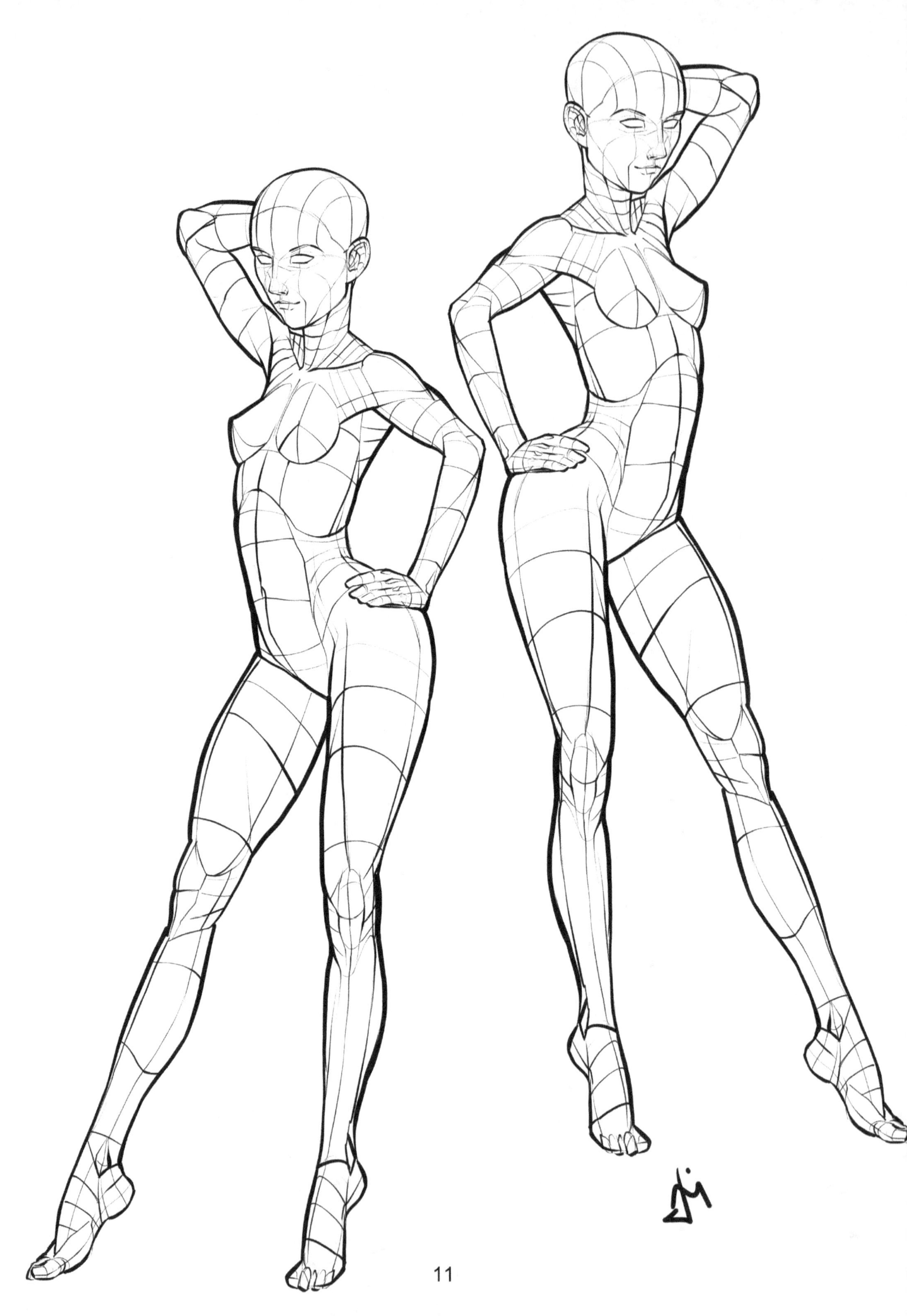

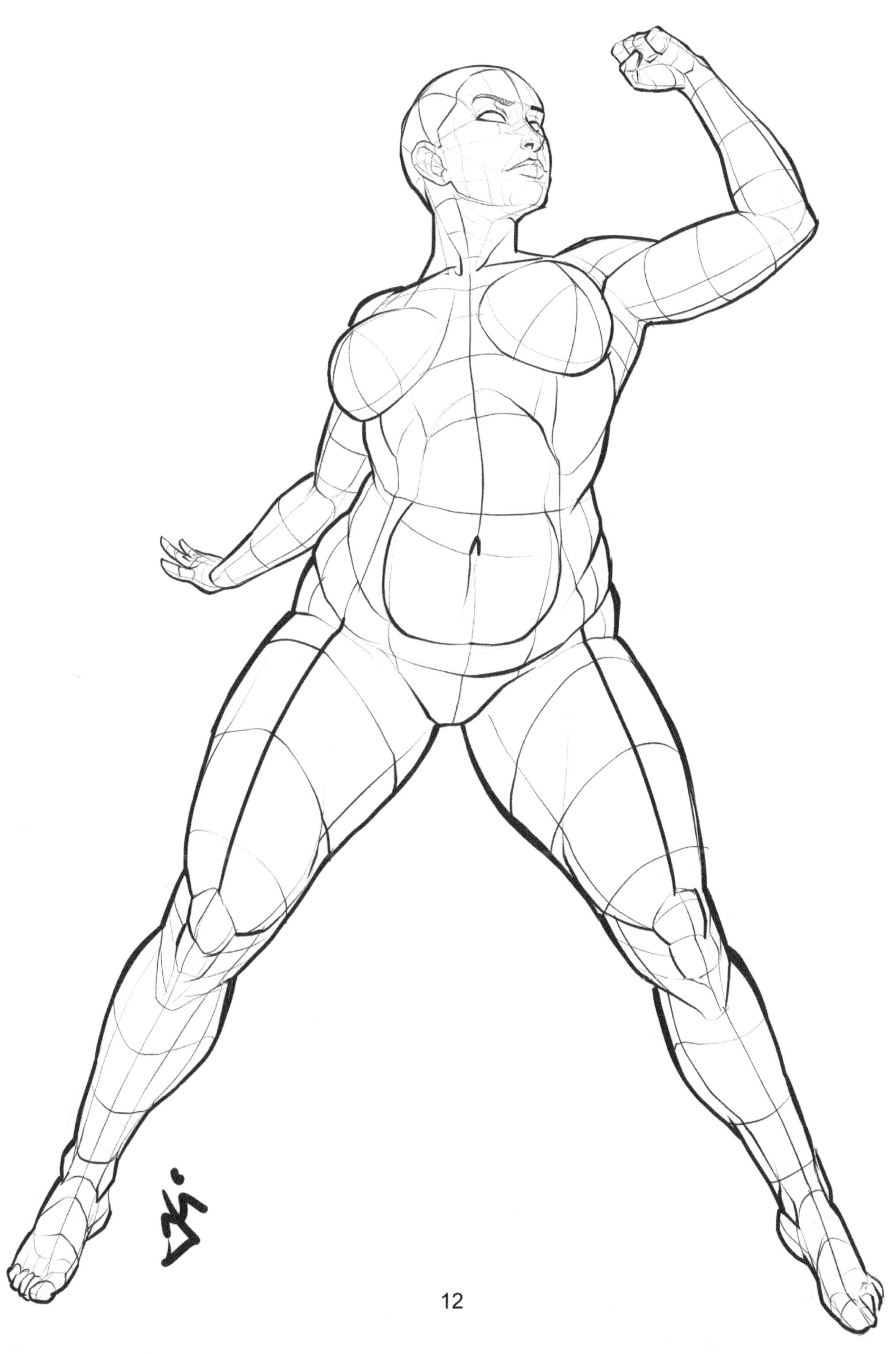

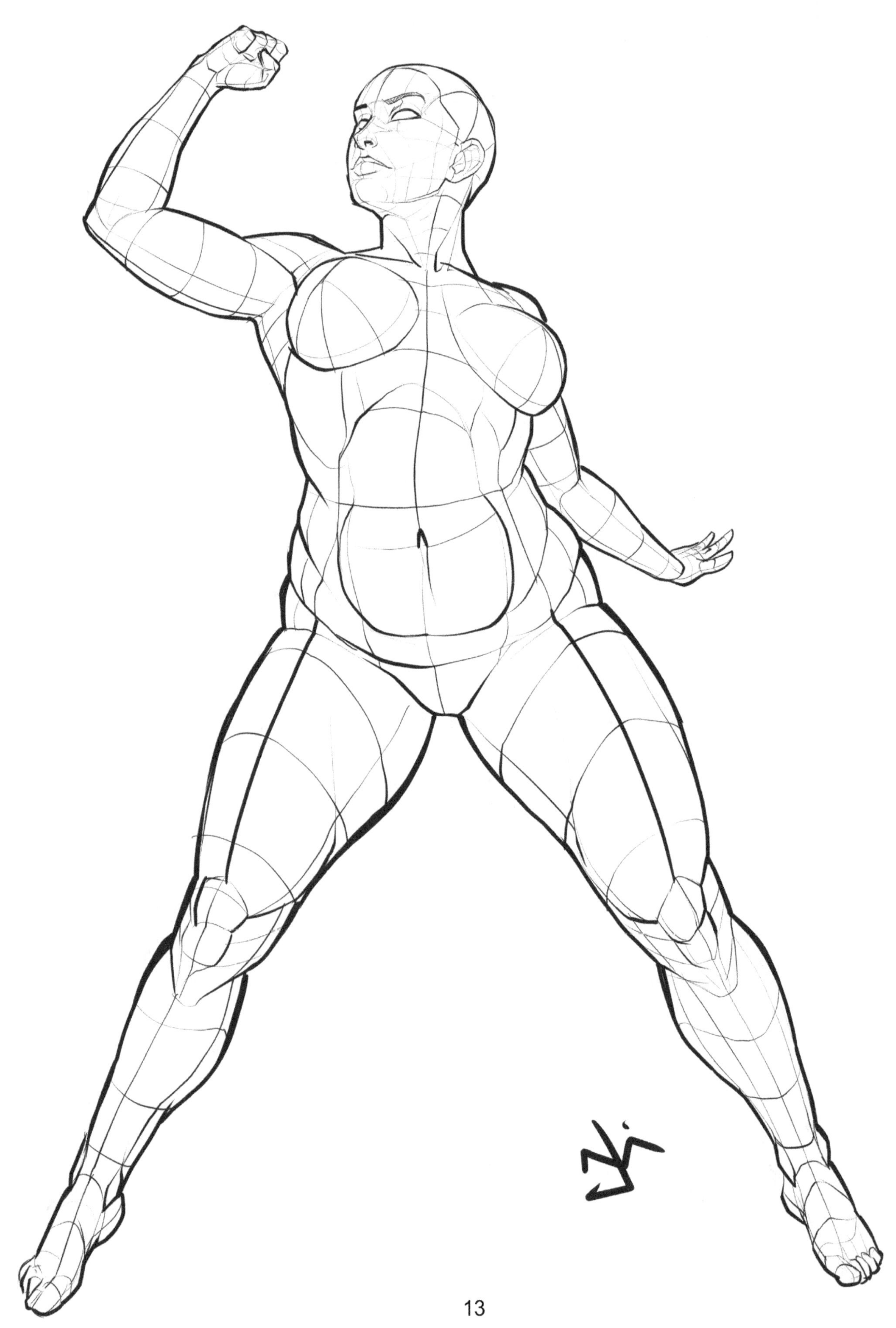

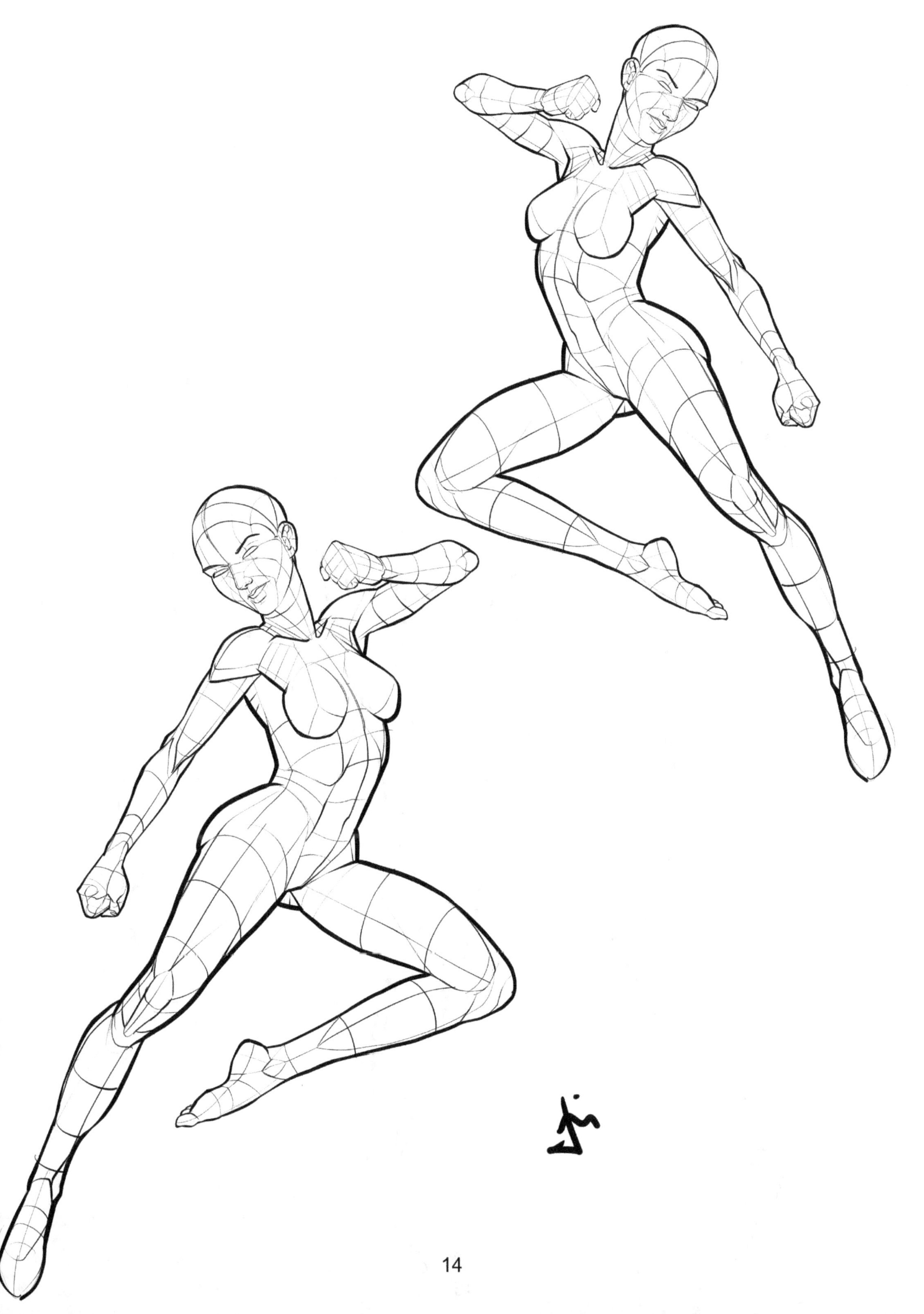

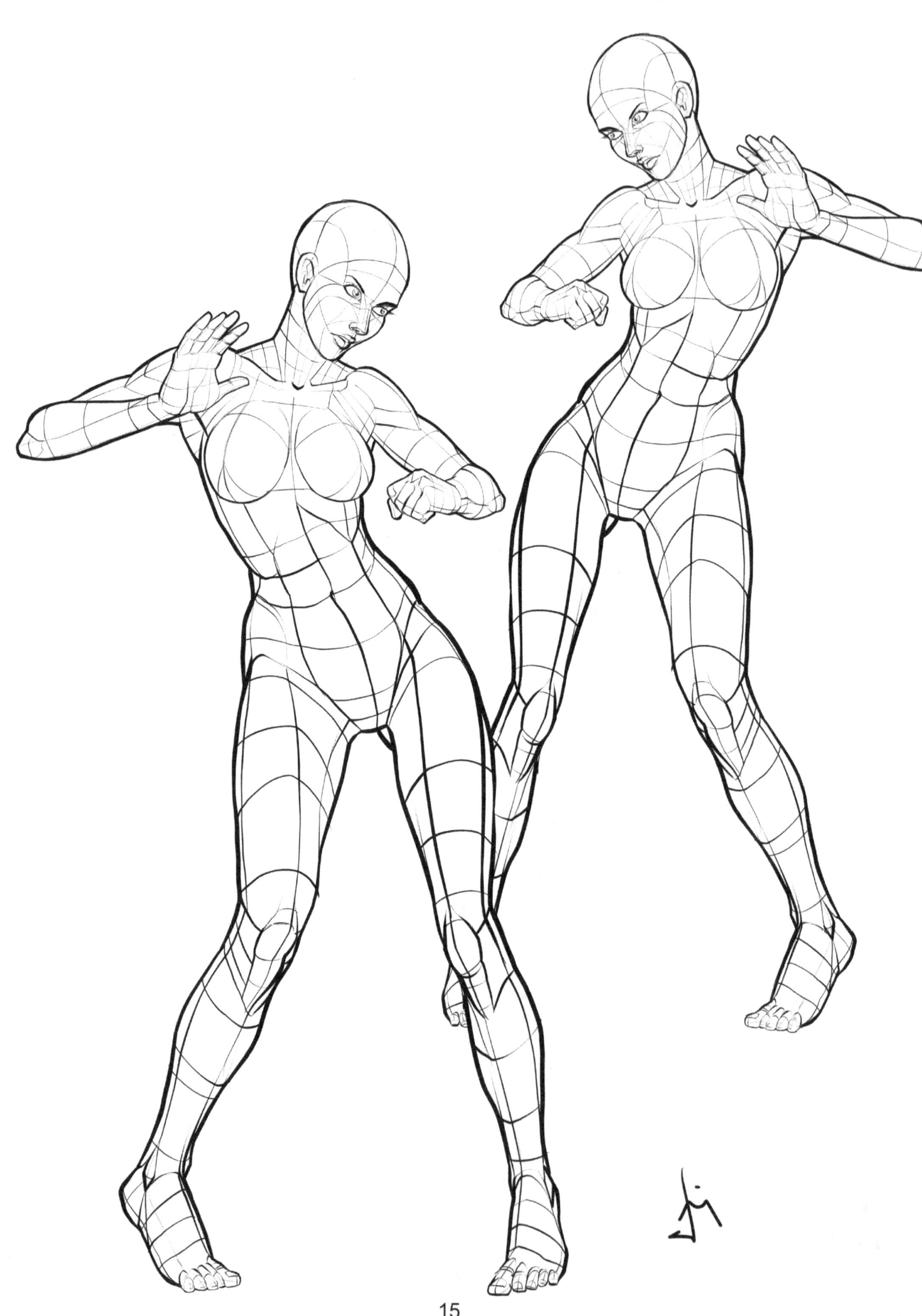

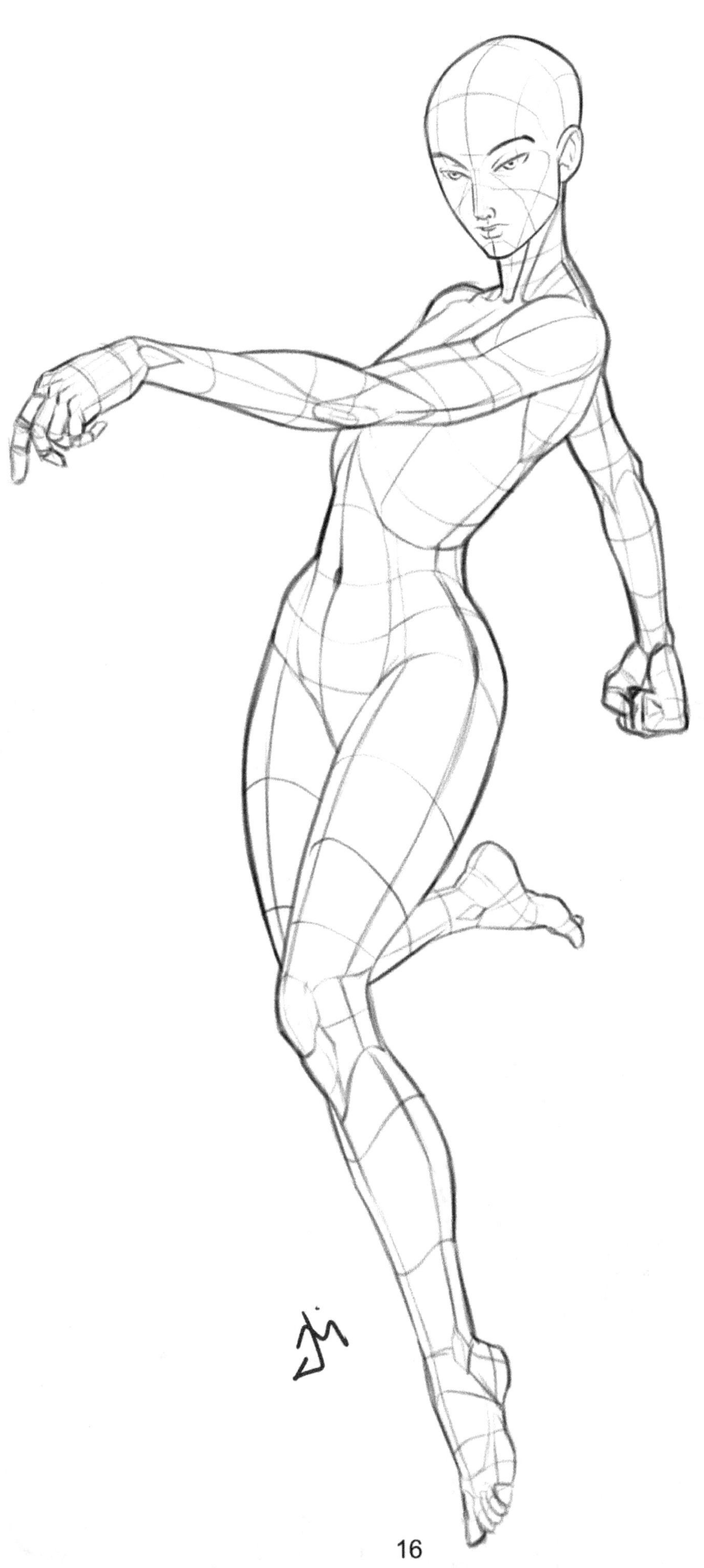

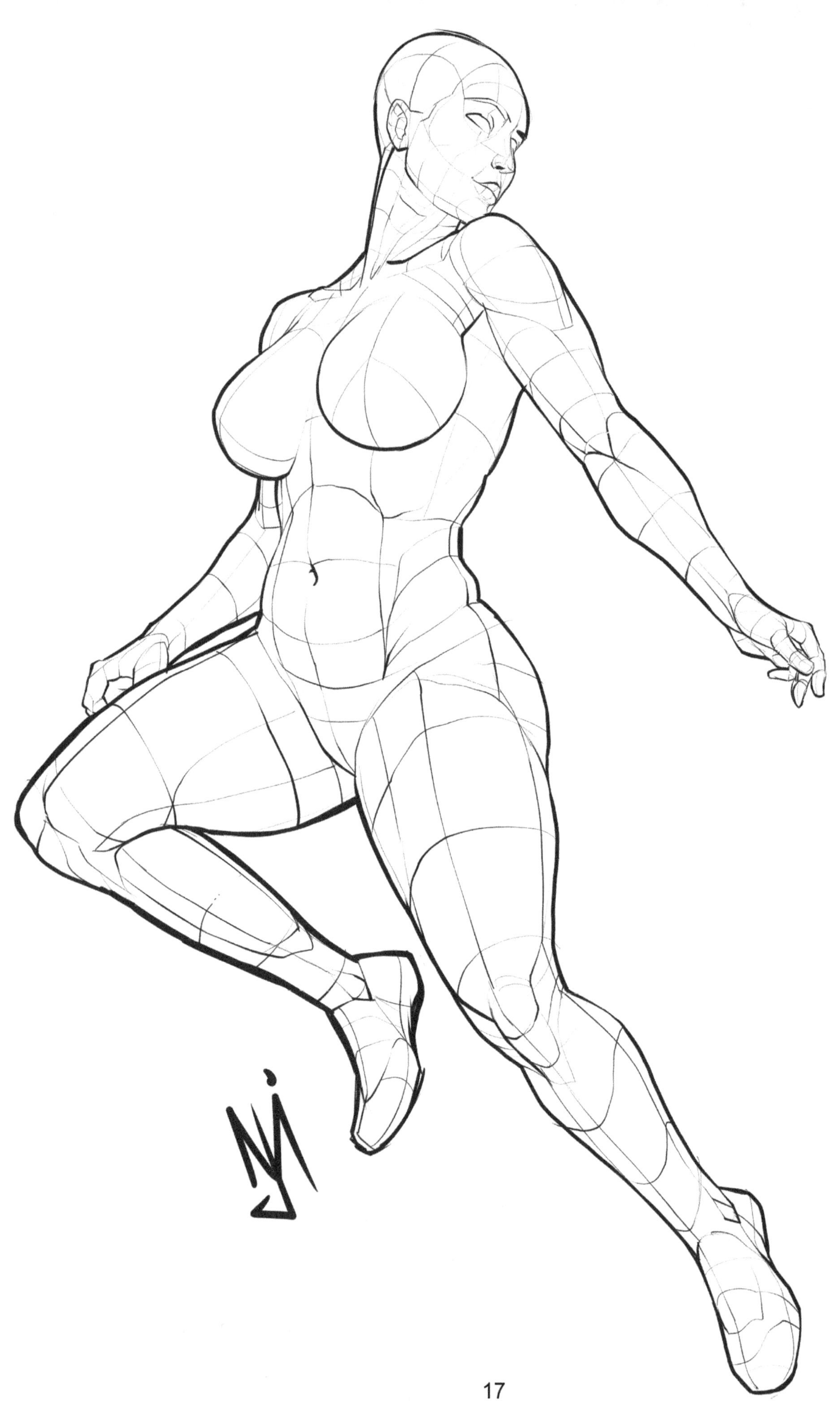

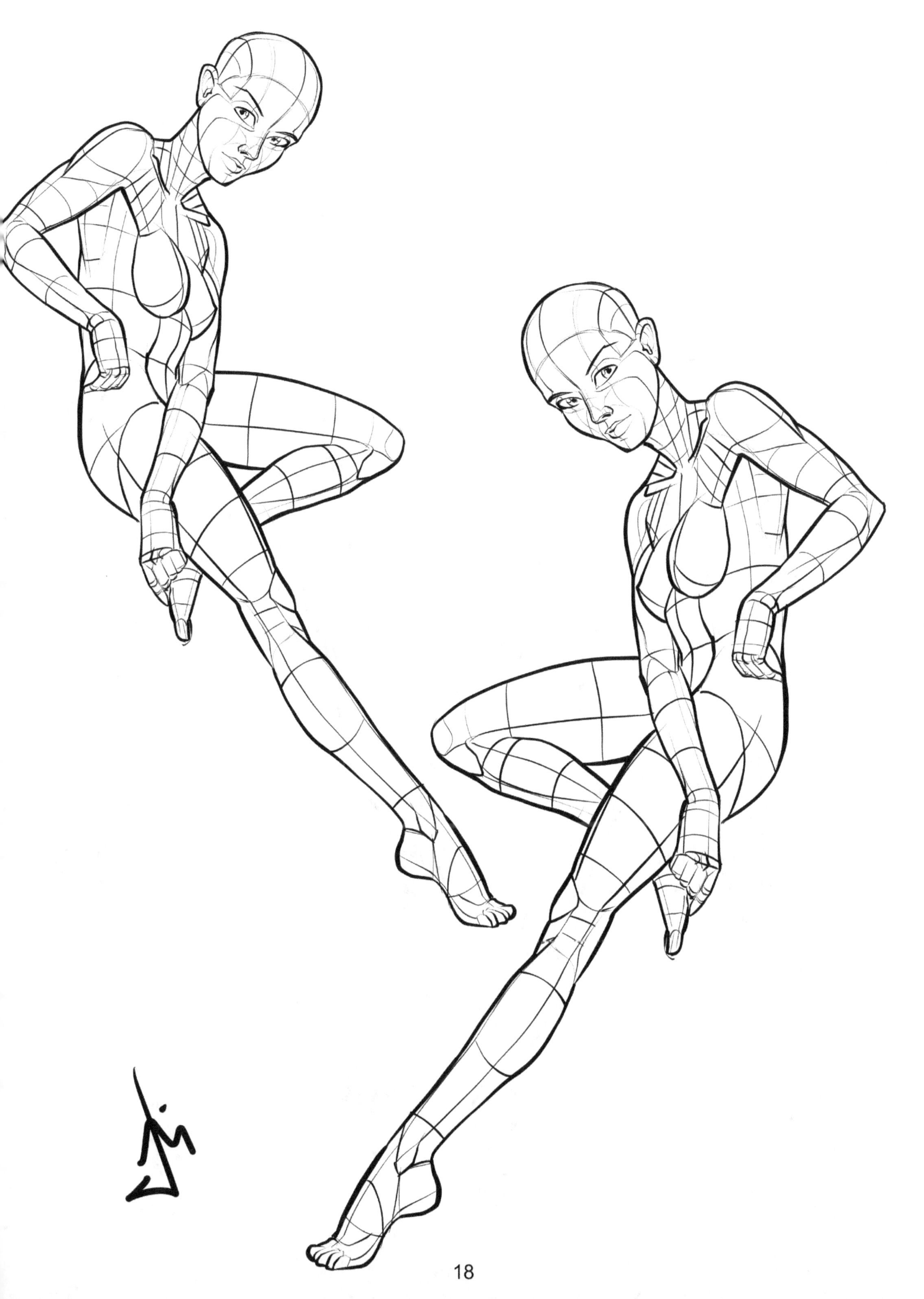

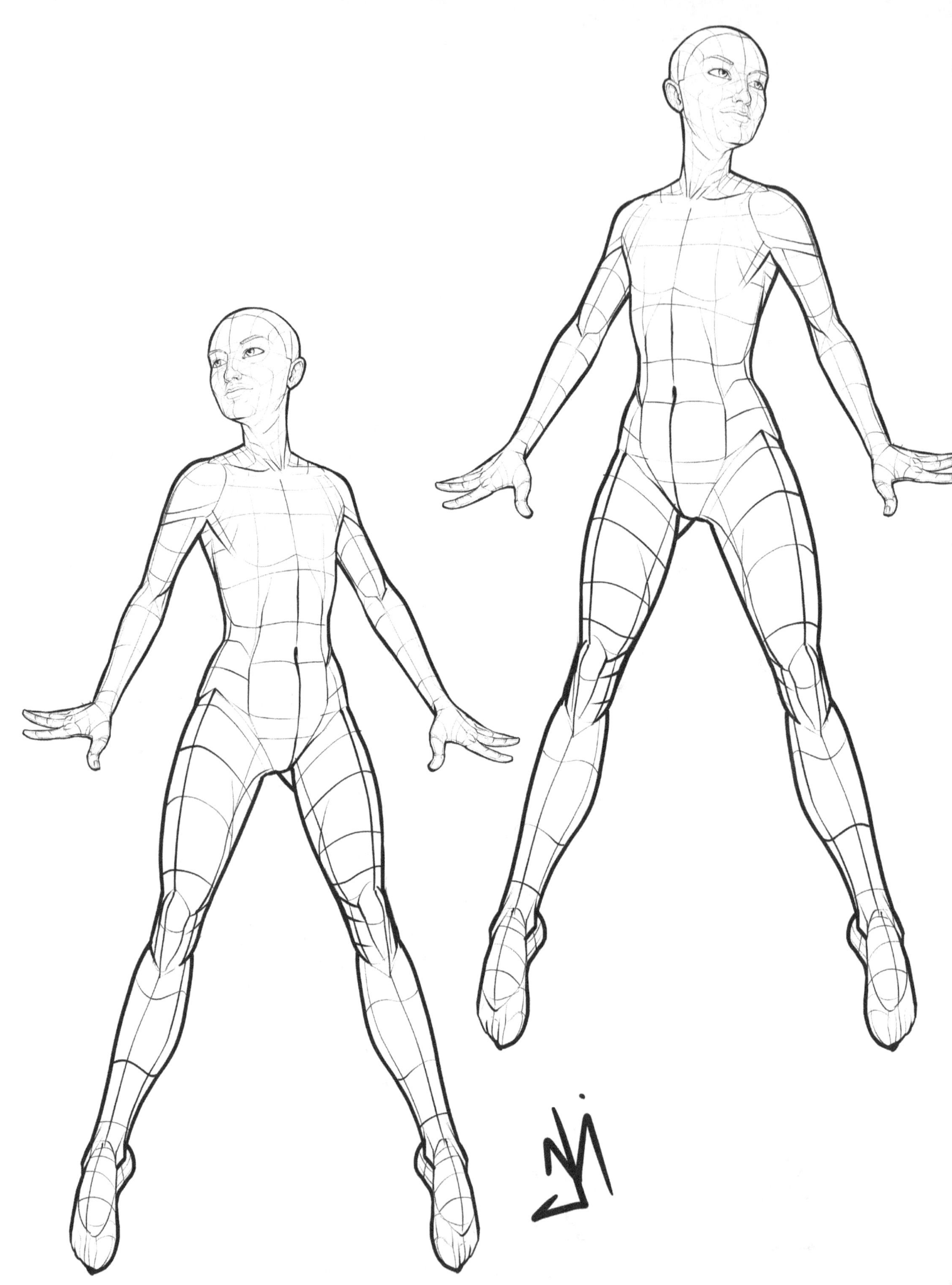

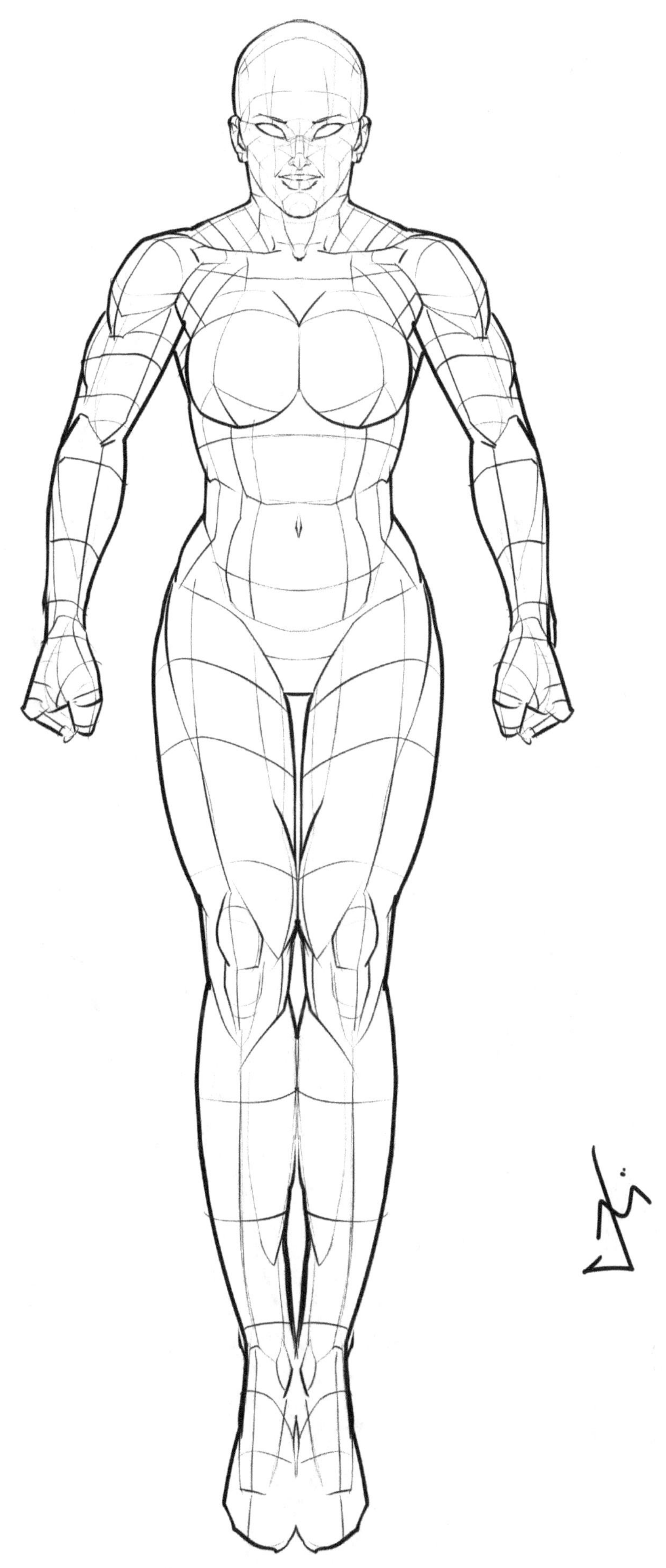

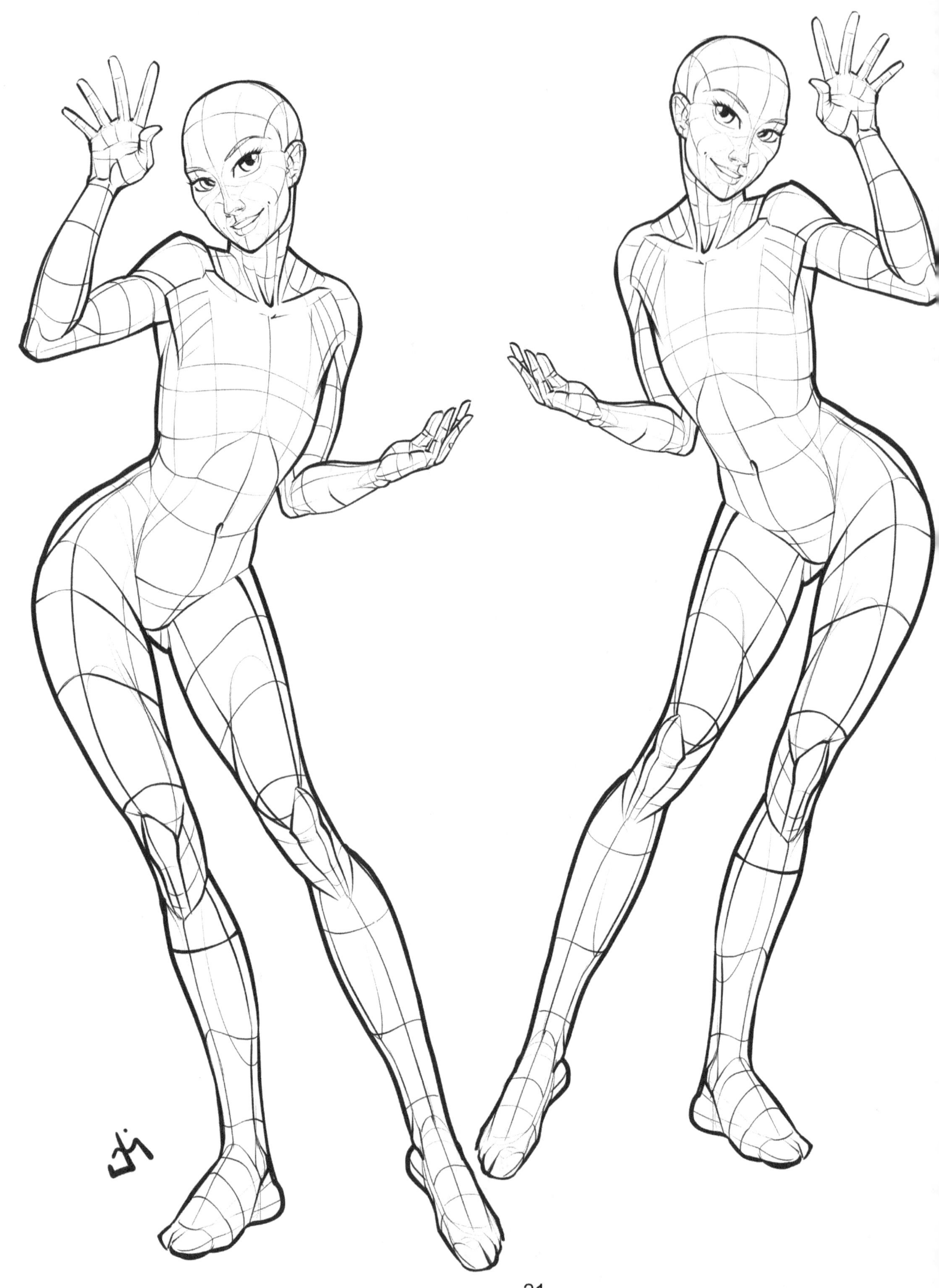

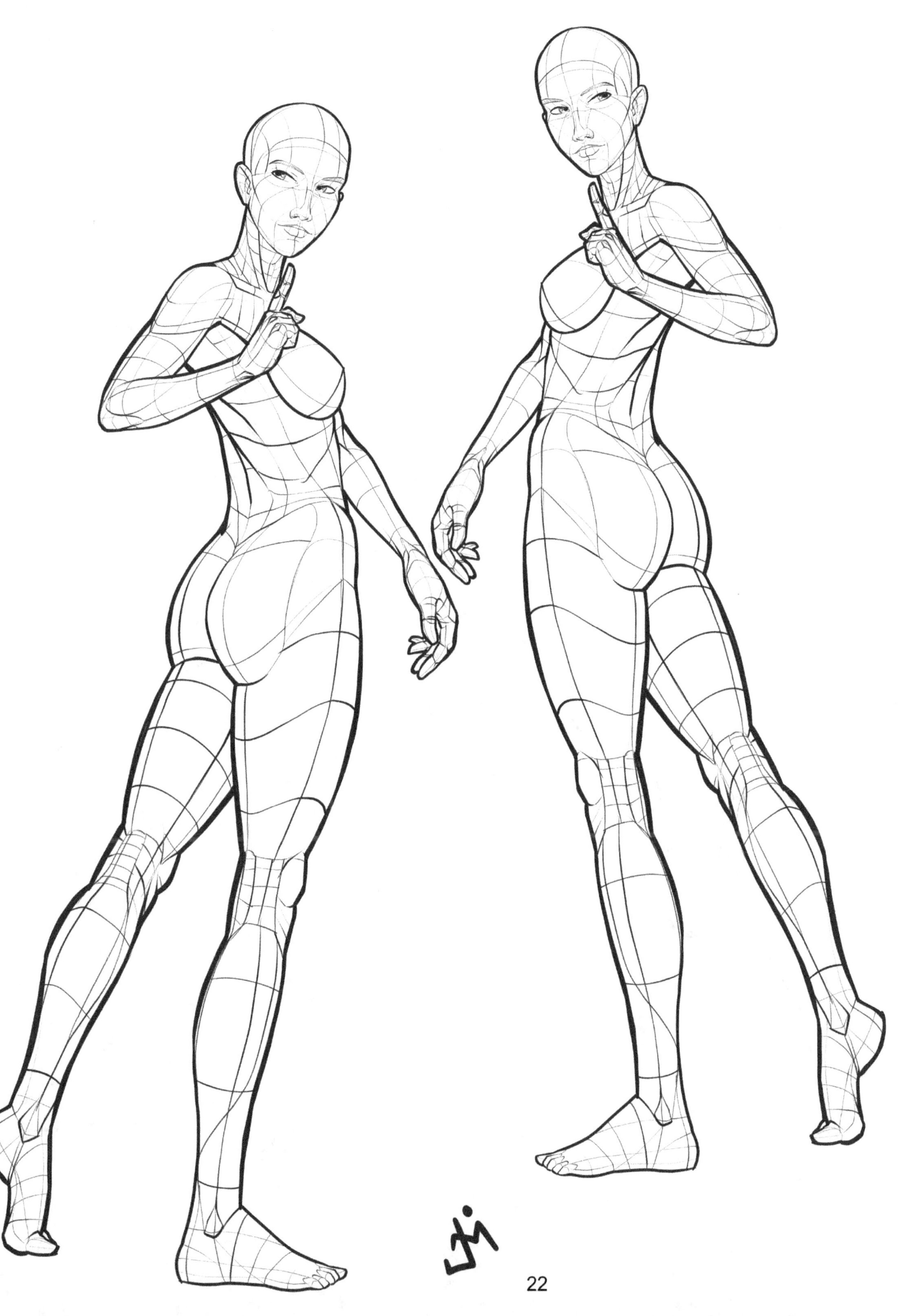

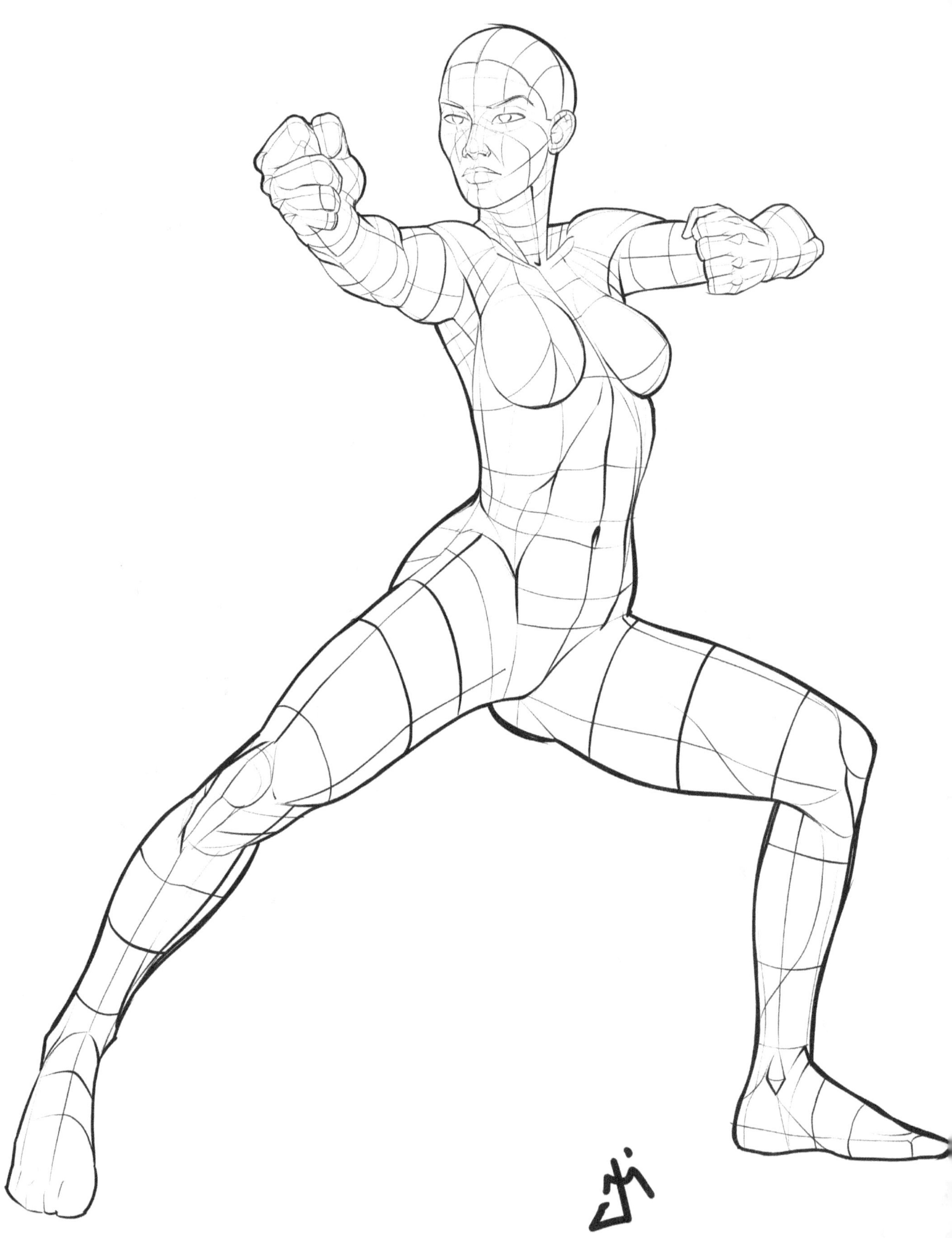

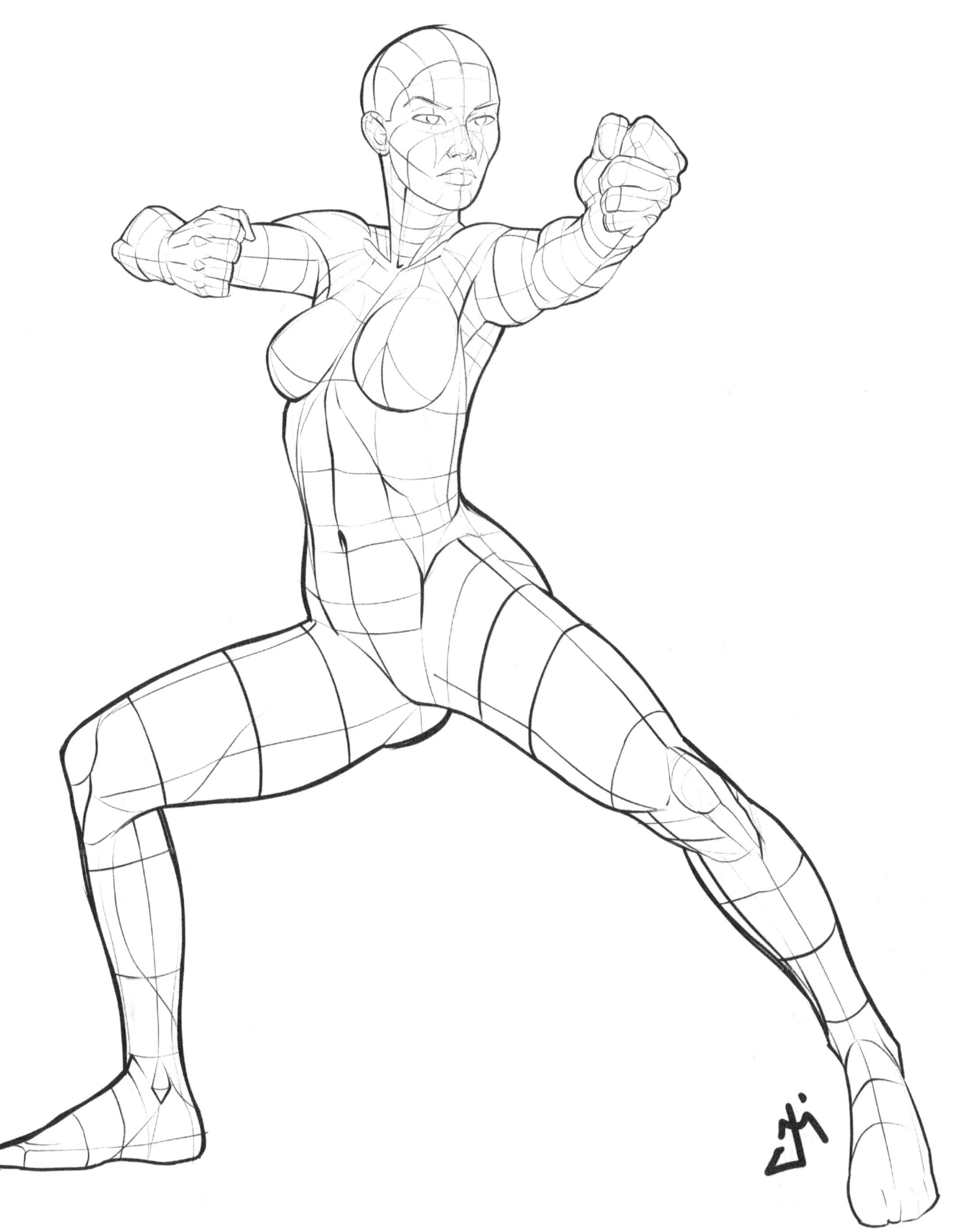

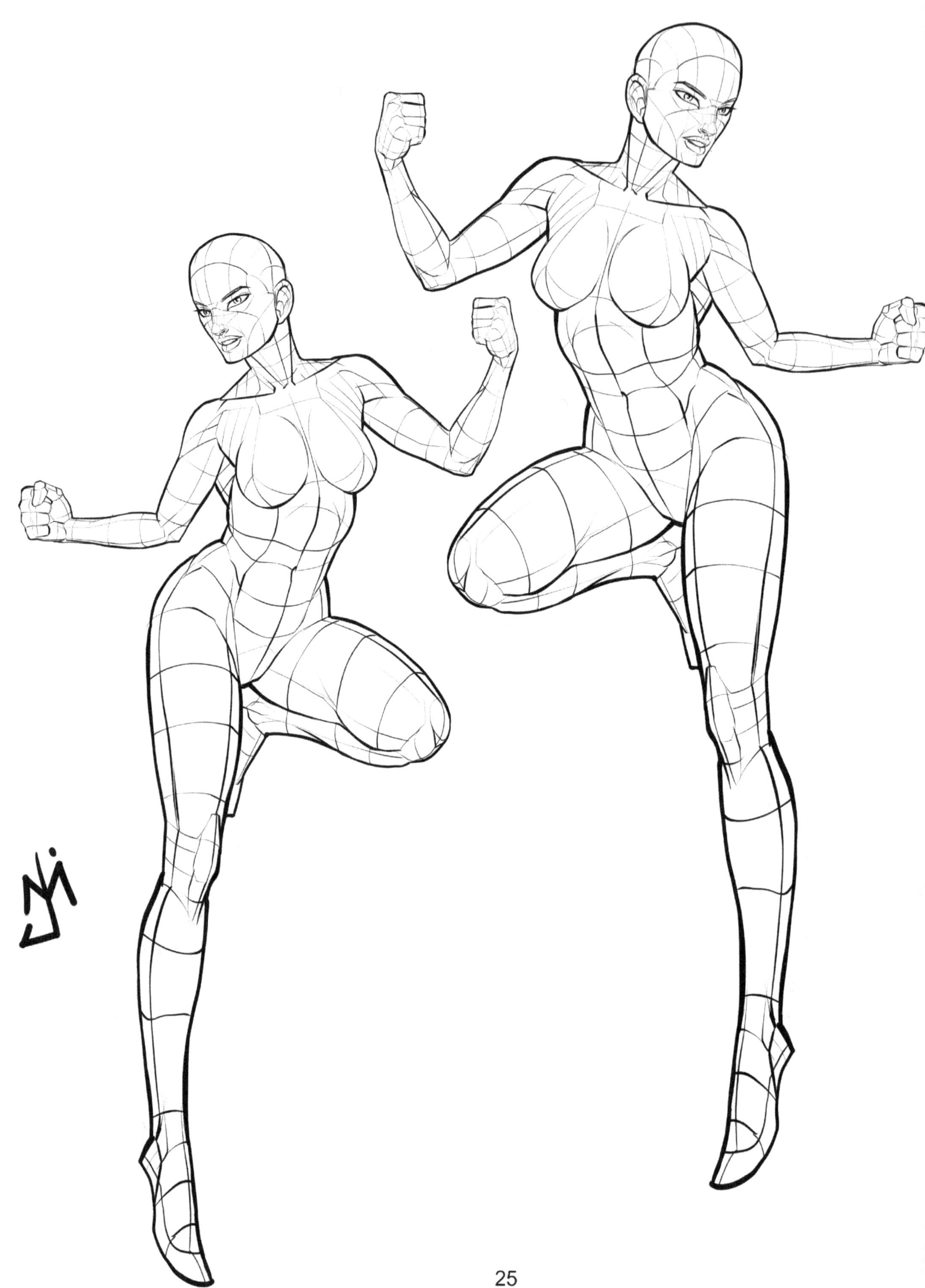

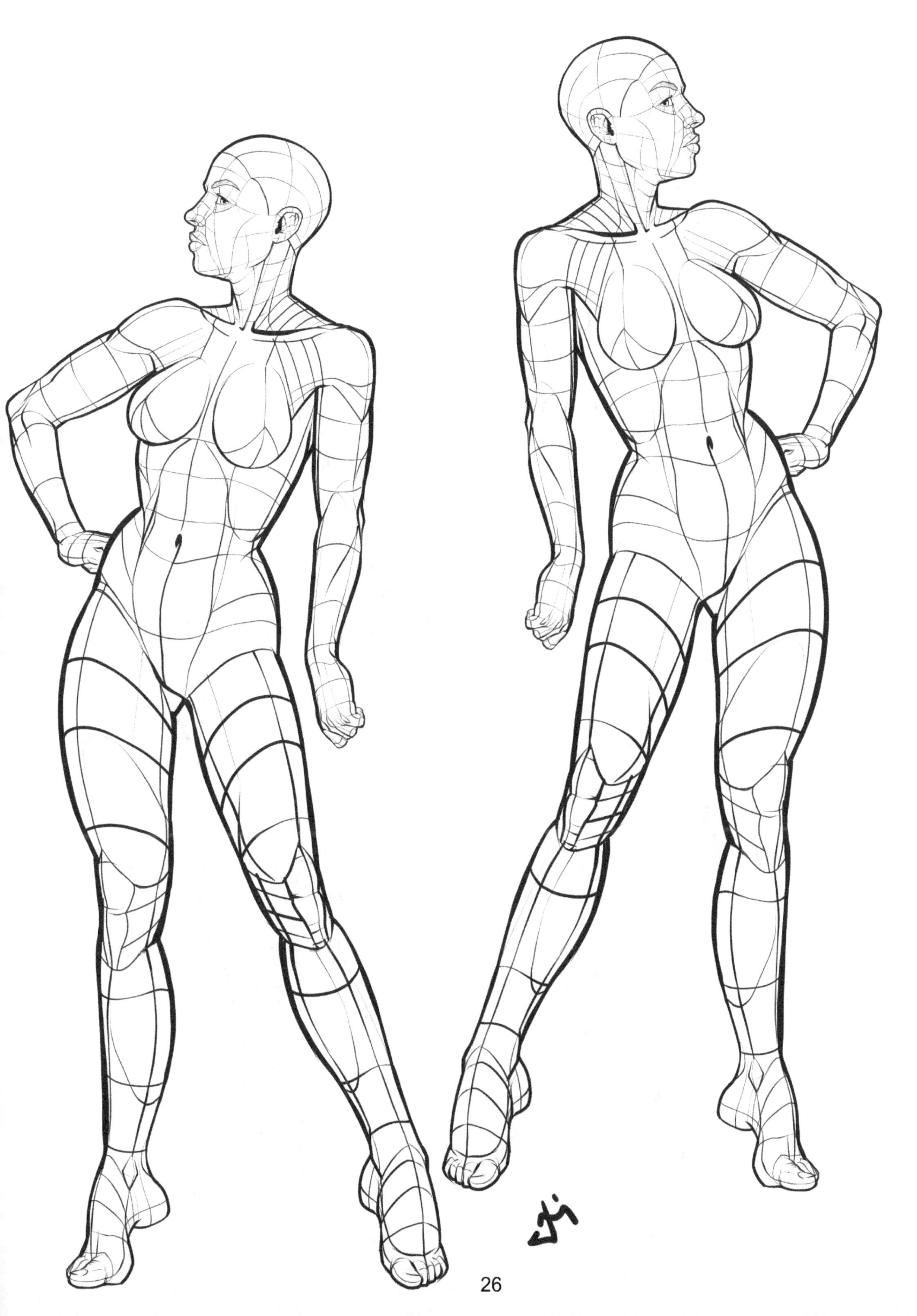

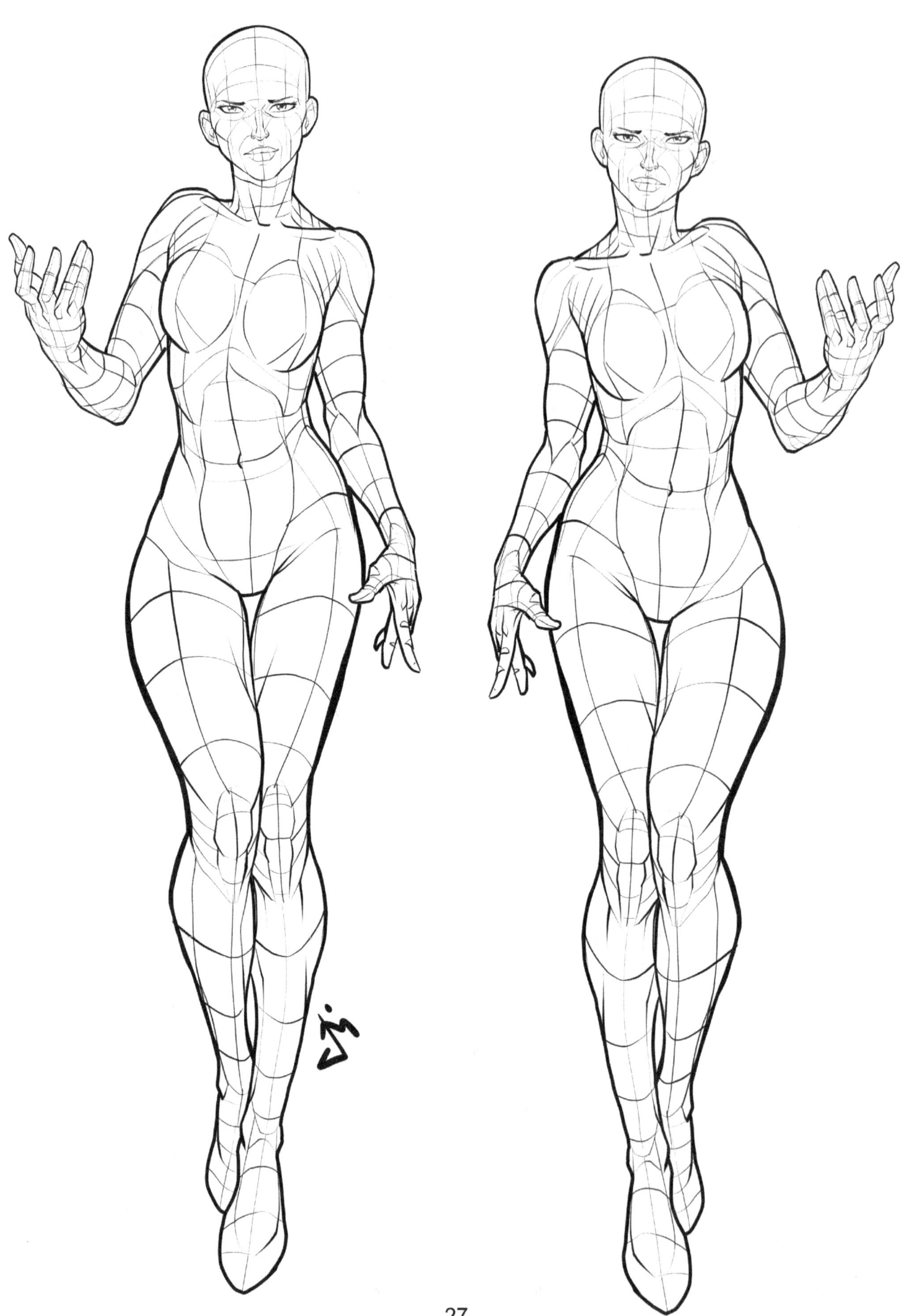

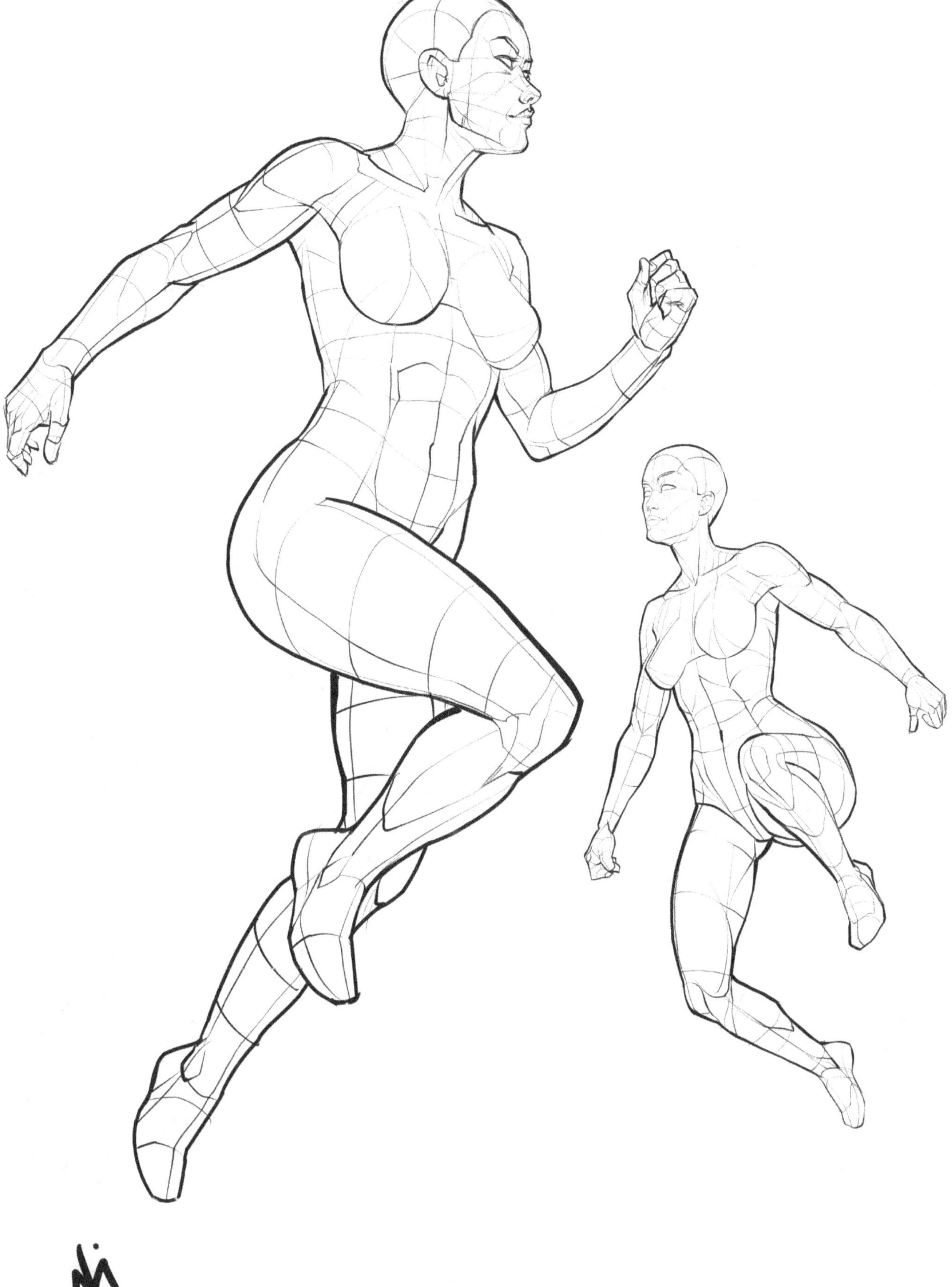

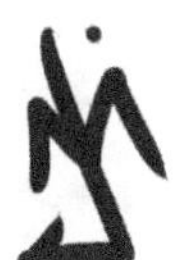

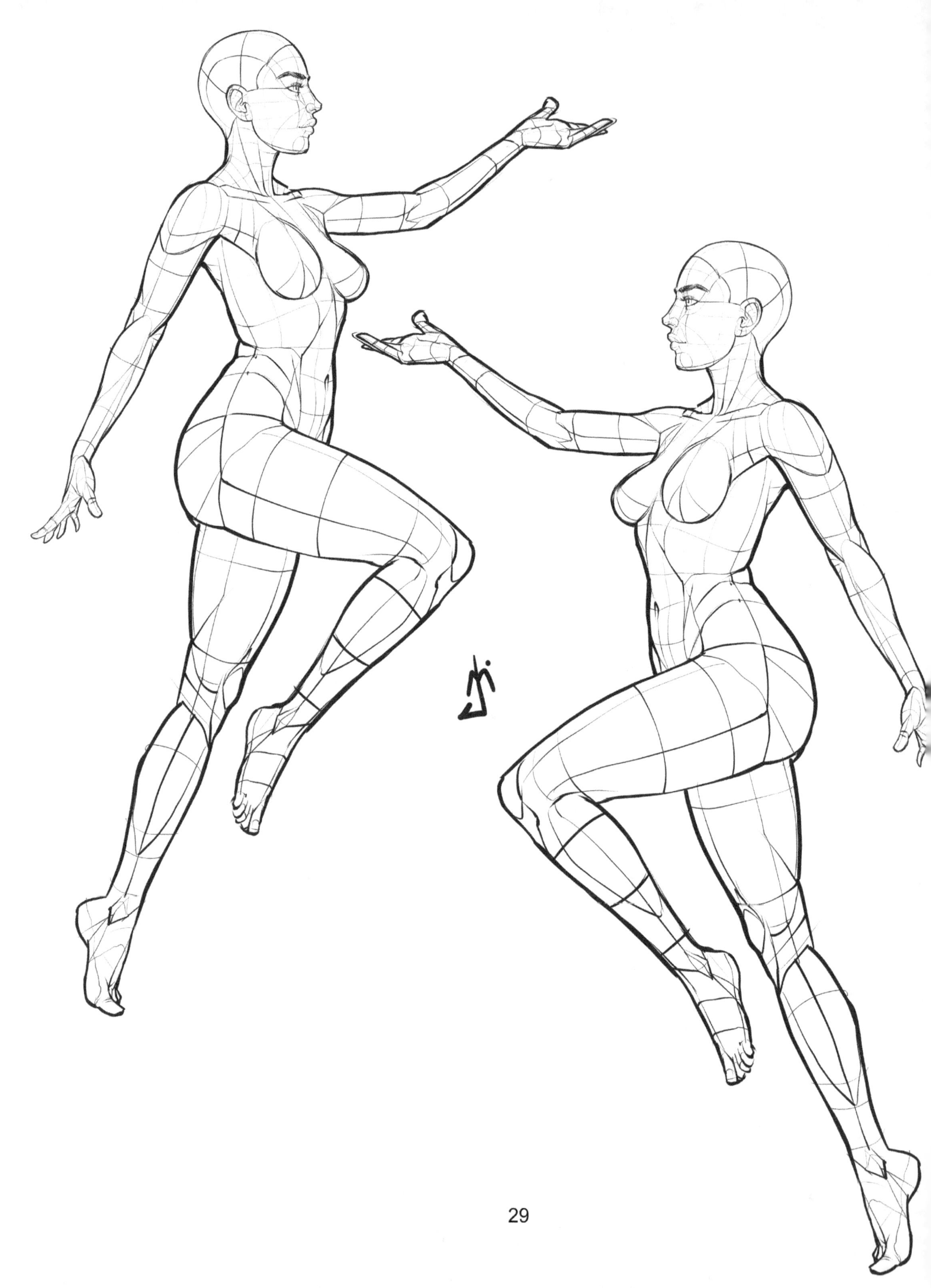

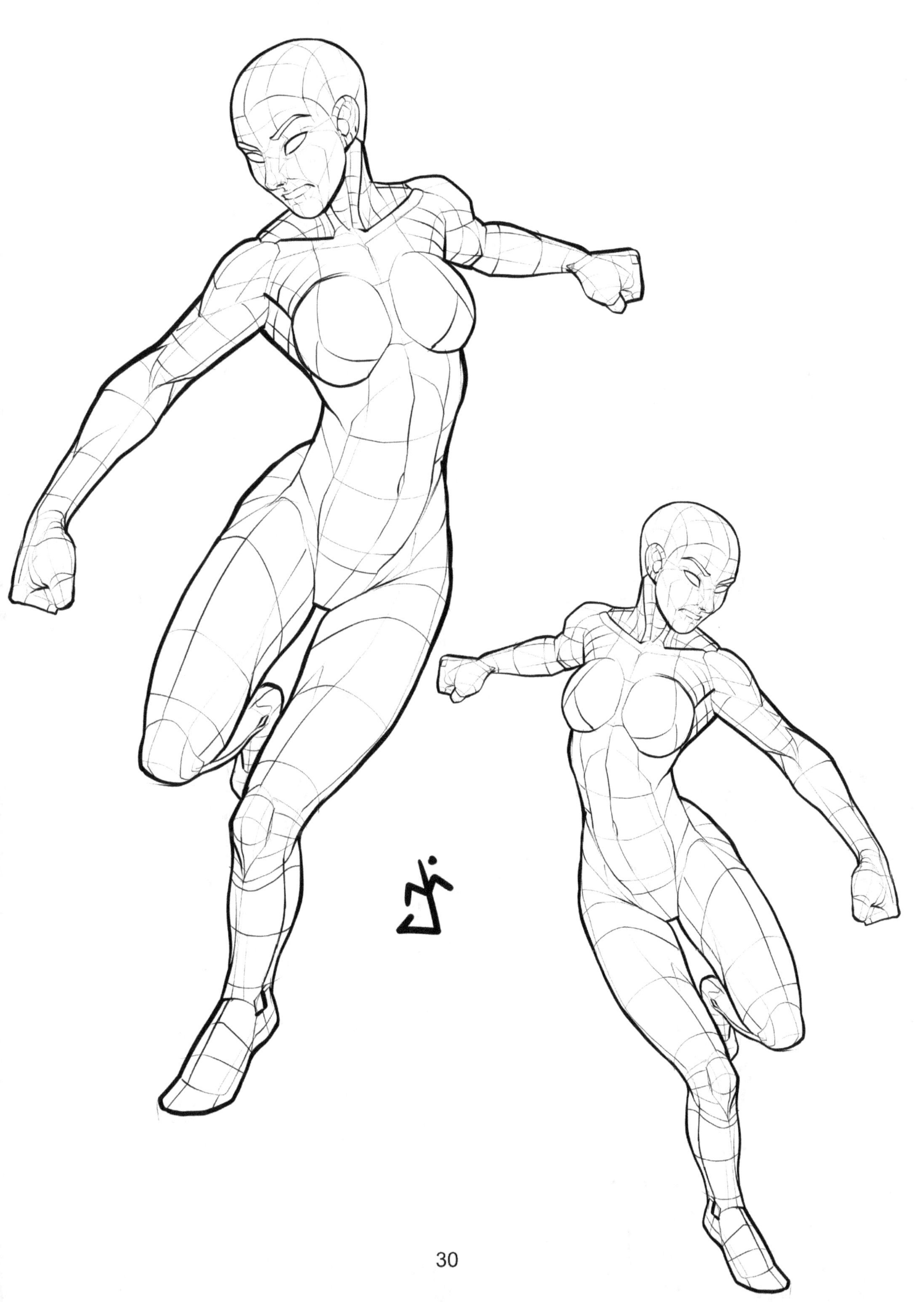

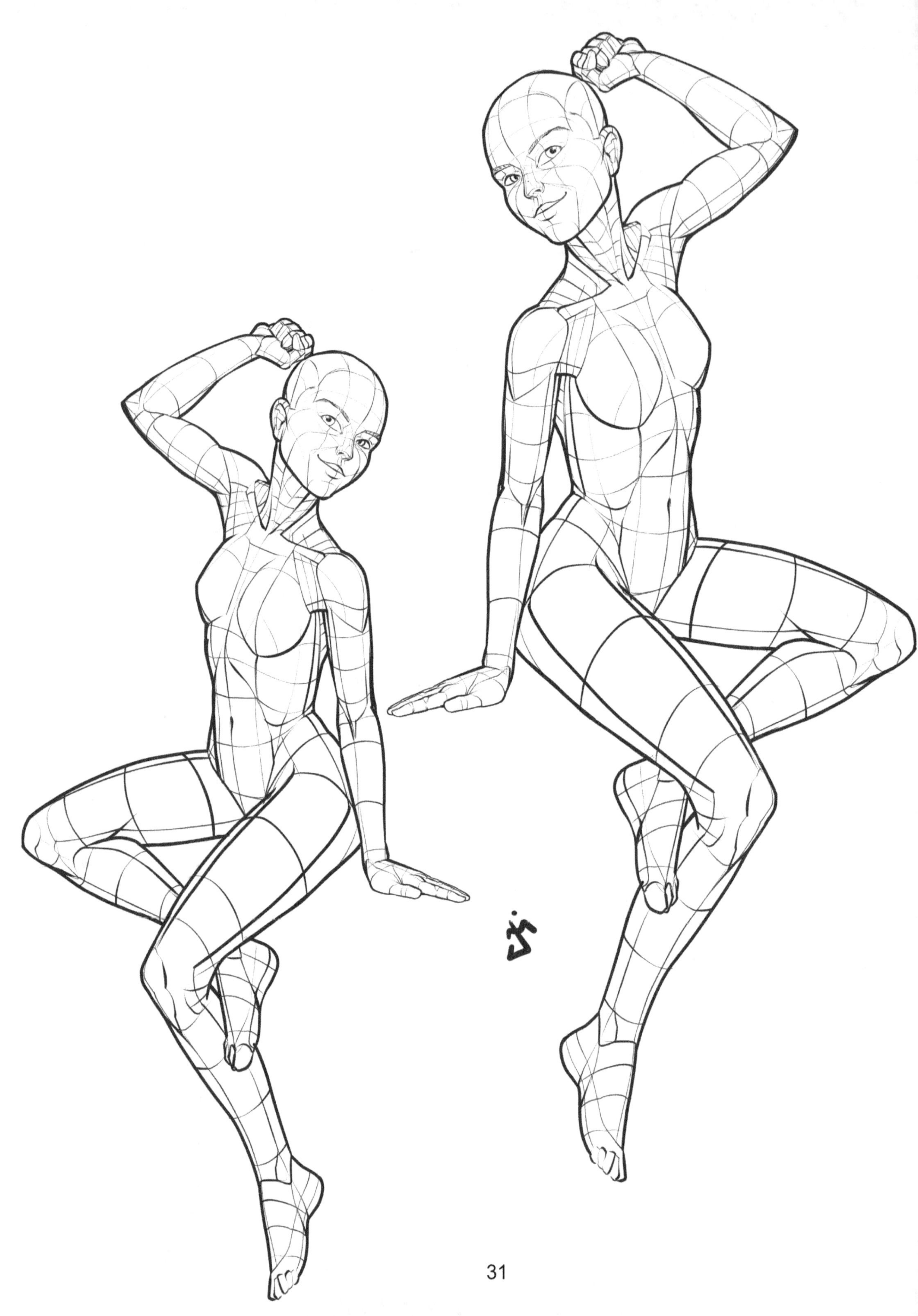

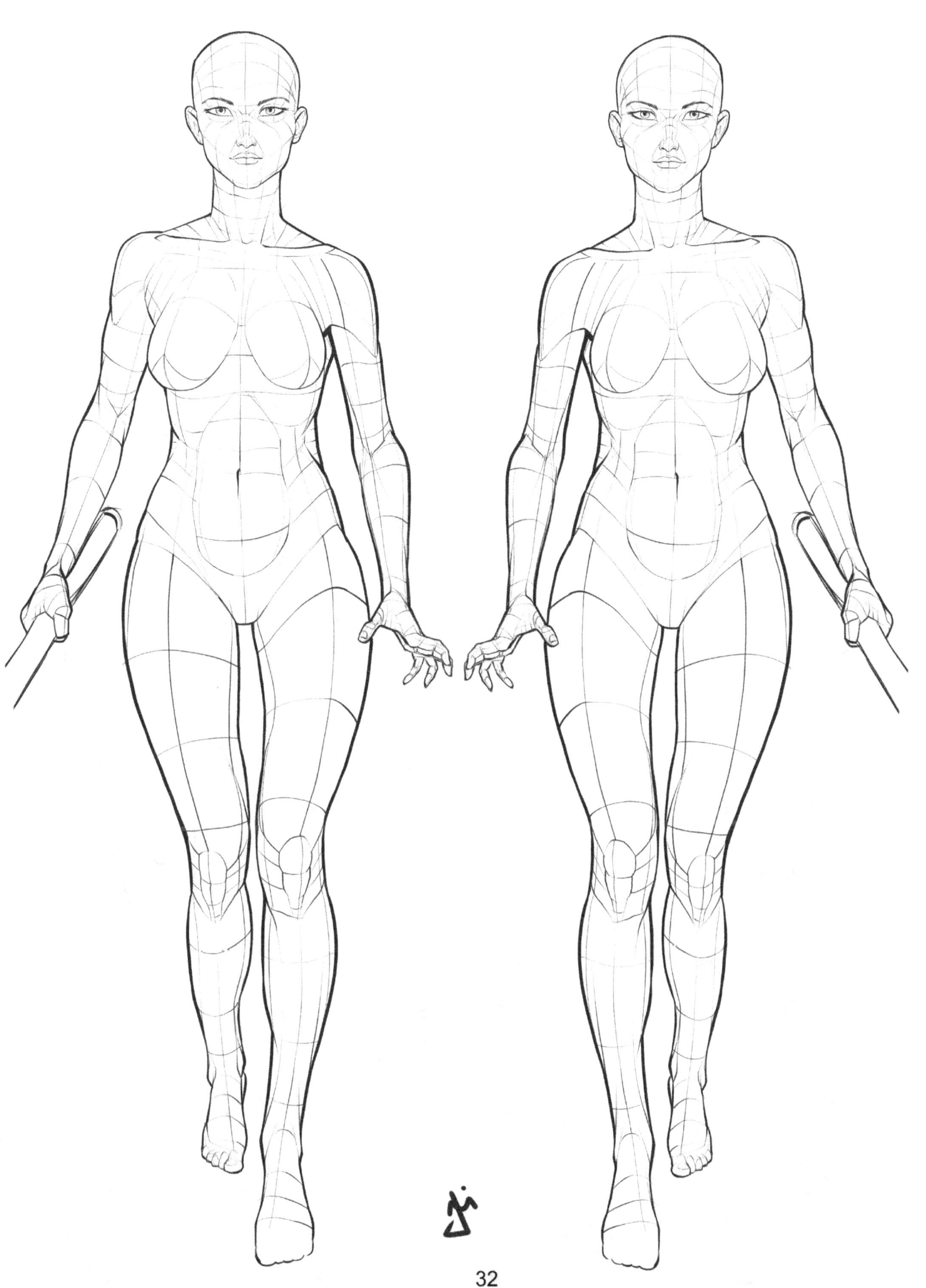

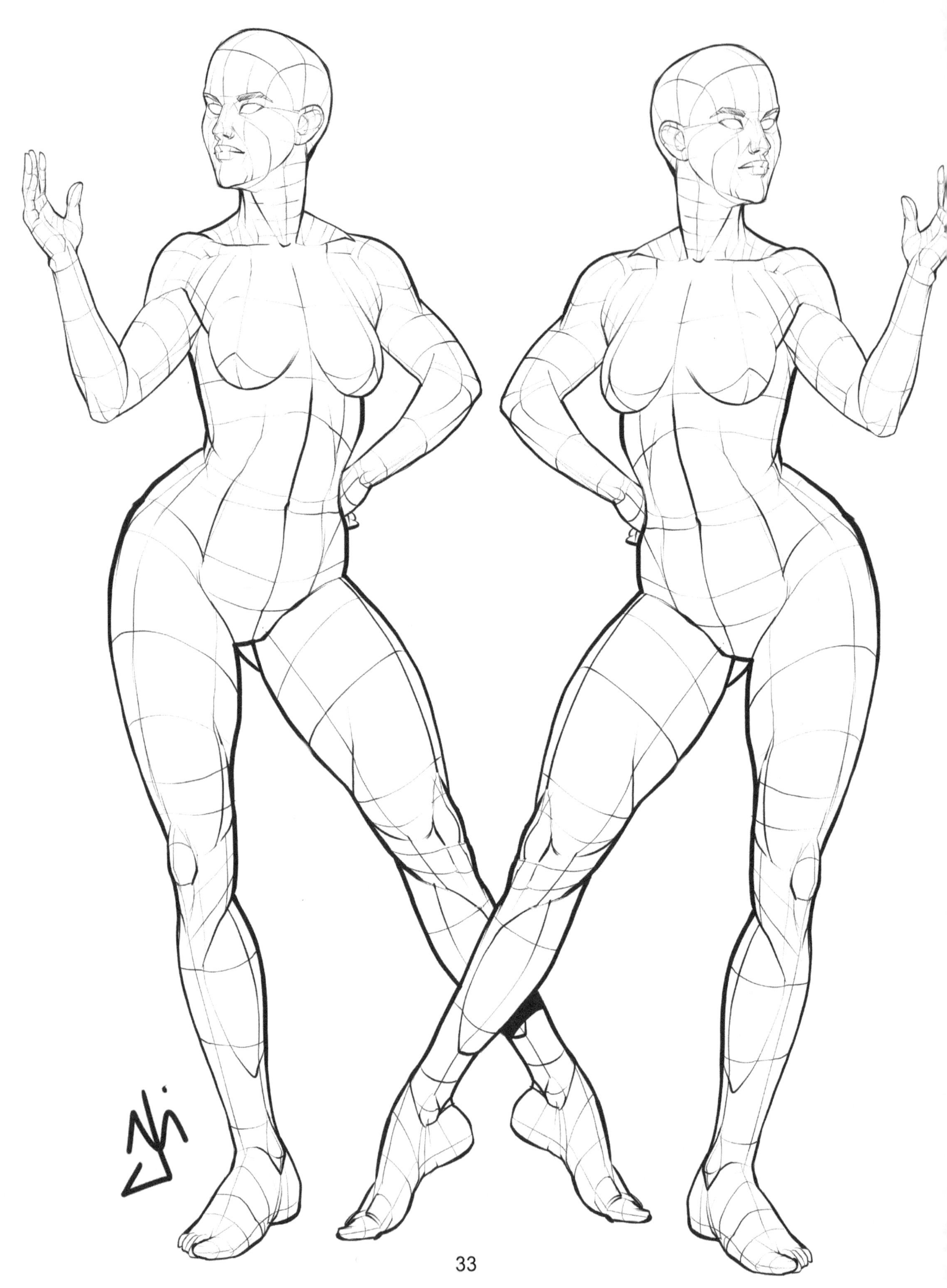

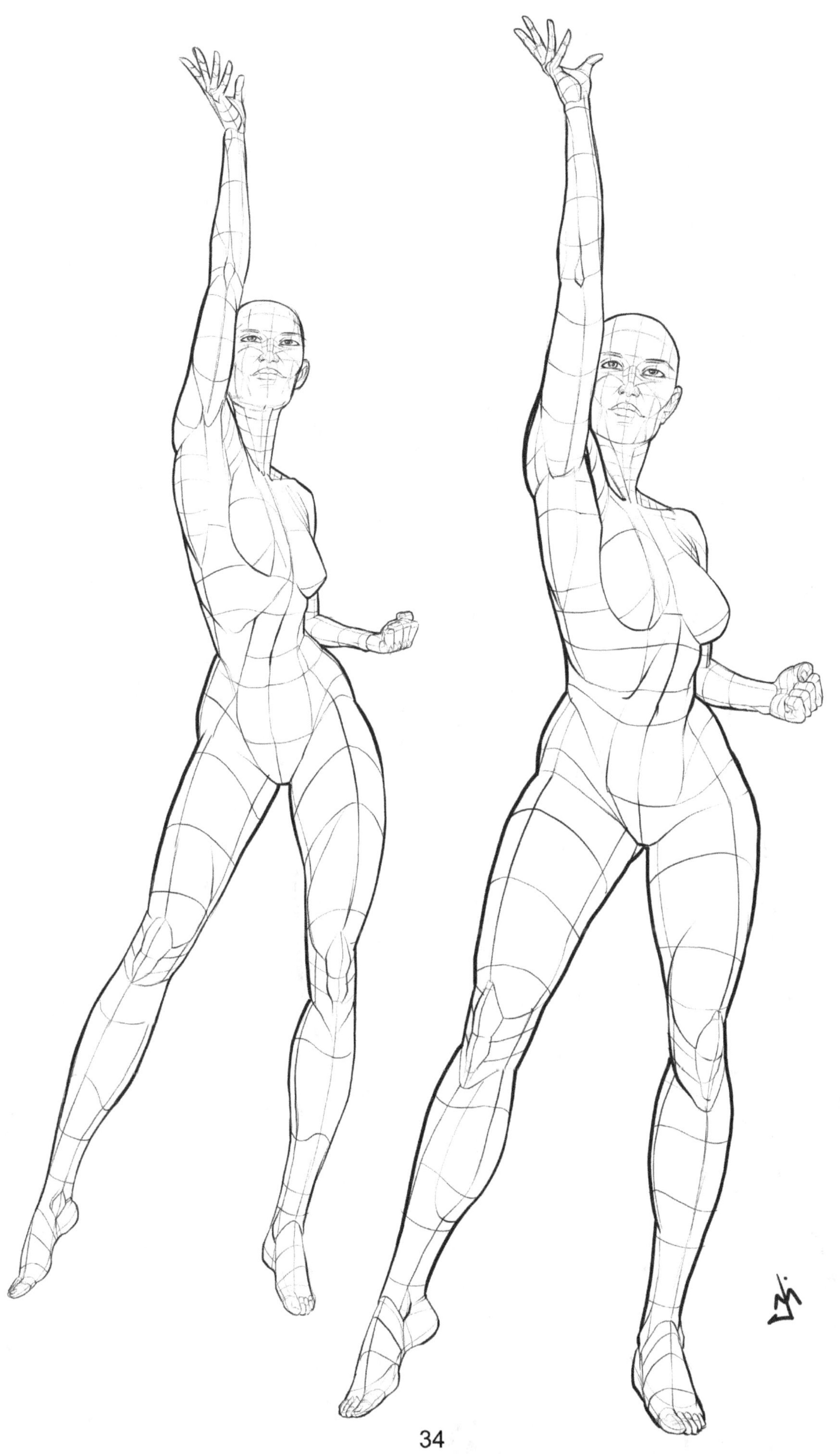

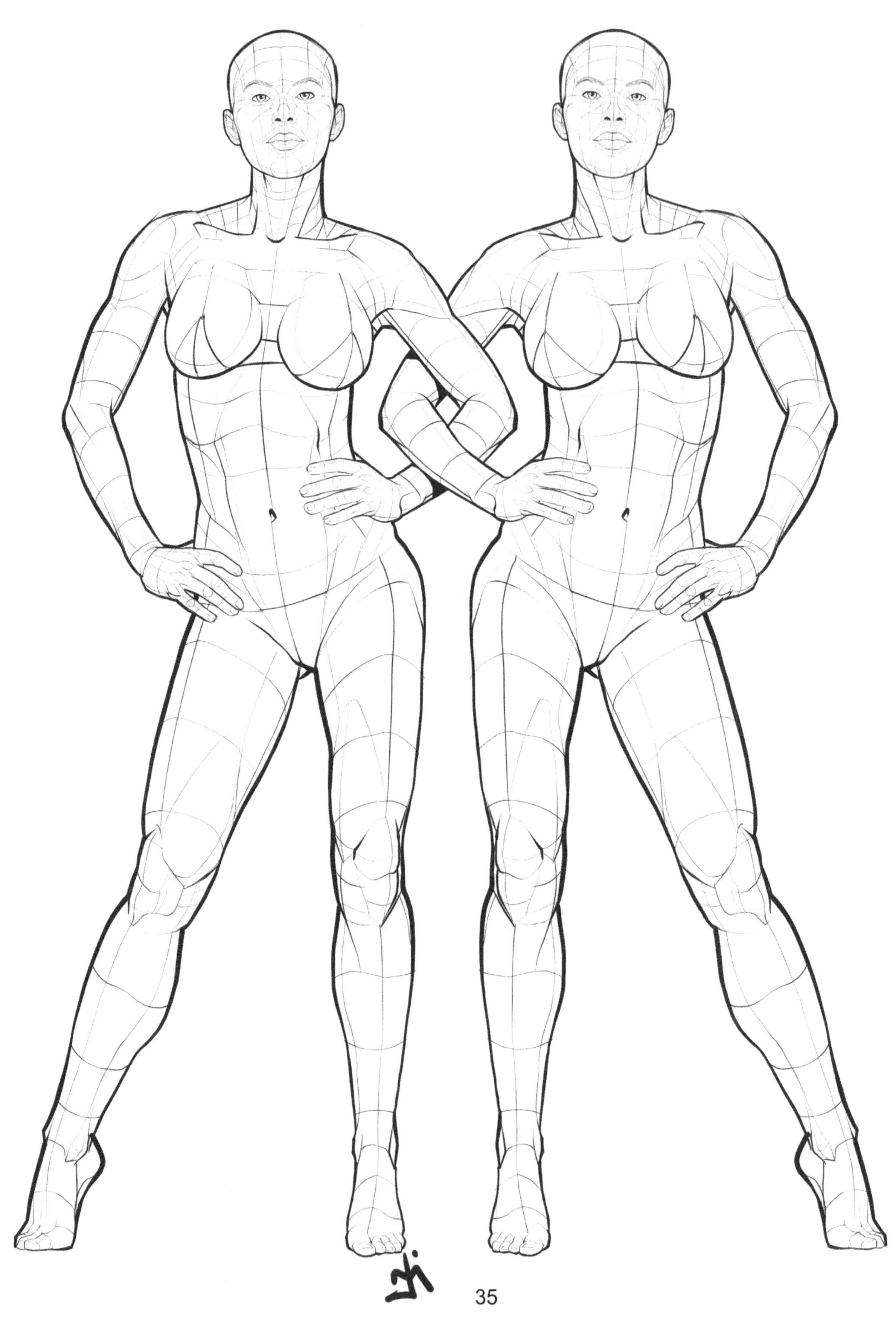

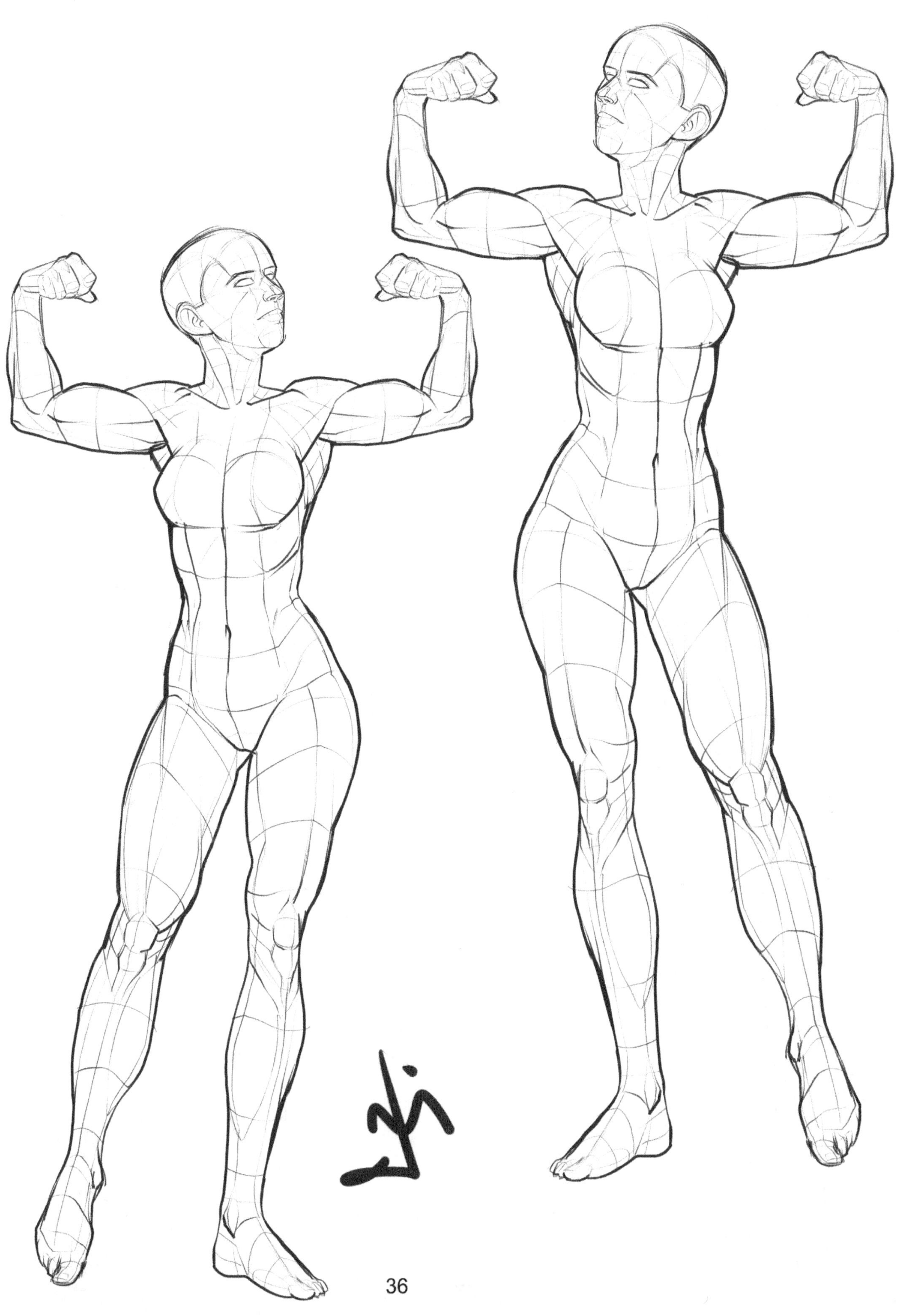

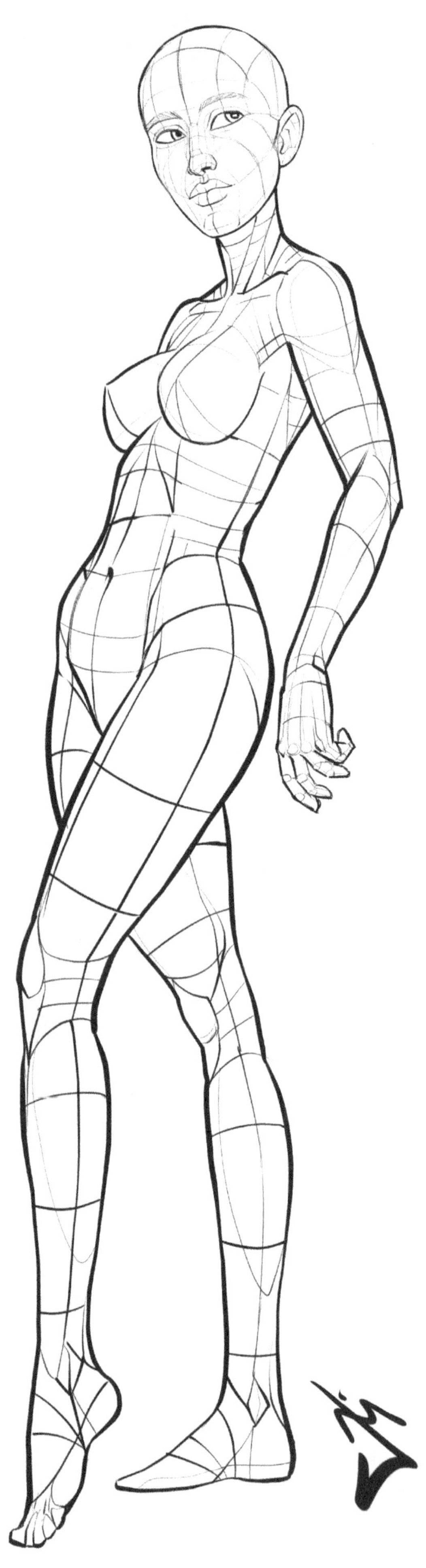
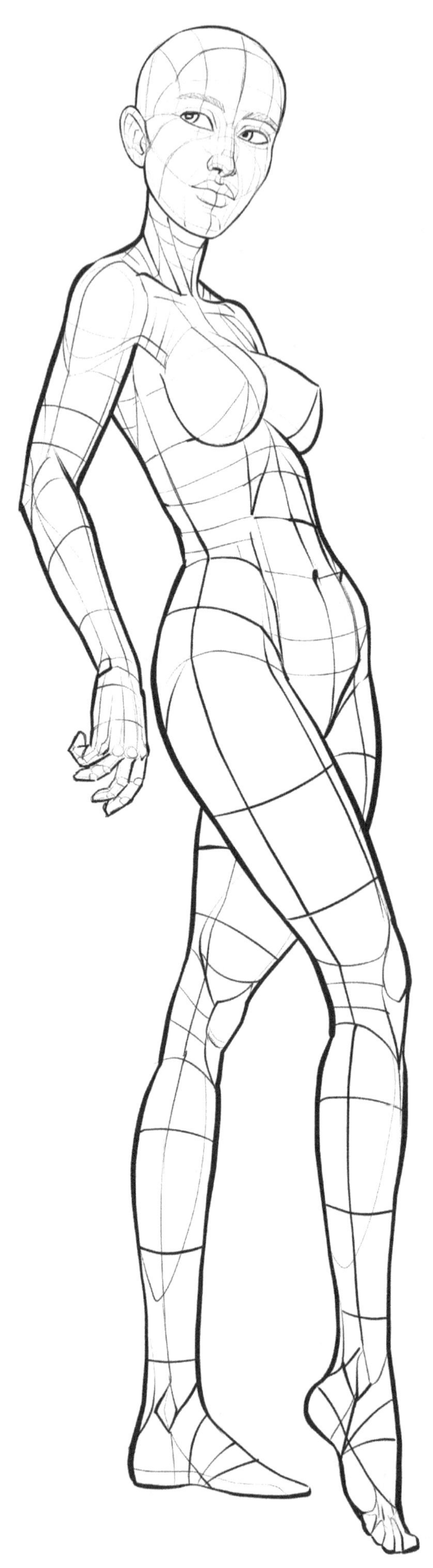

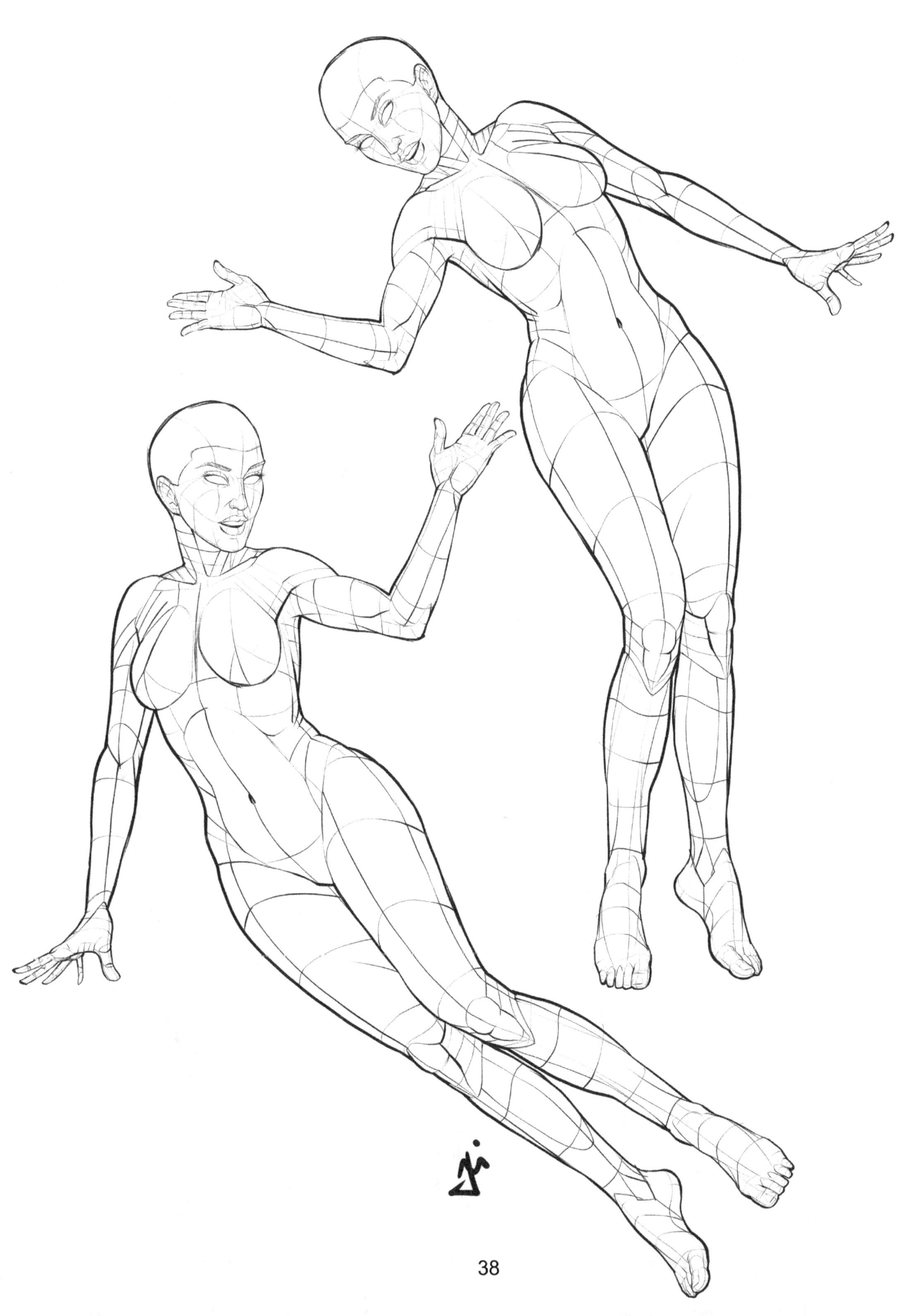

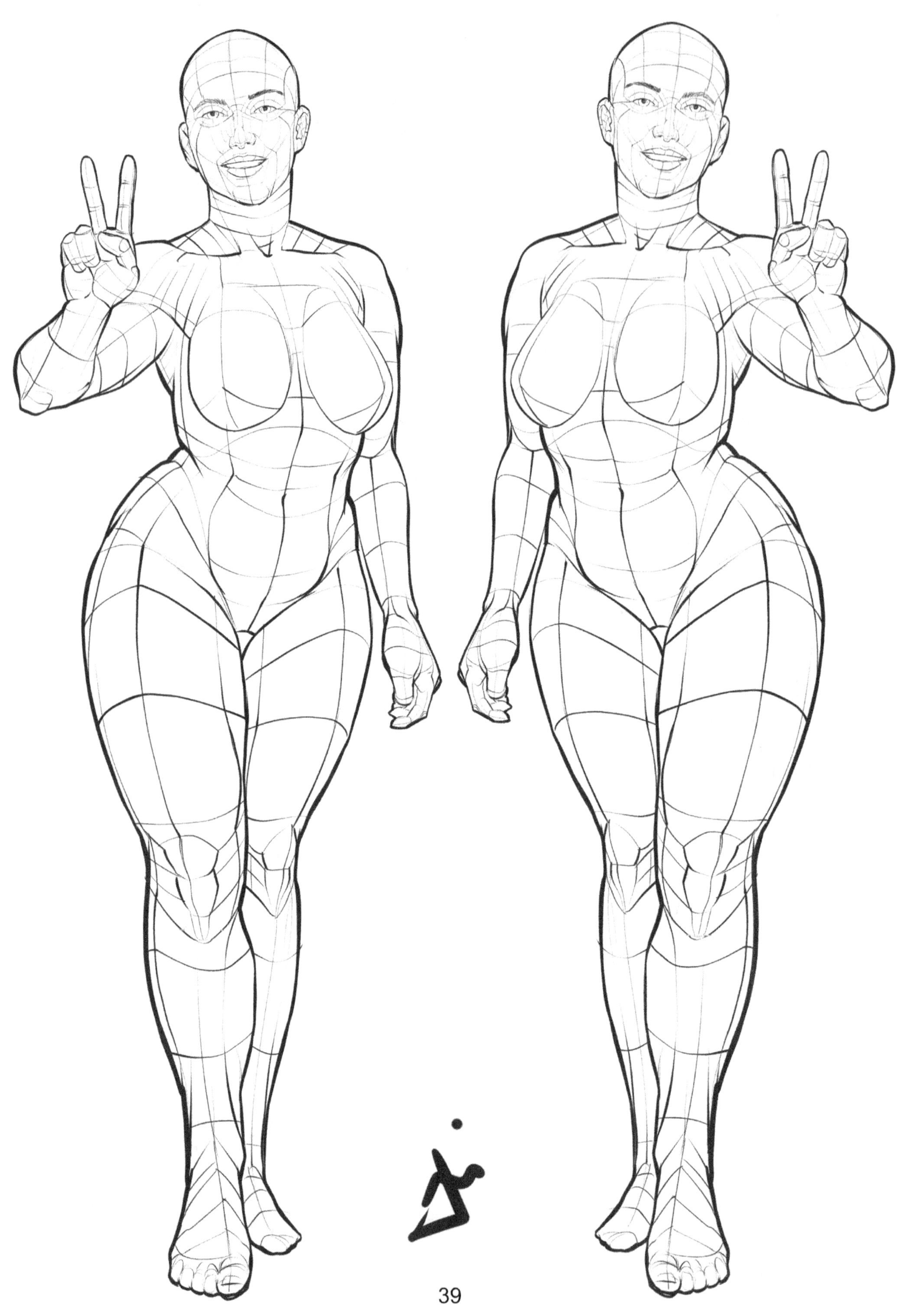

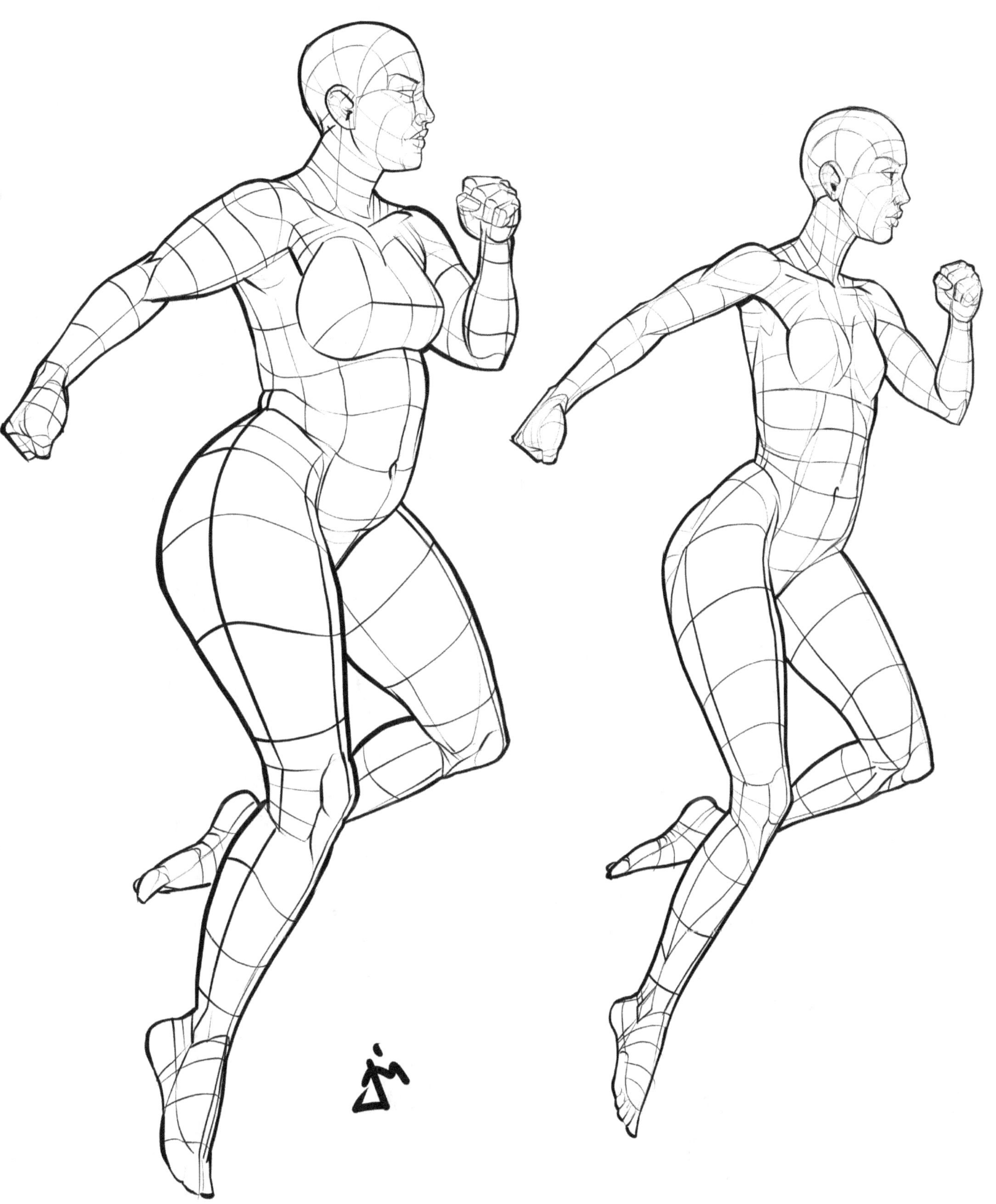

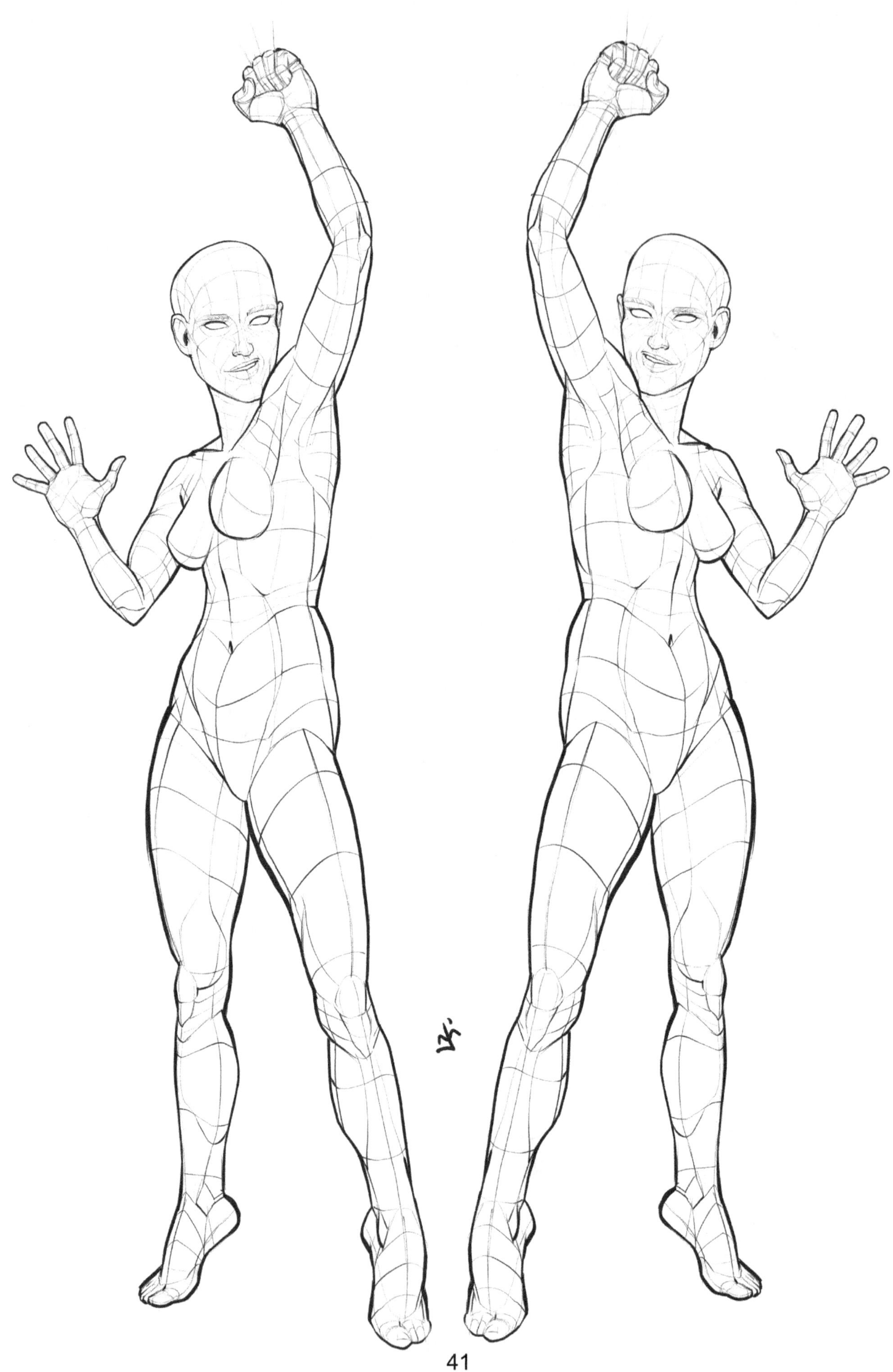

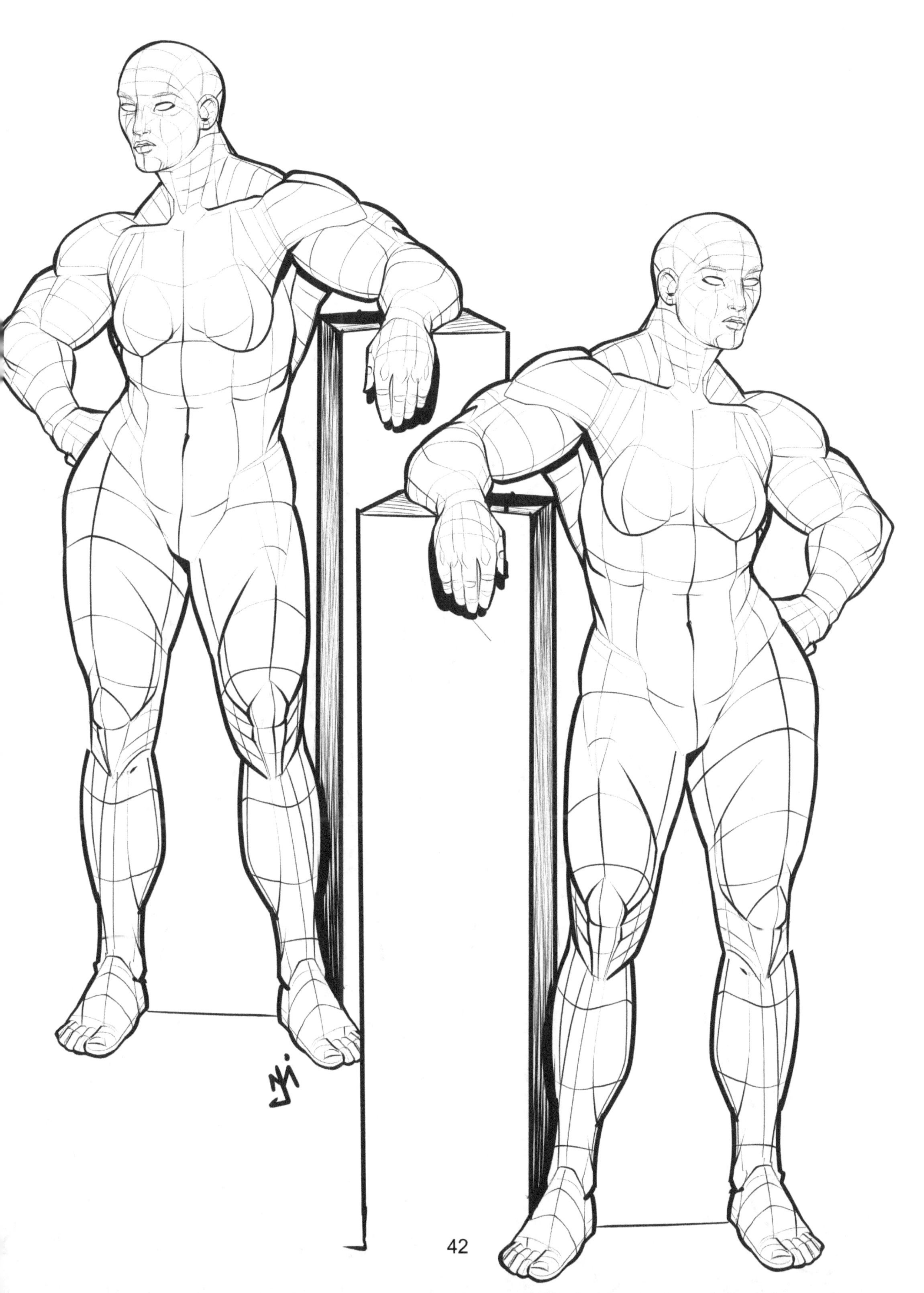

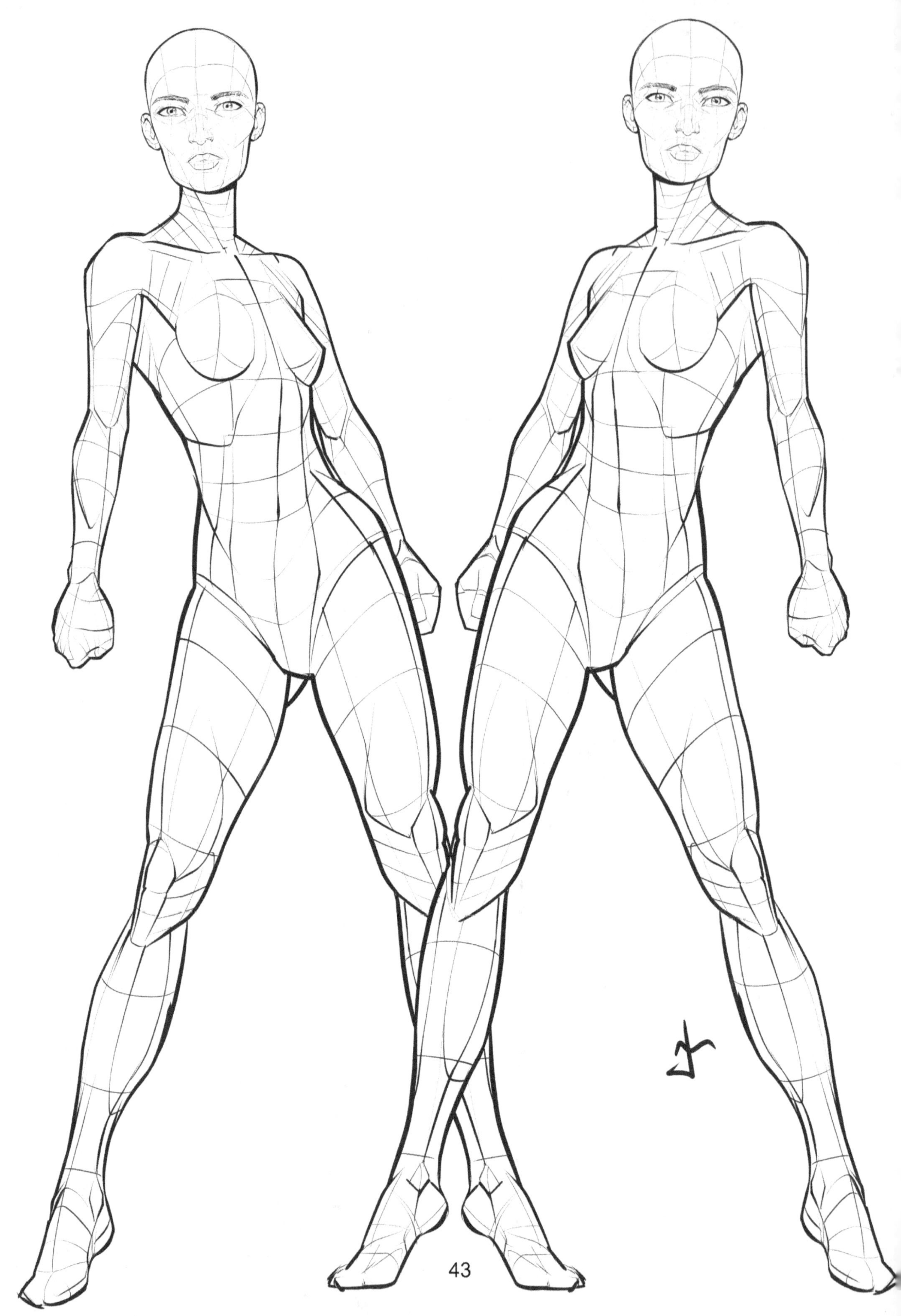

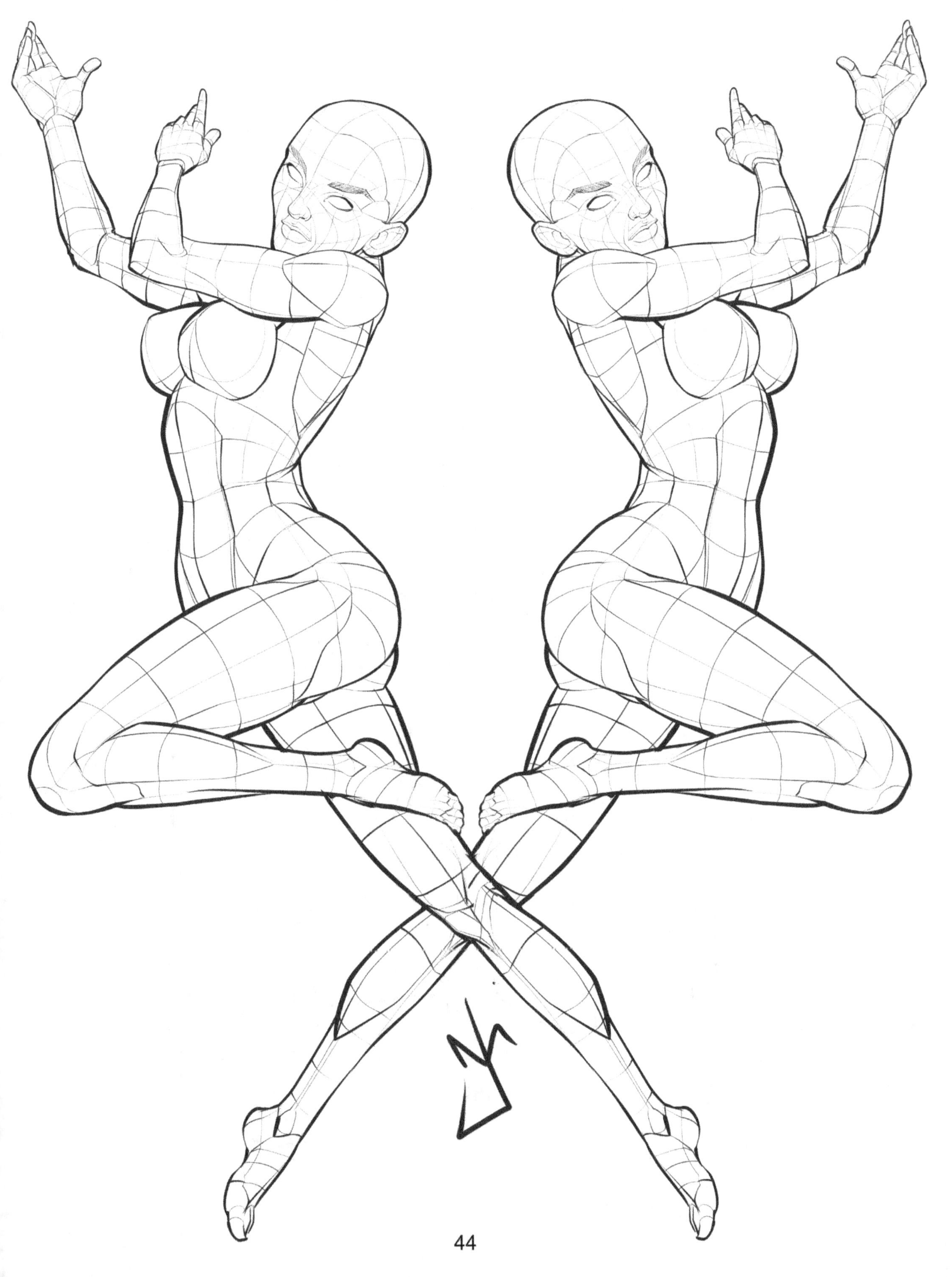

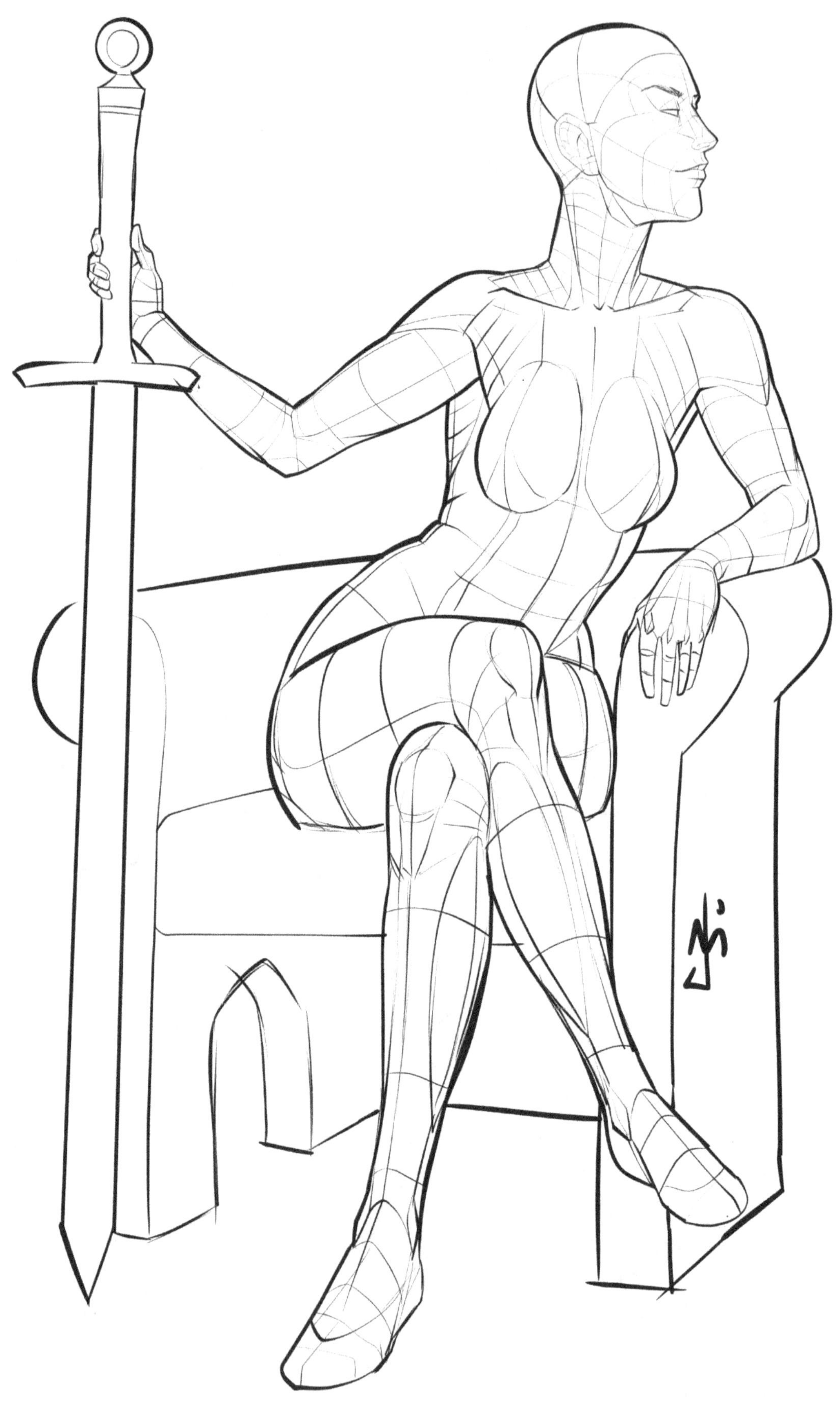

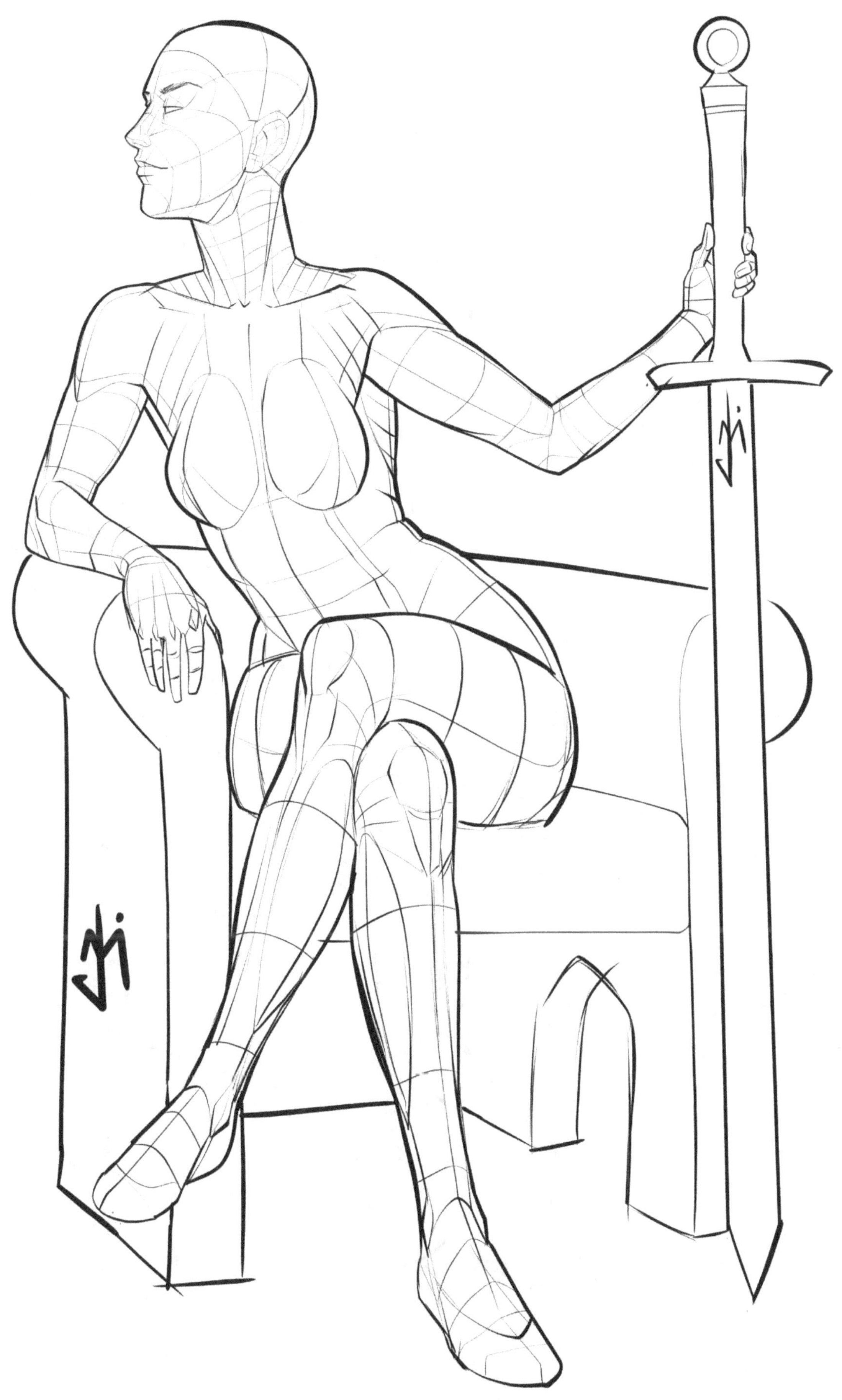

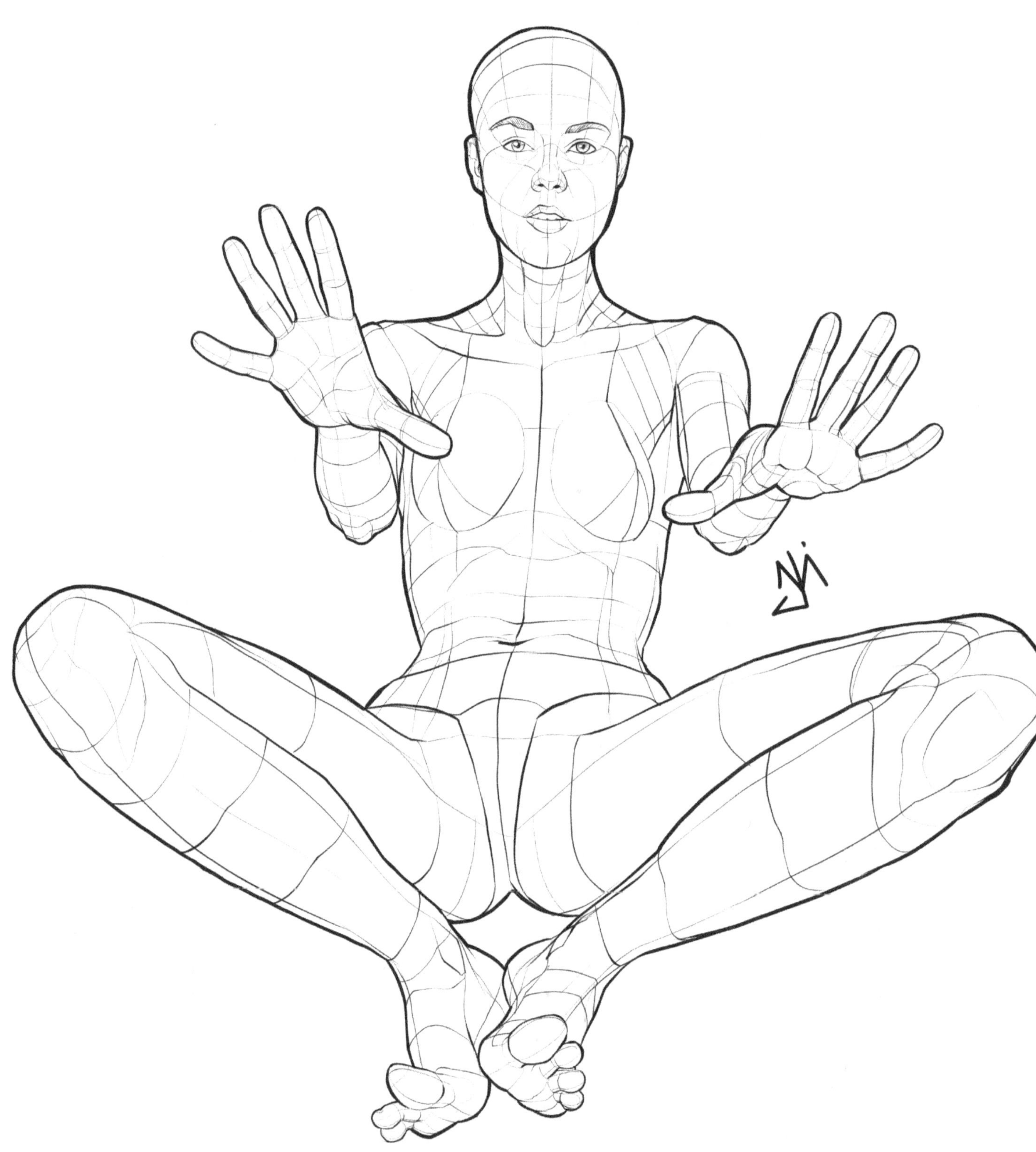

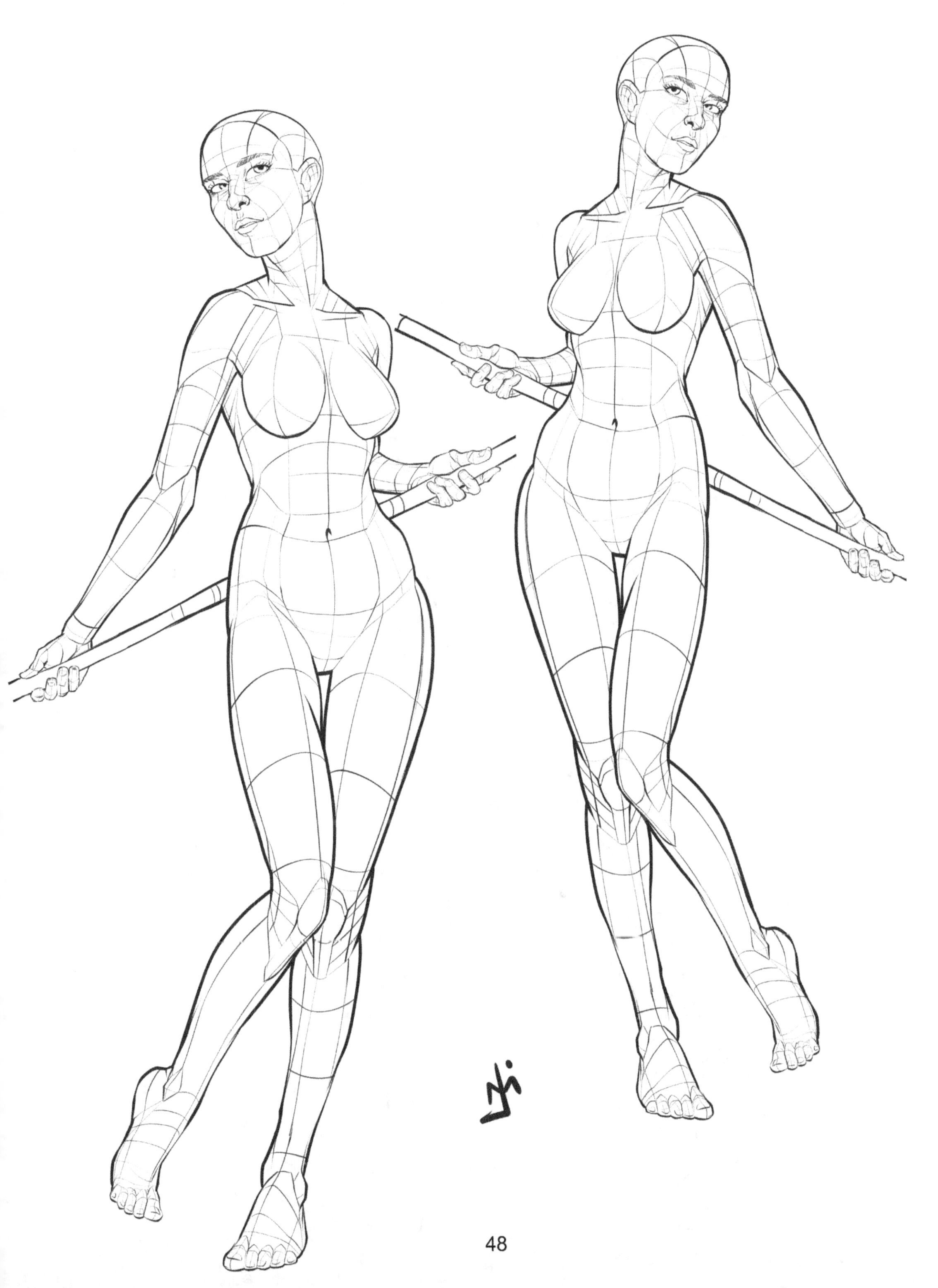

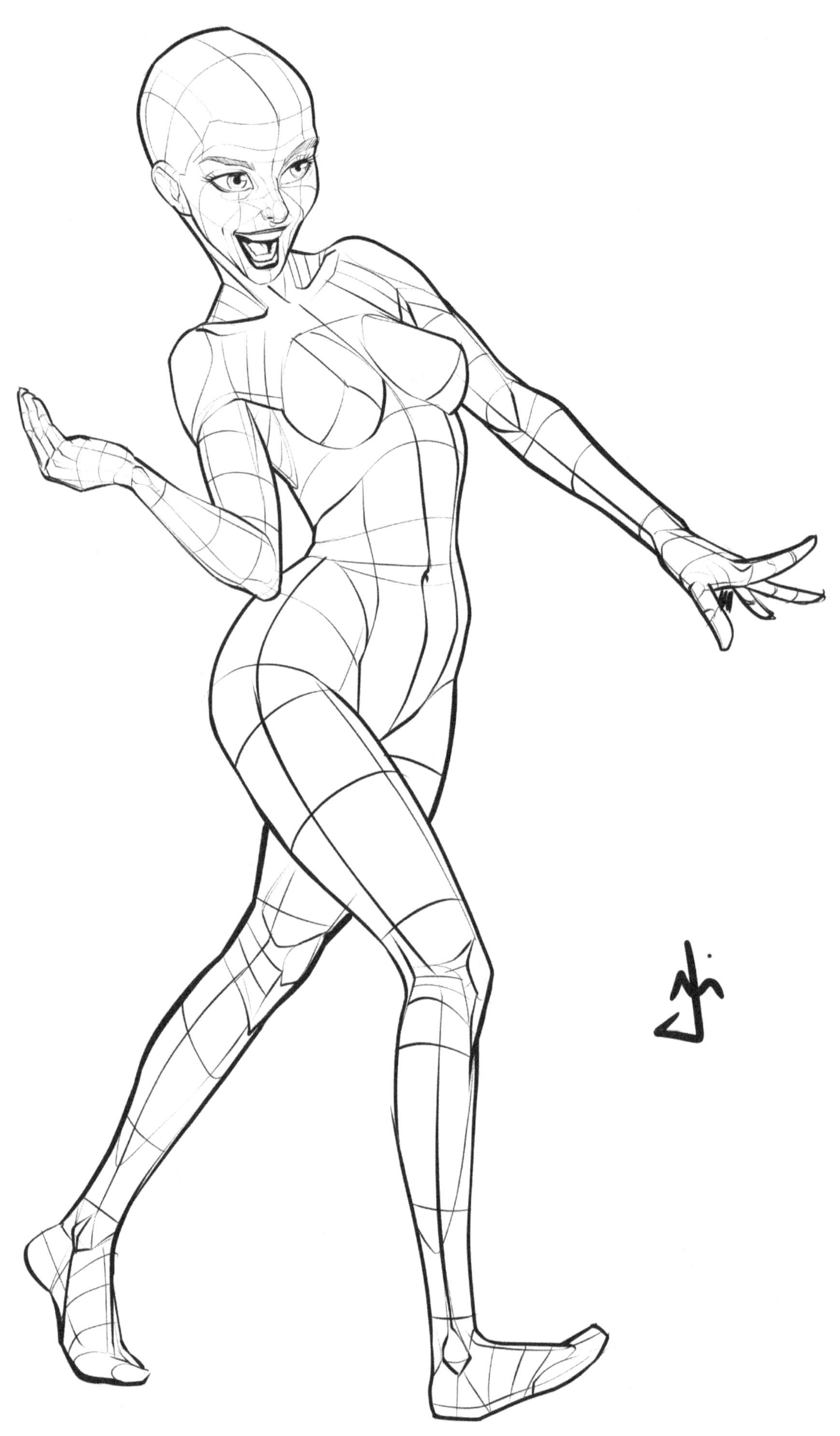

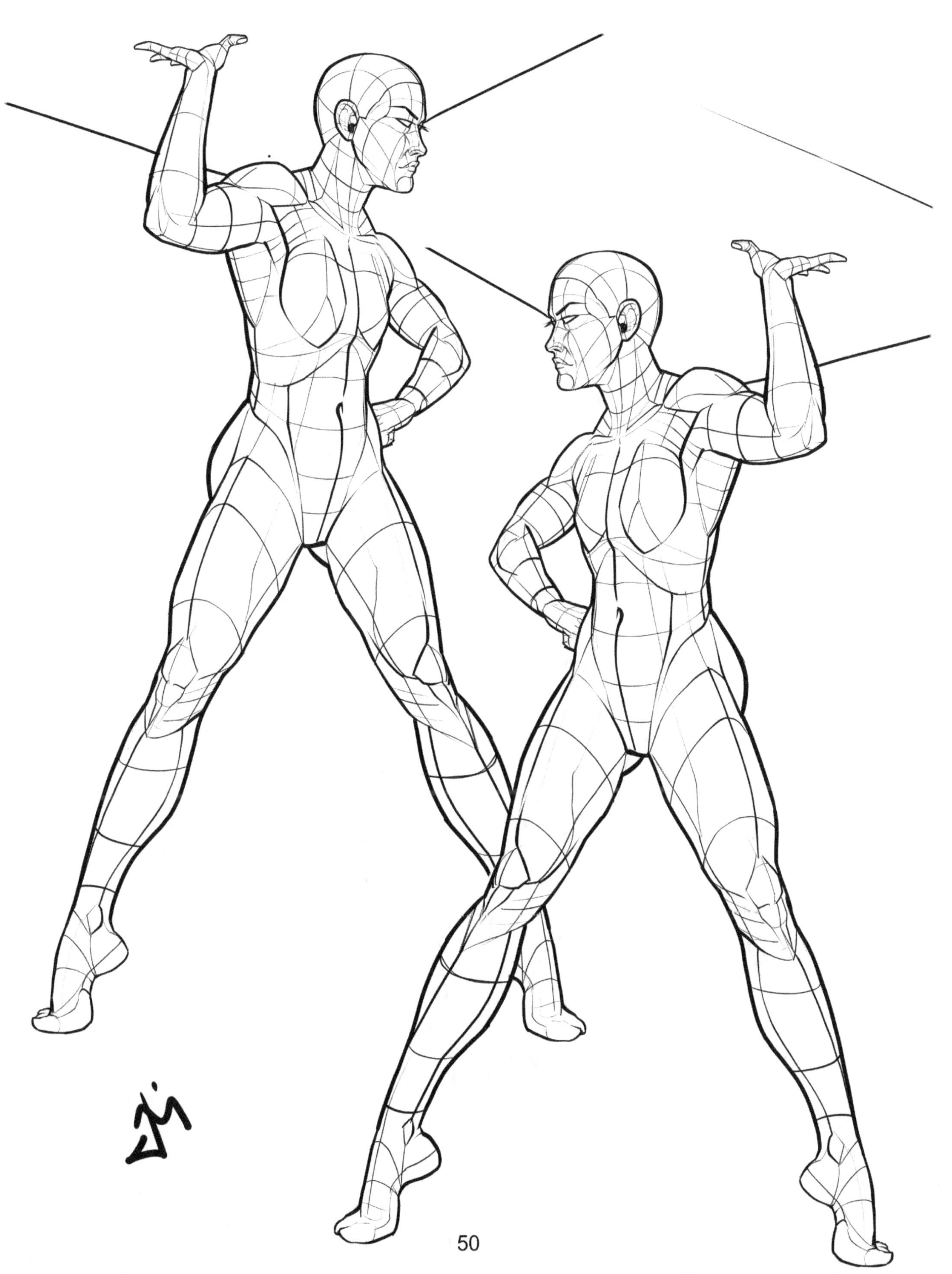

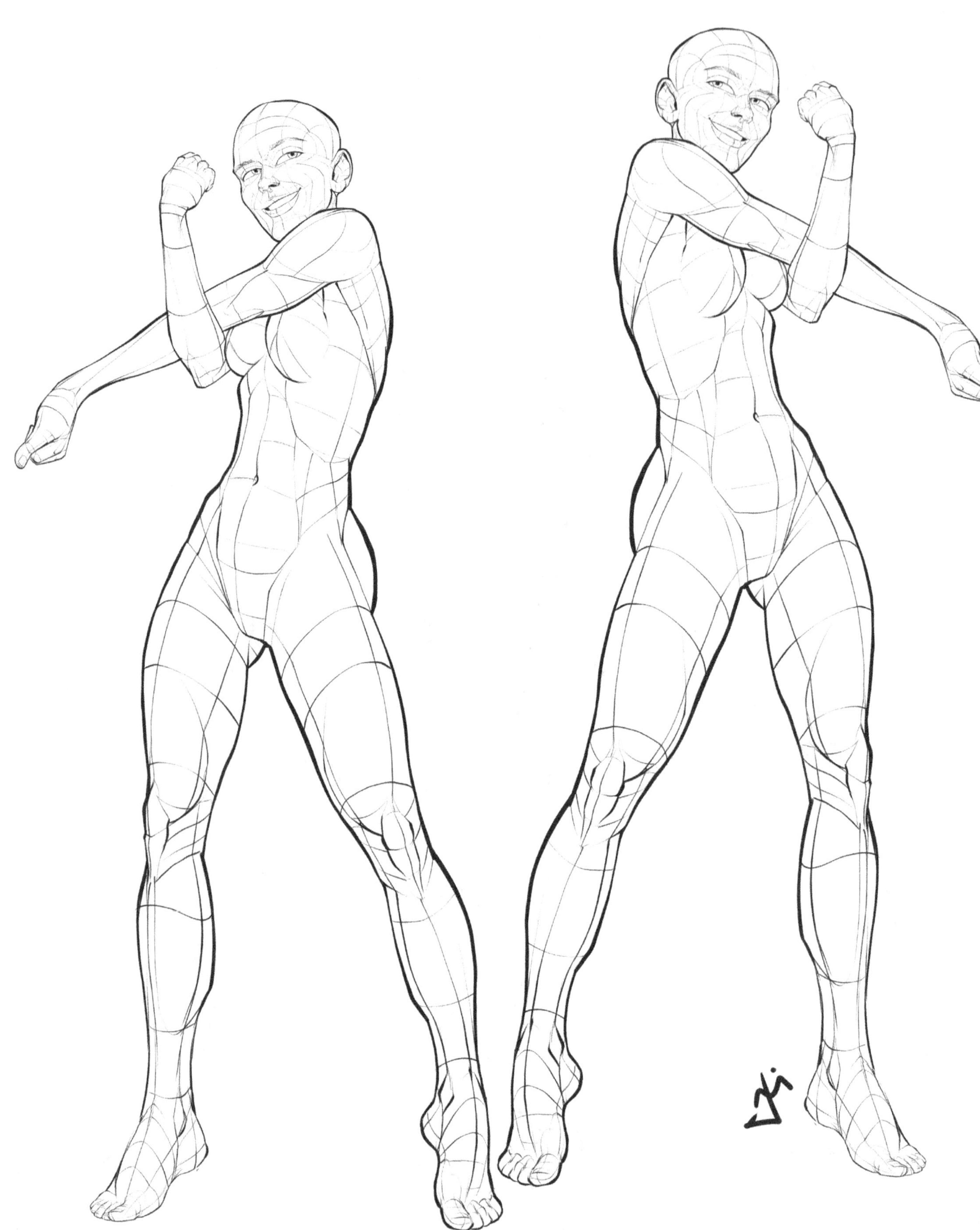

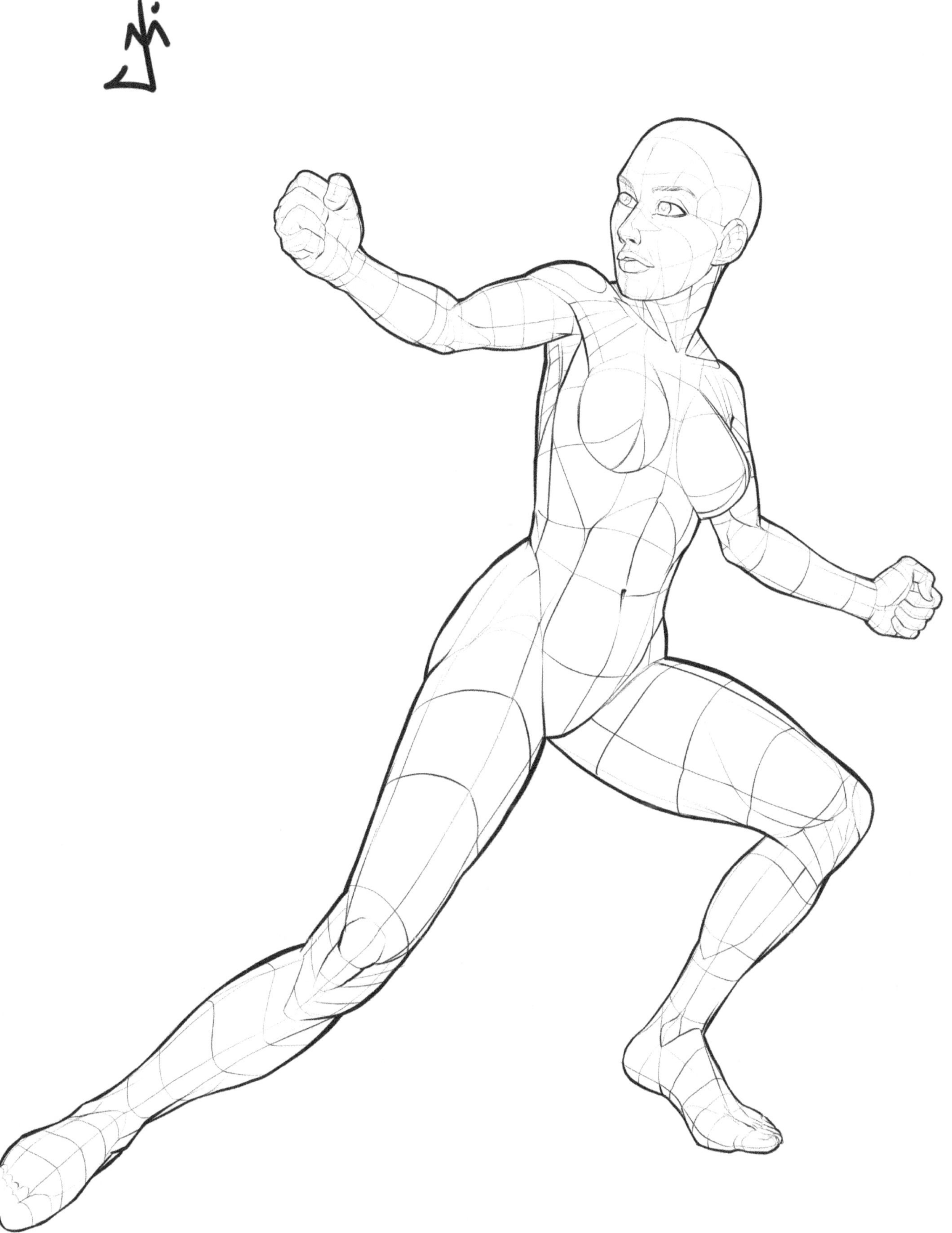

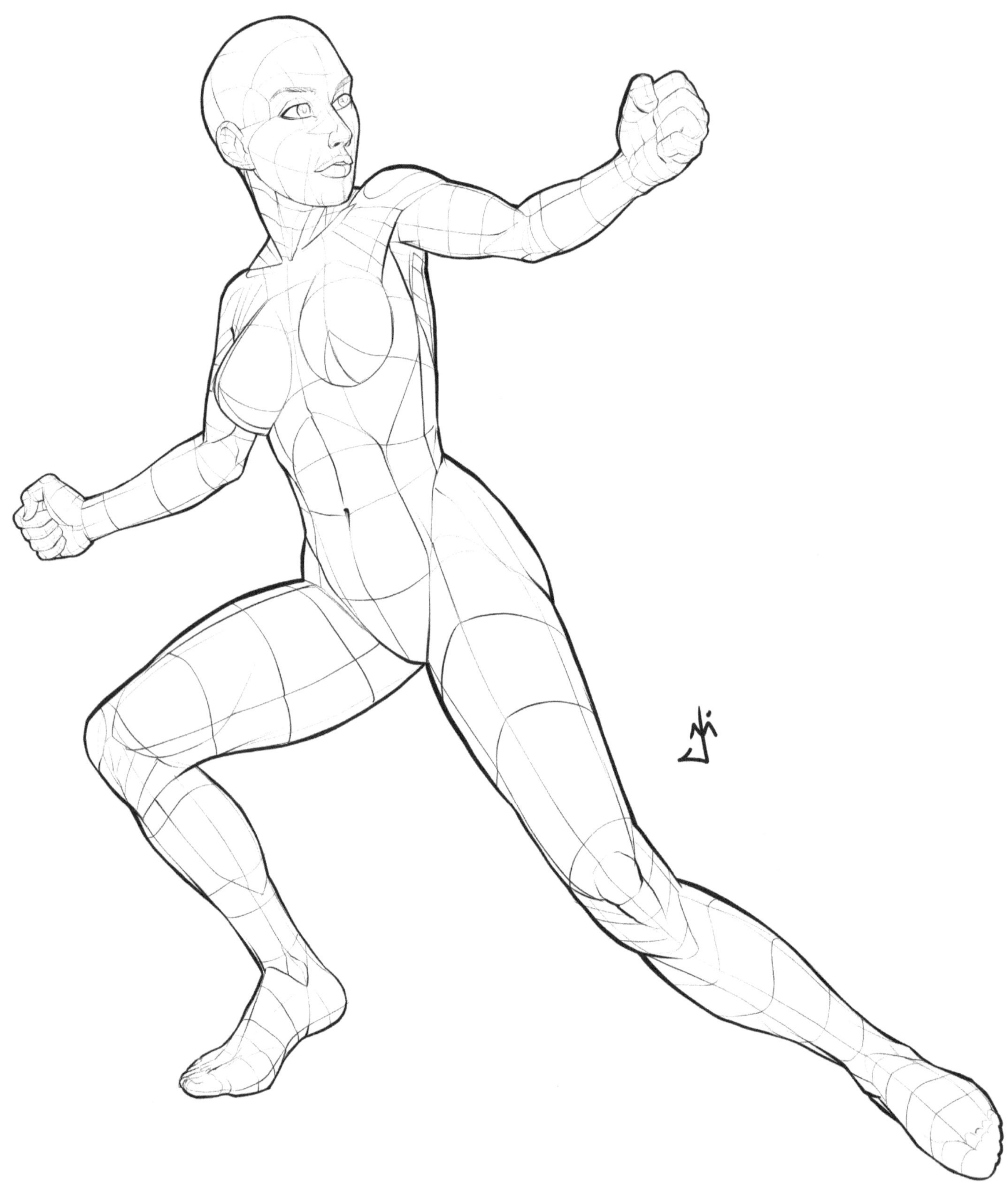

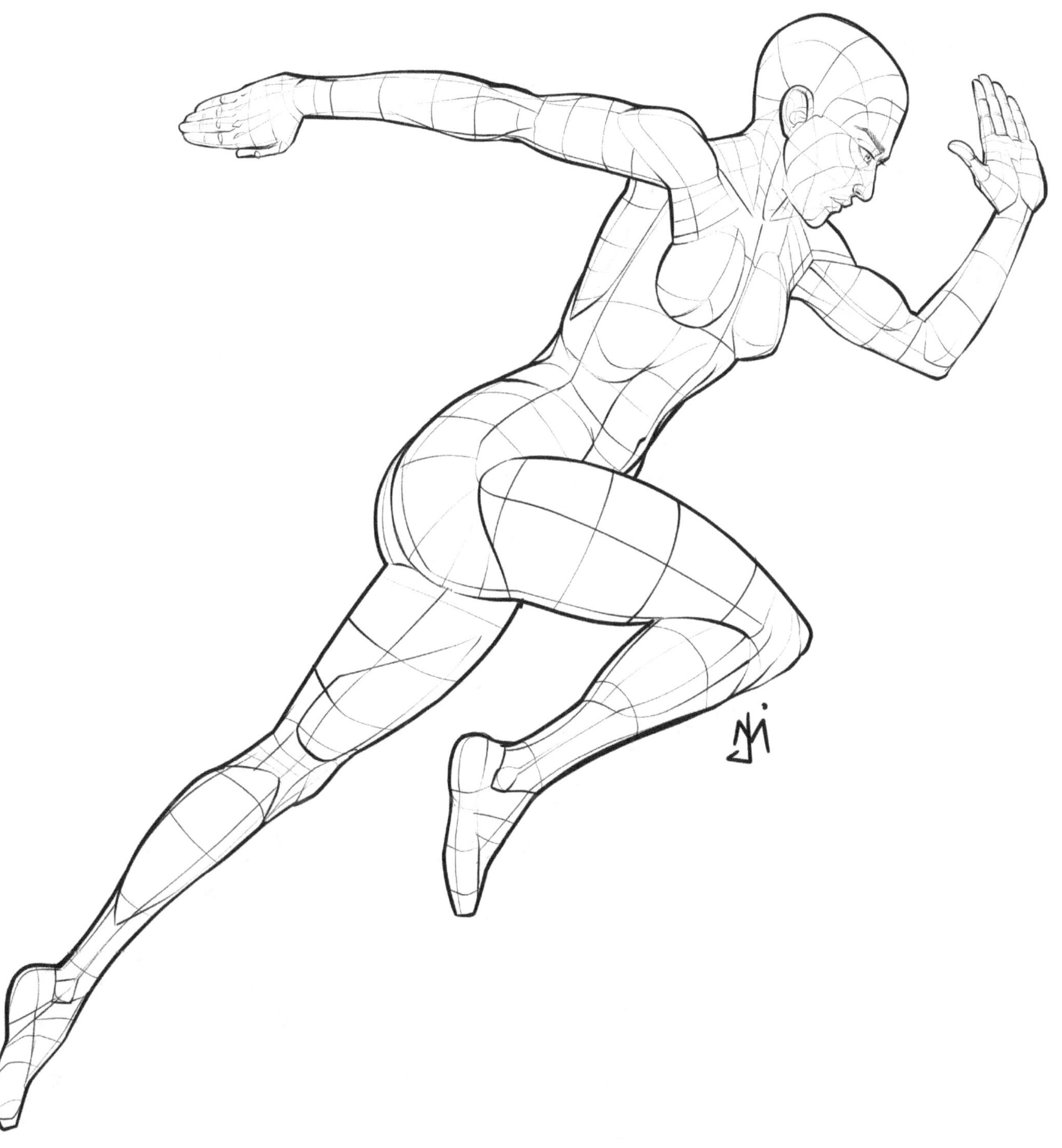

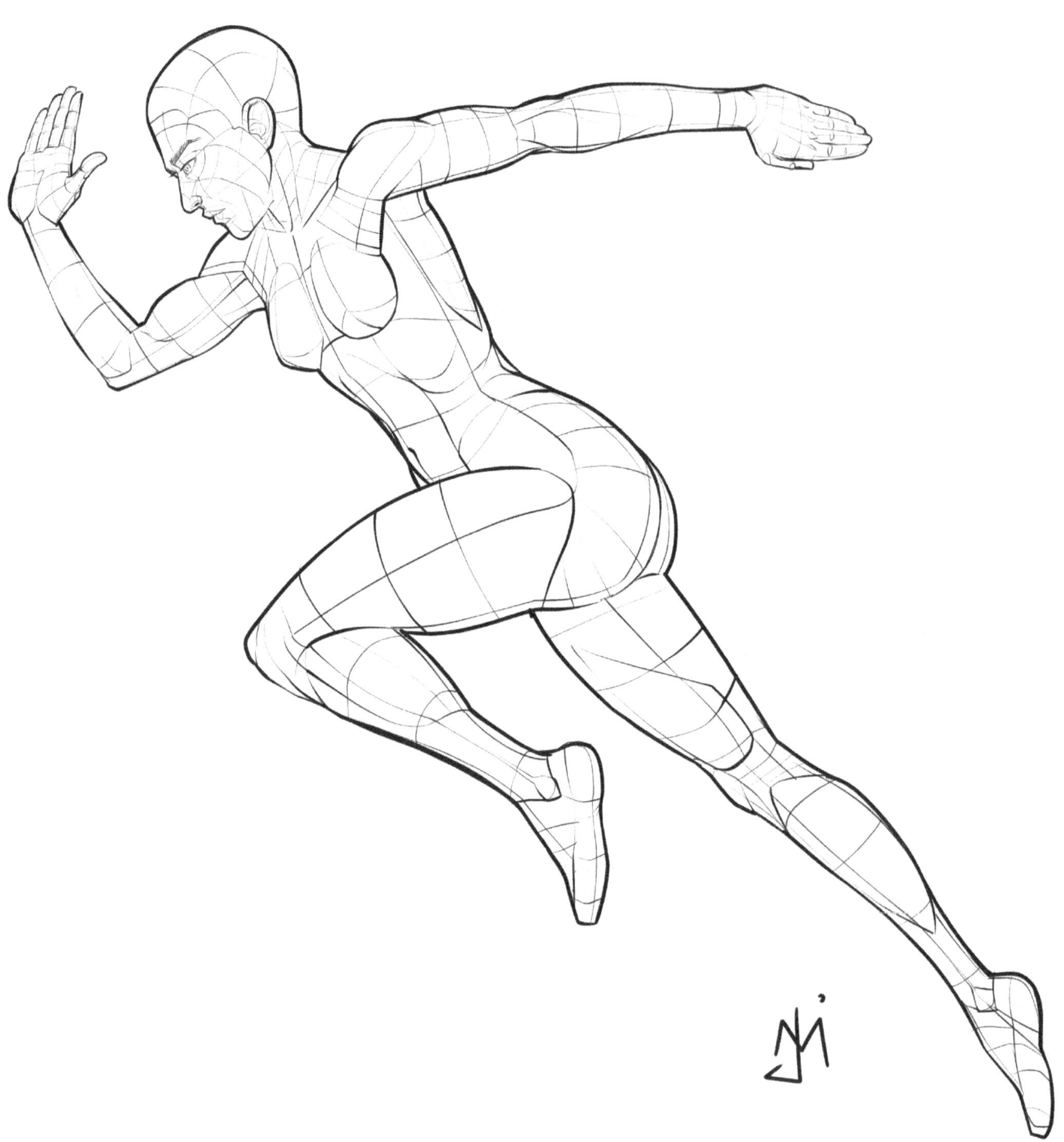

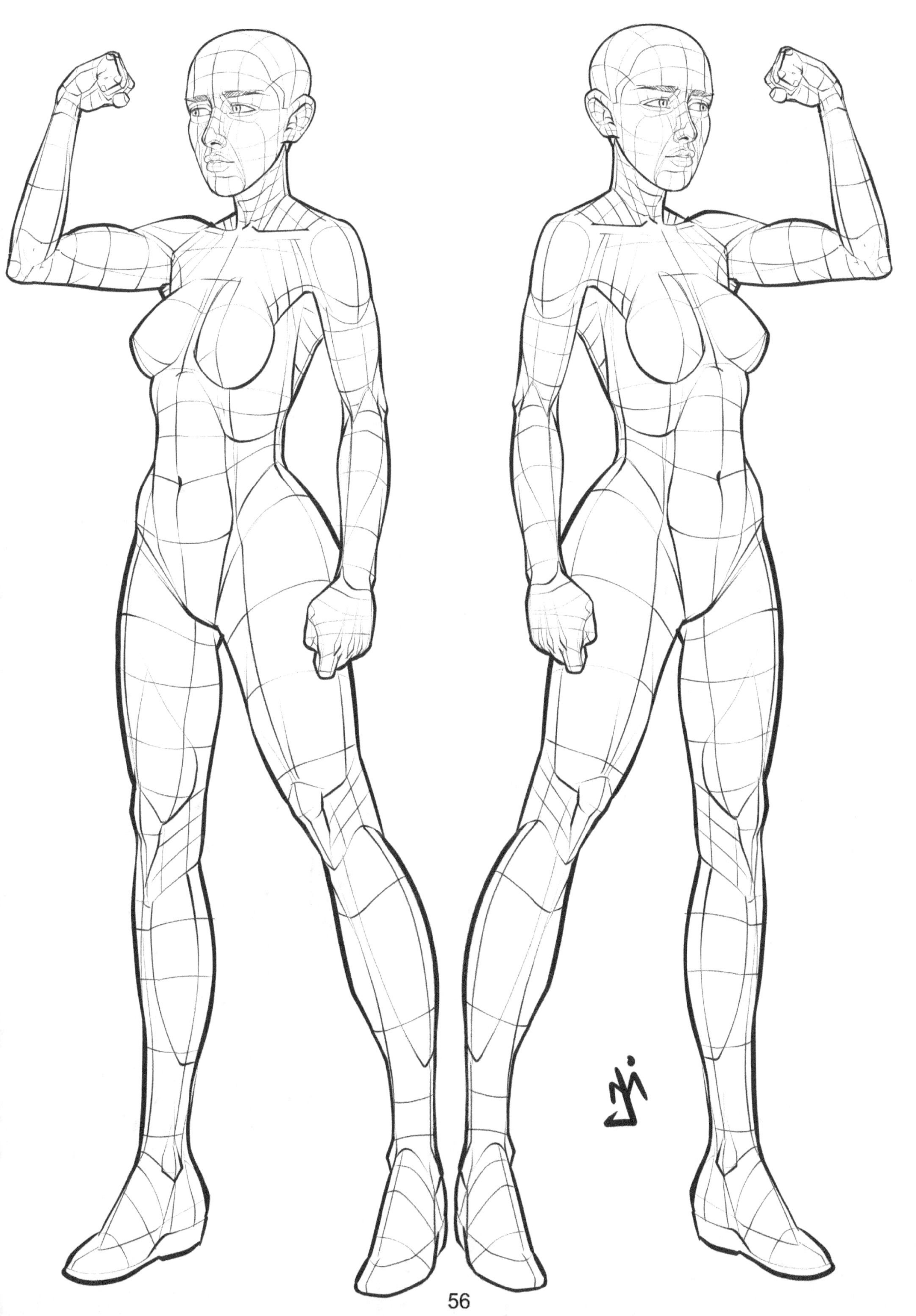

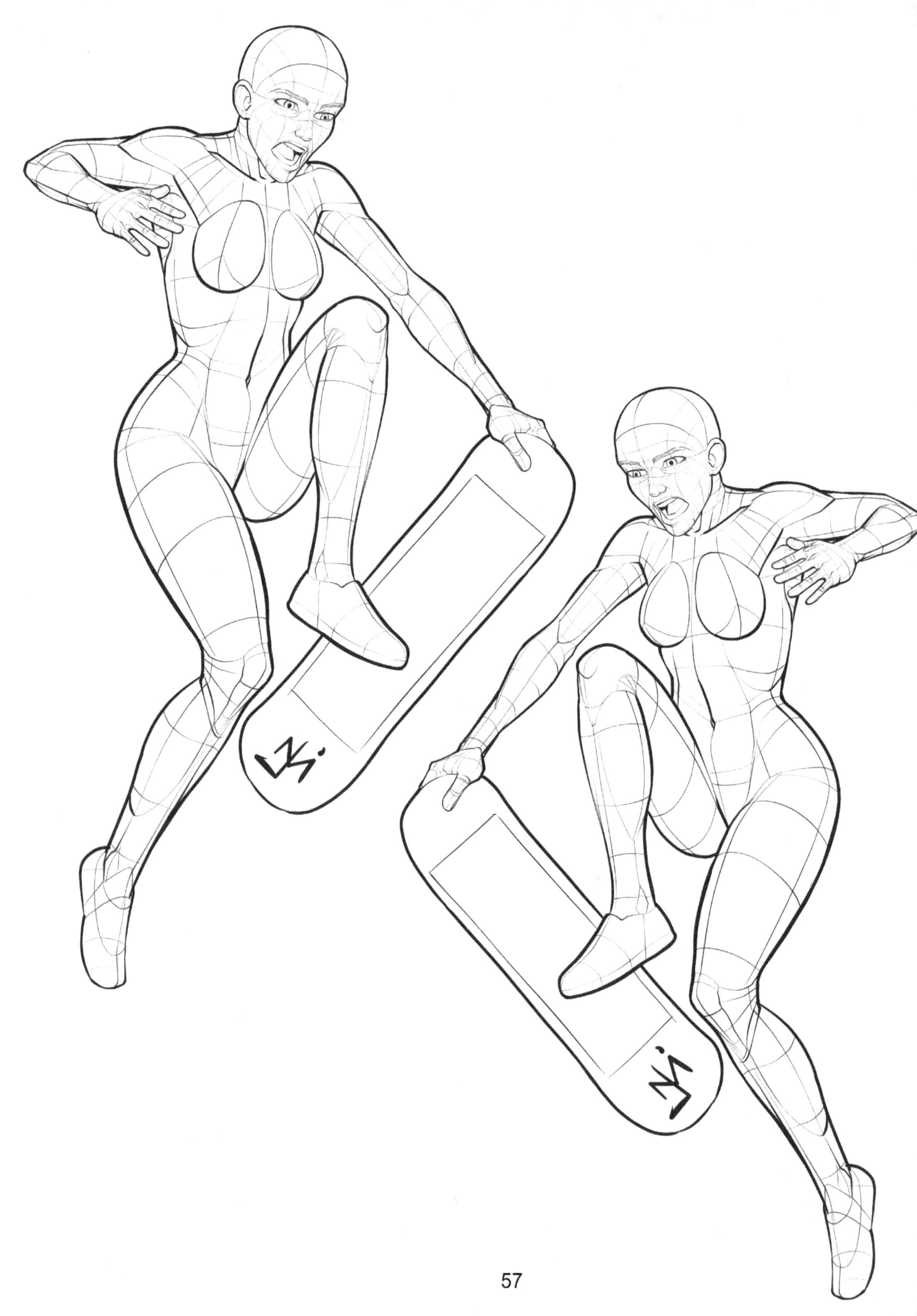

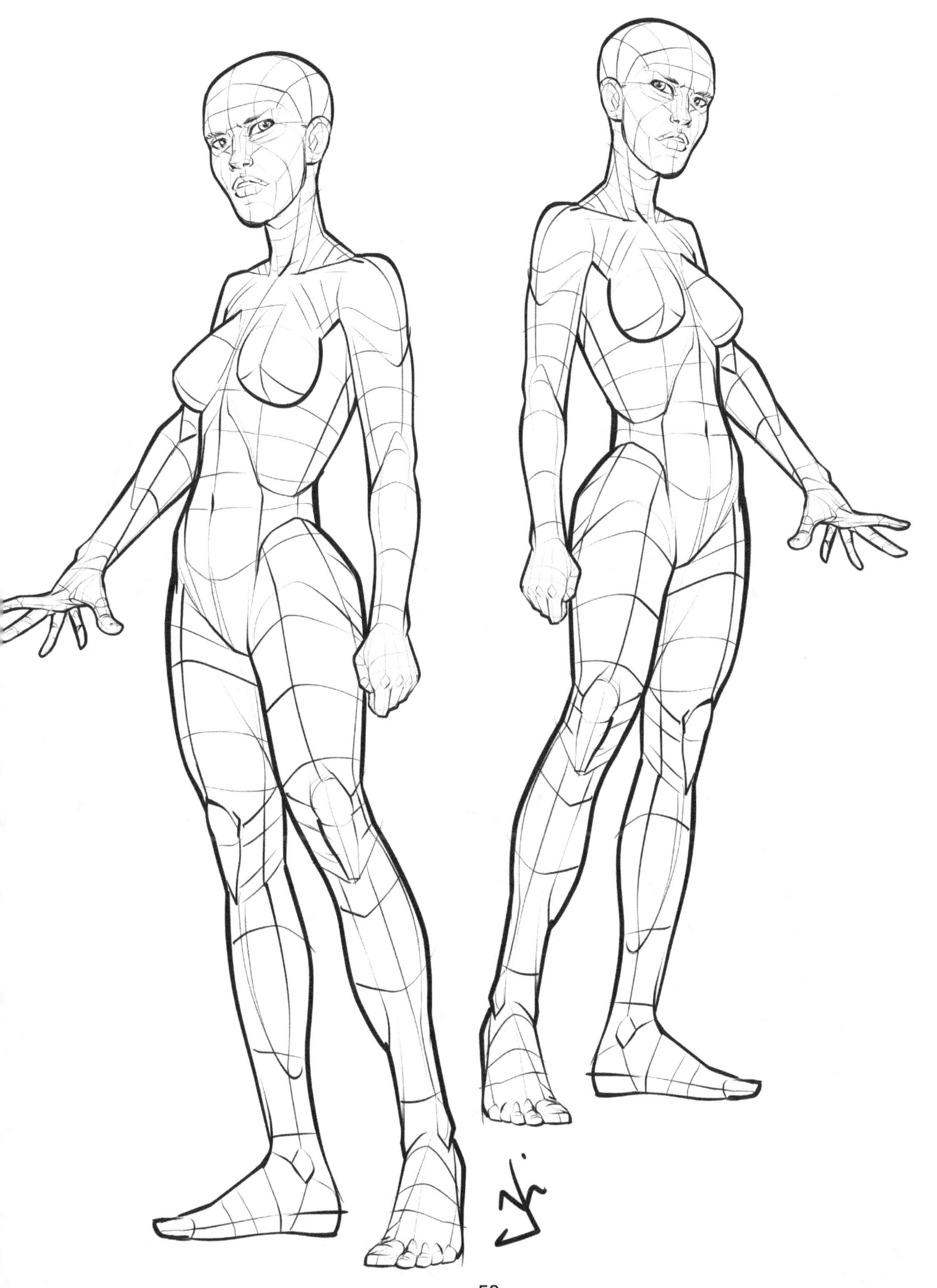

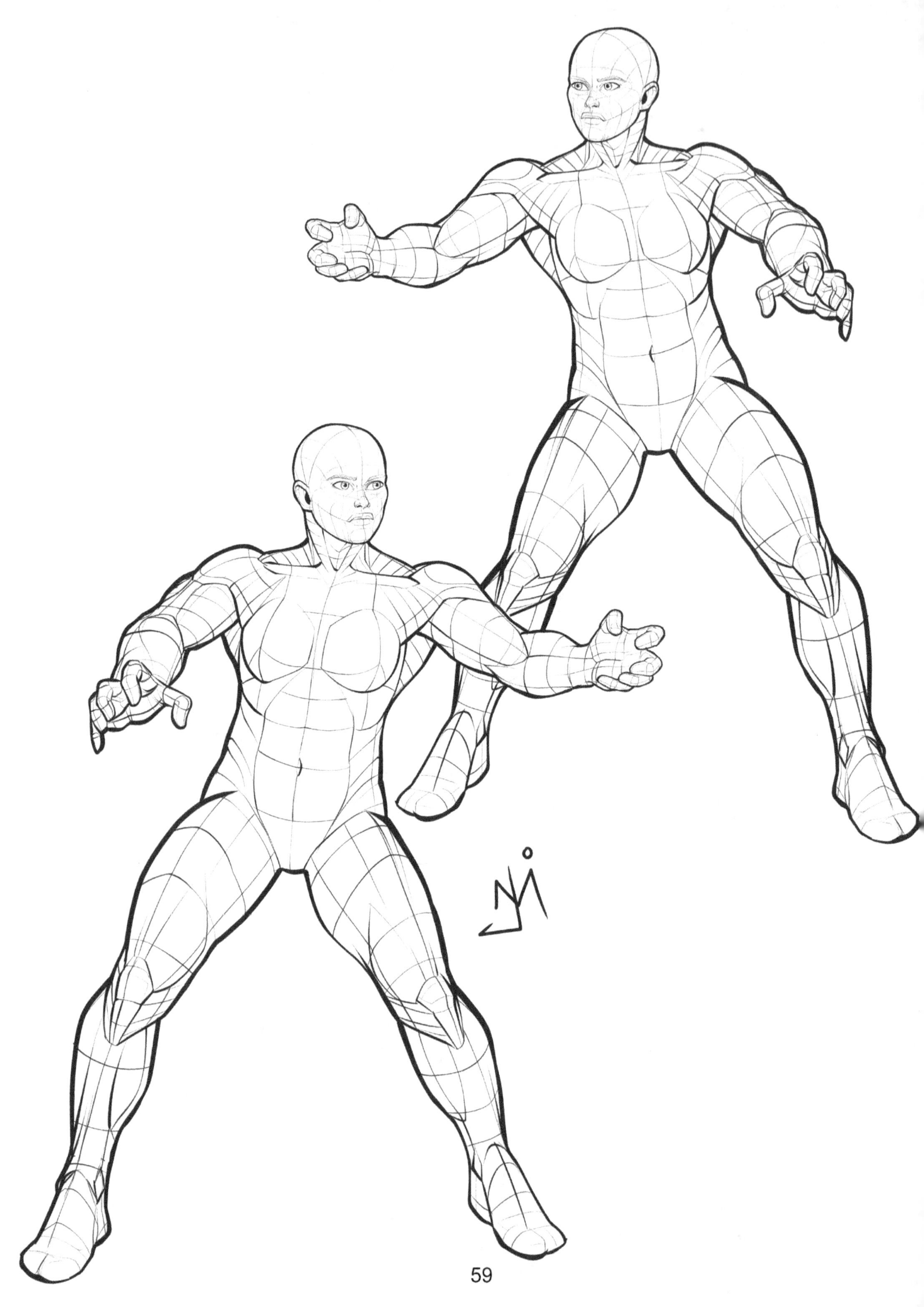

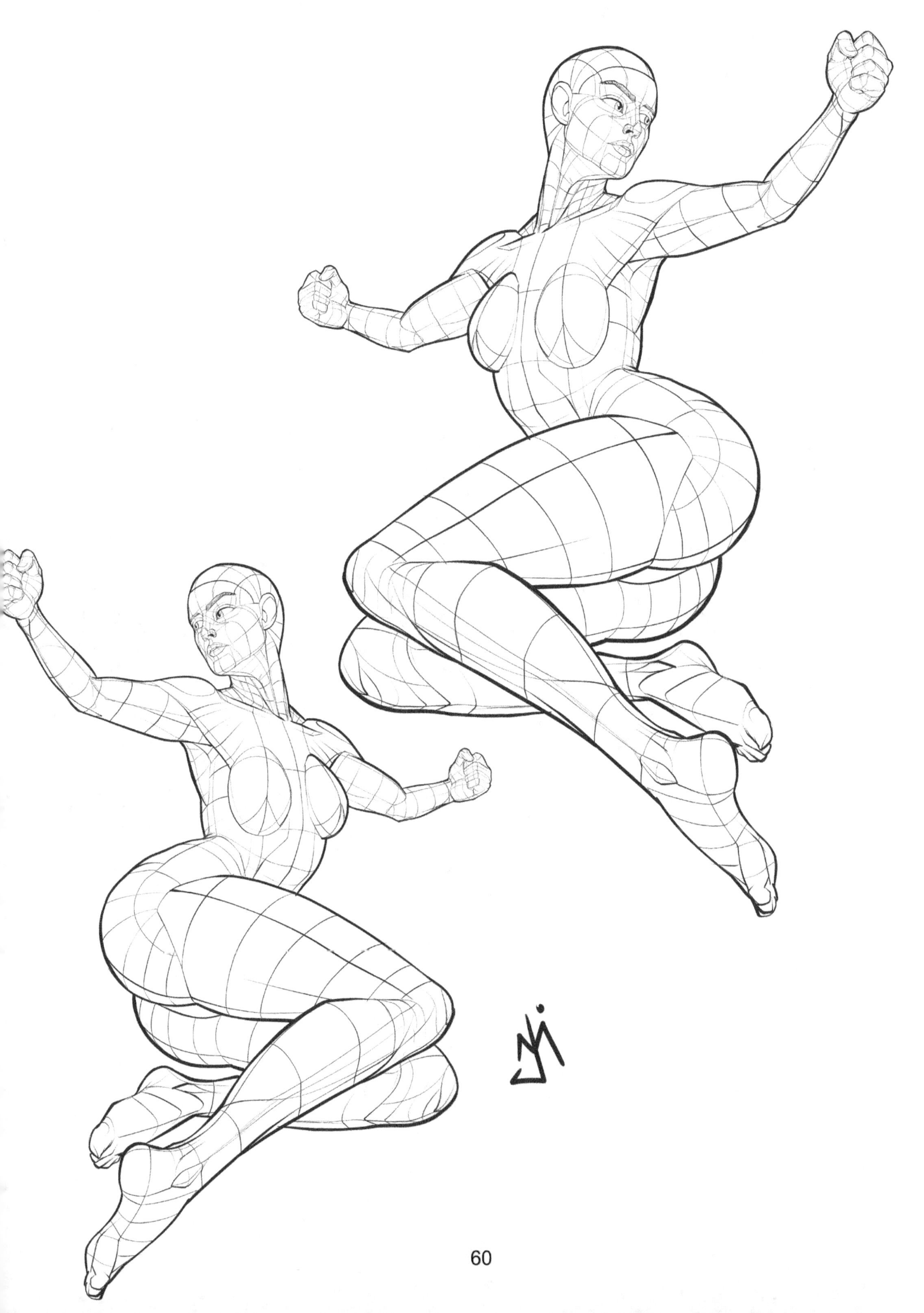

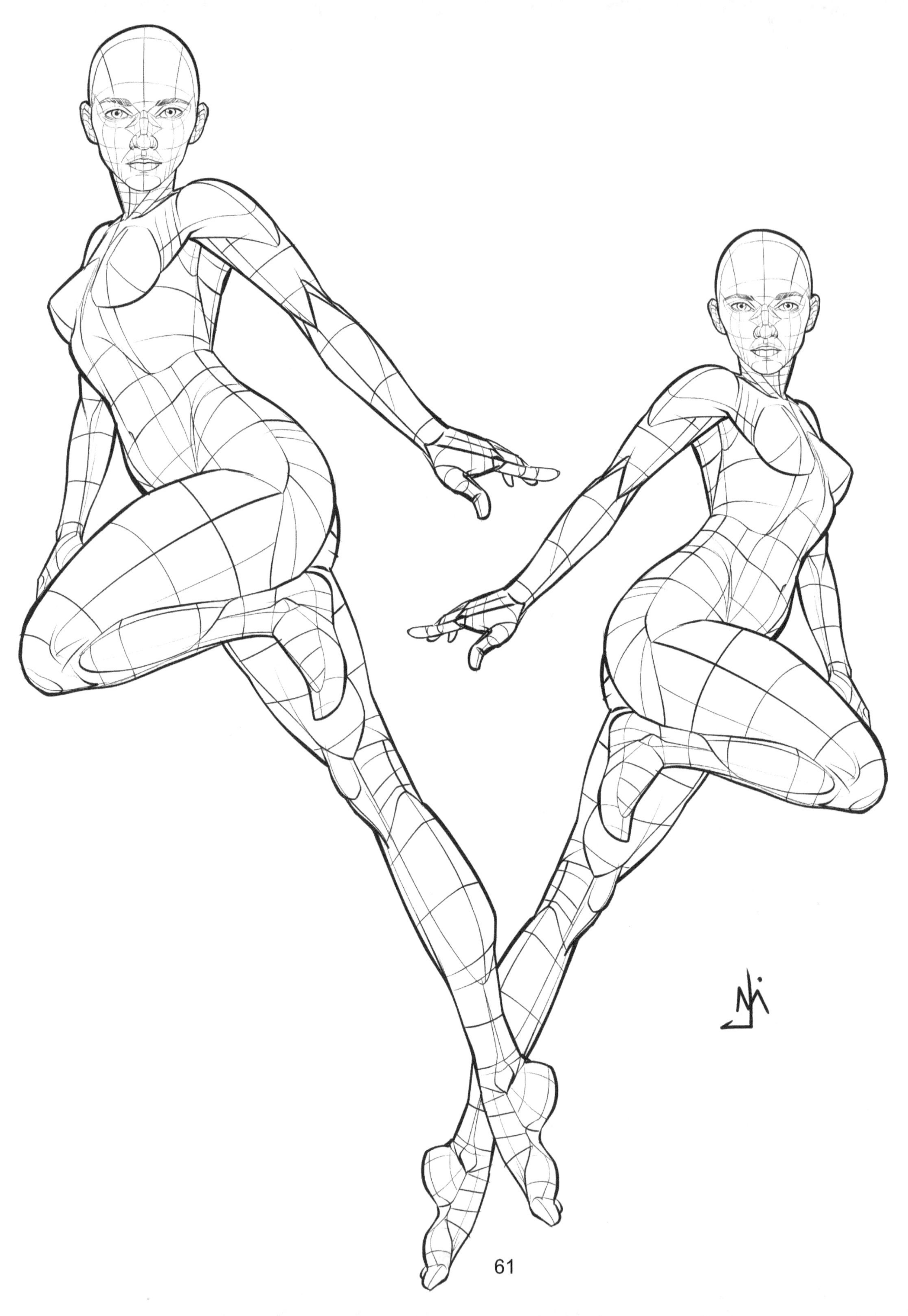

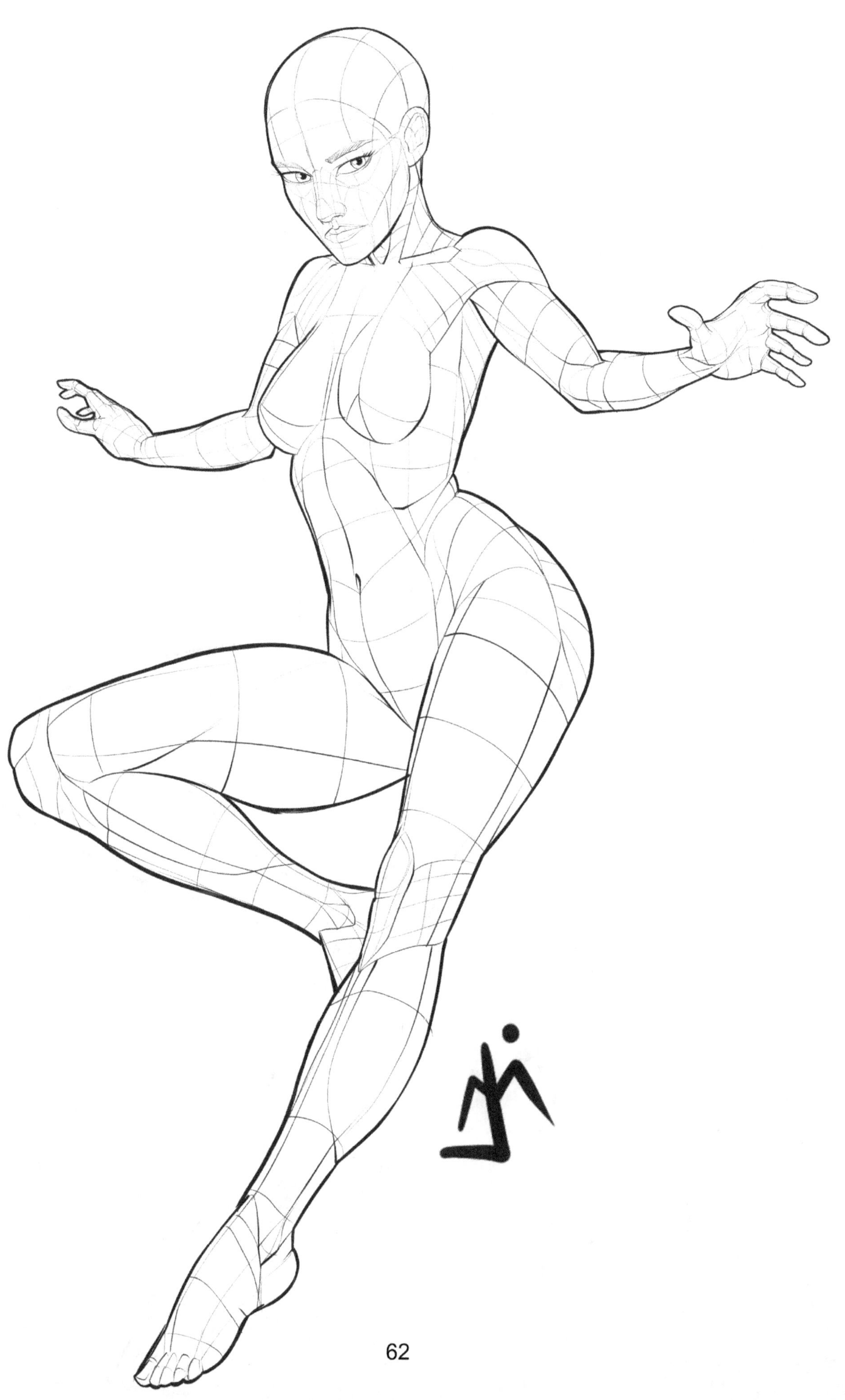

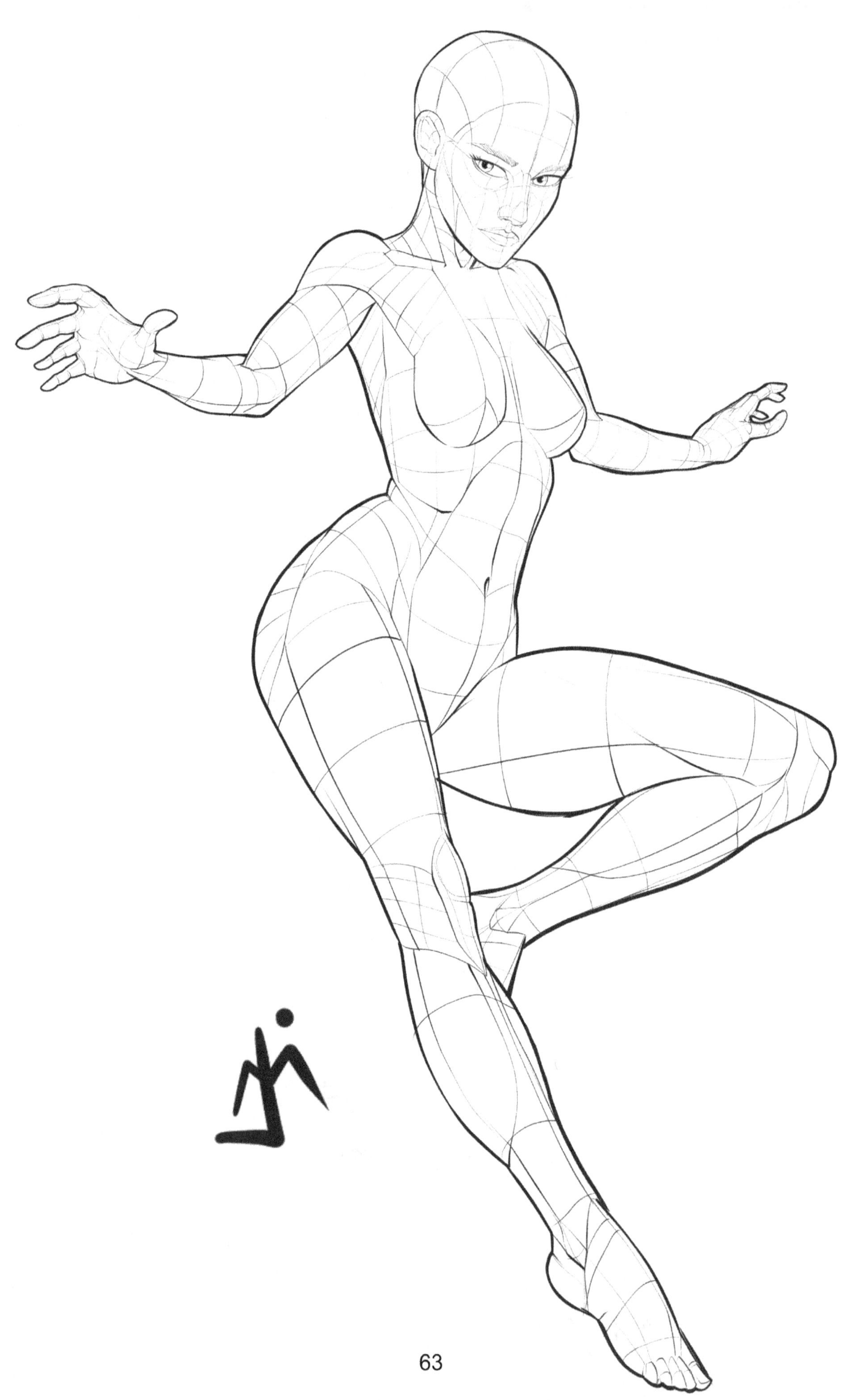

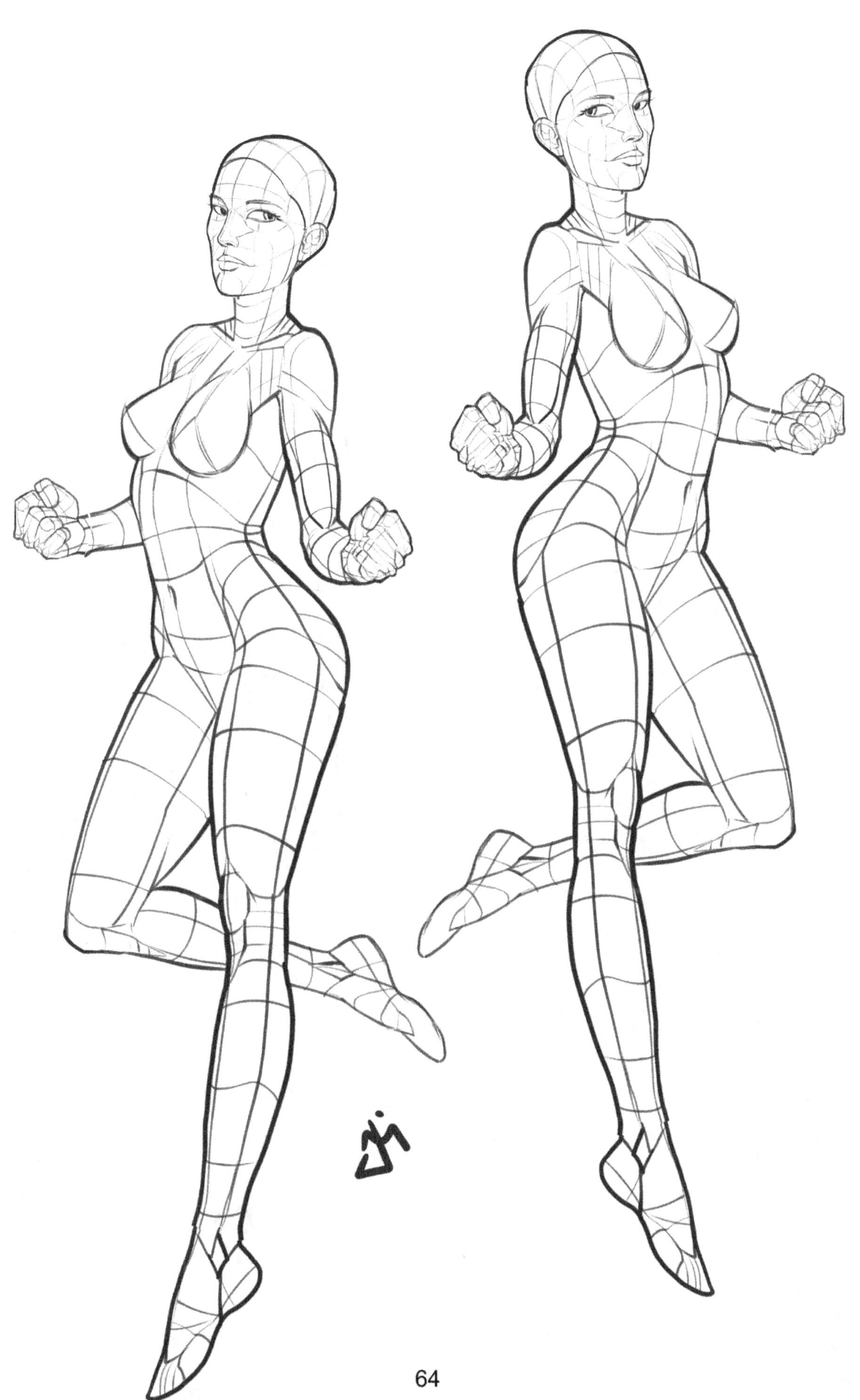

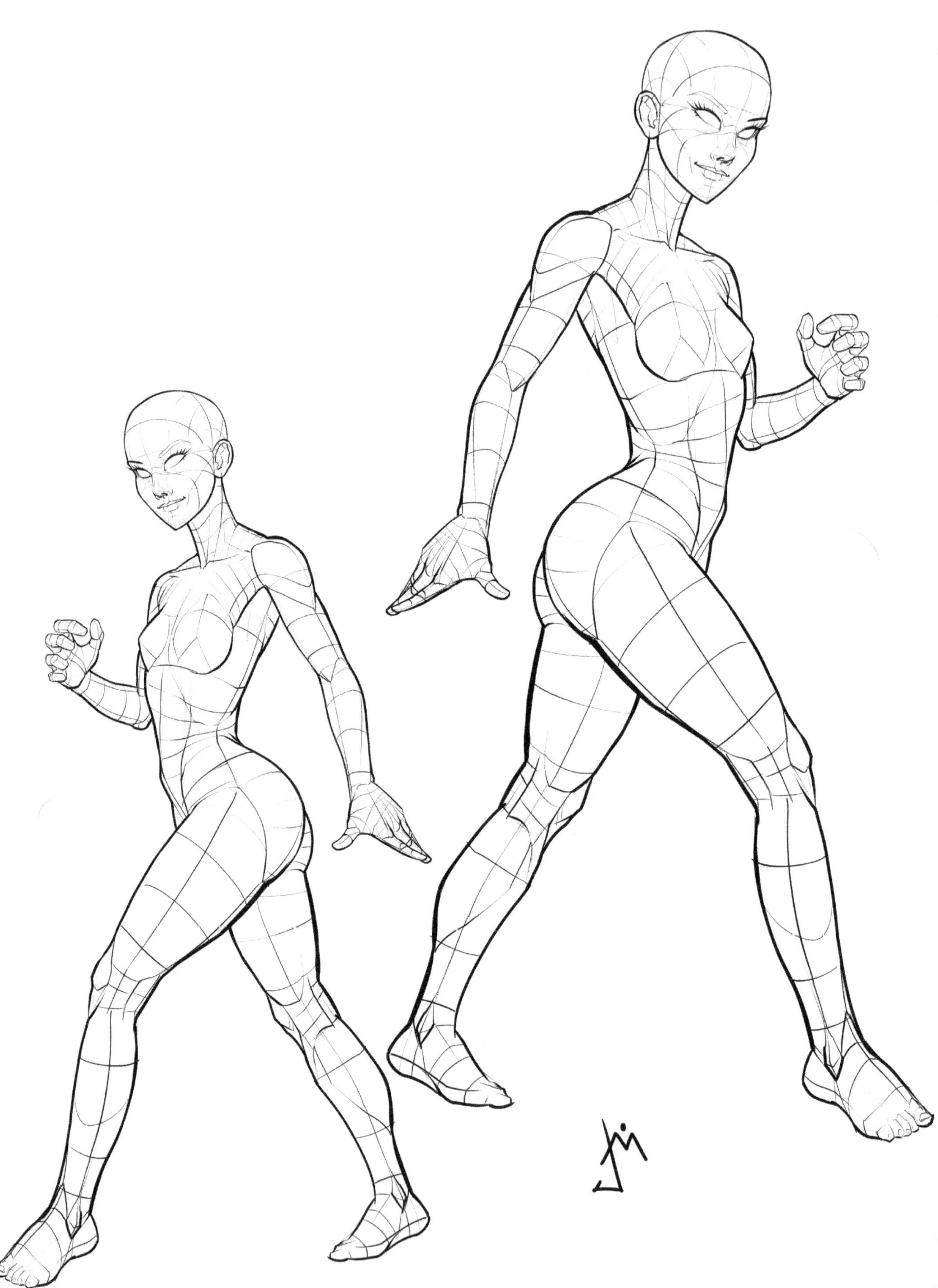

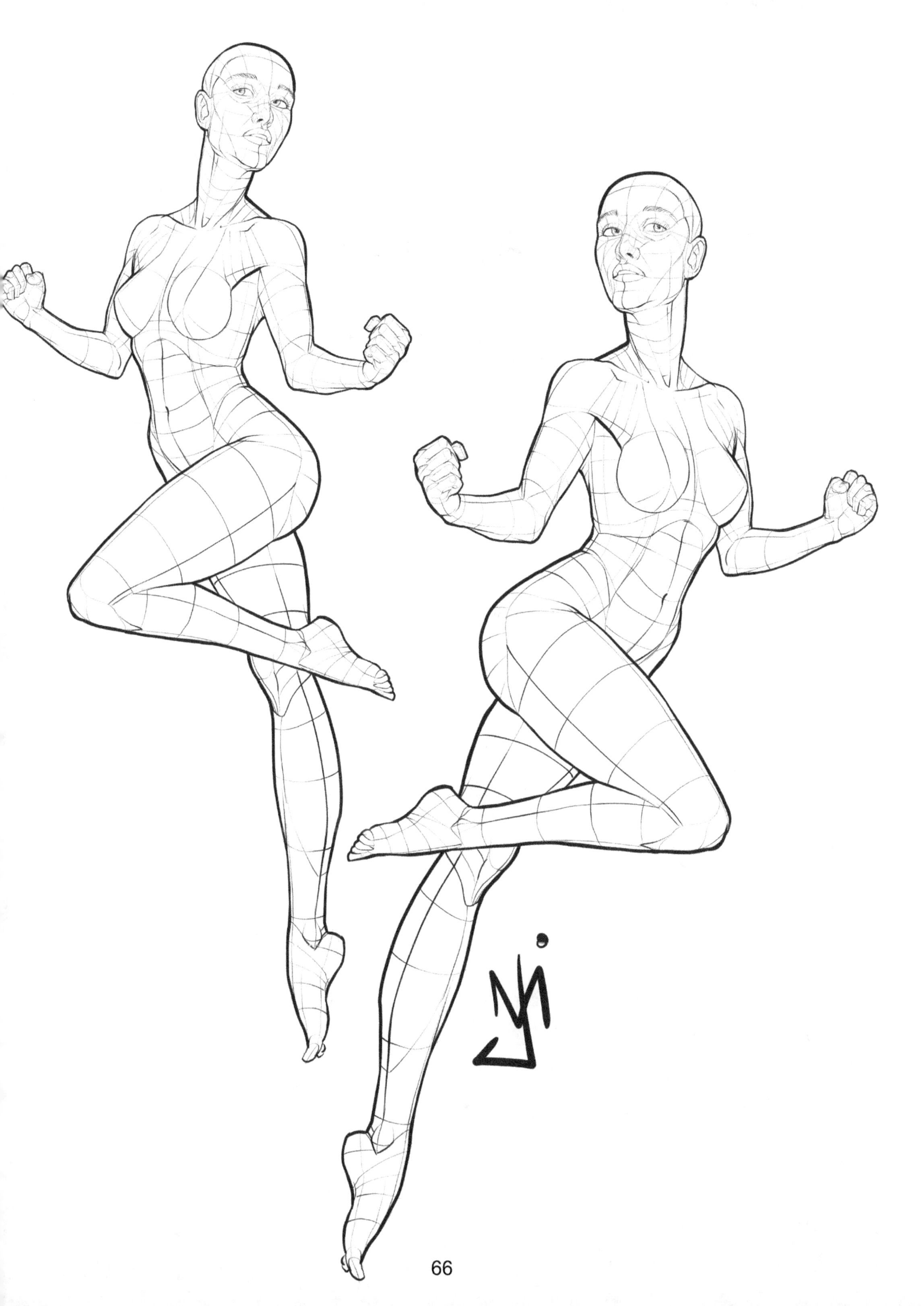

Part Two
Masculine

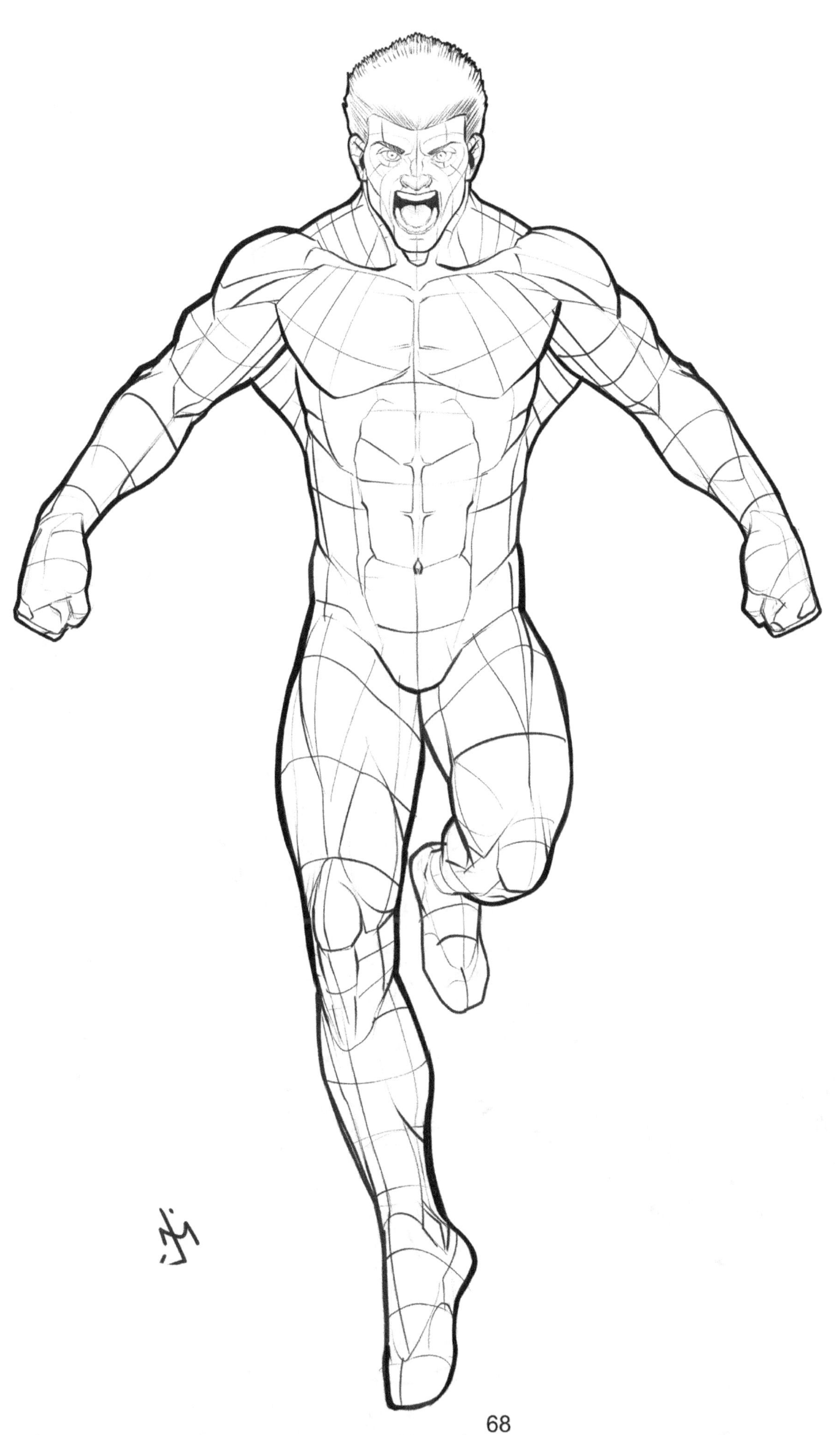

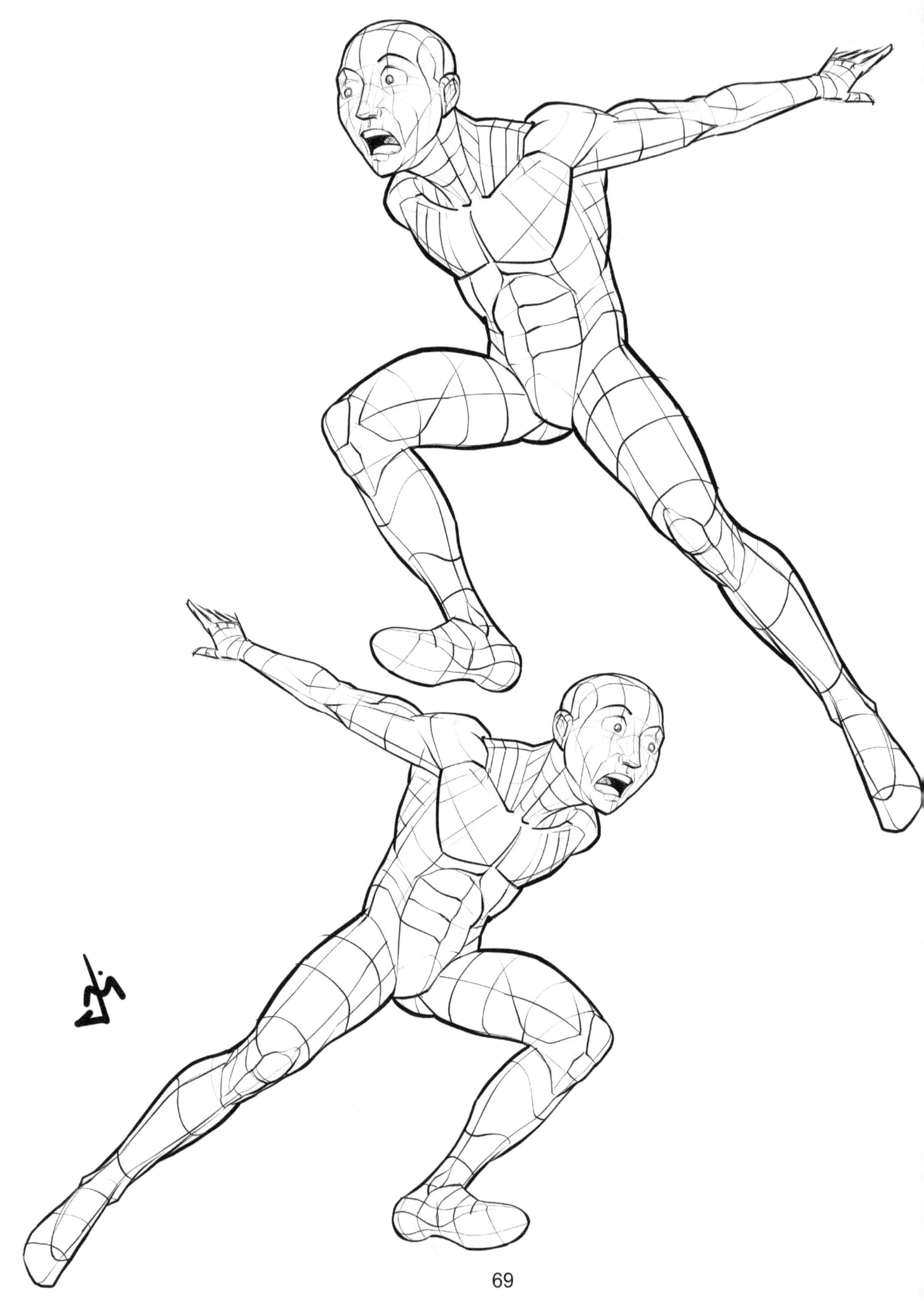

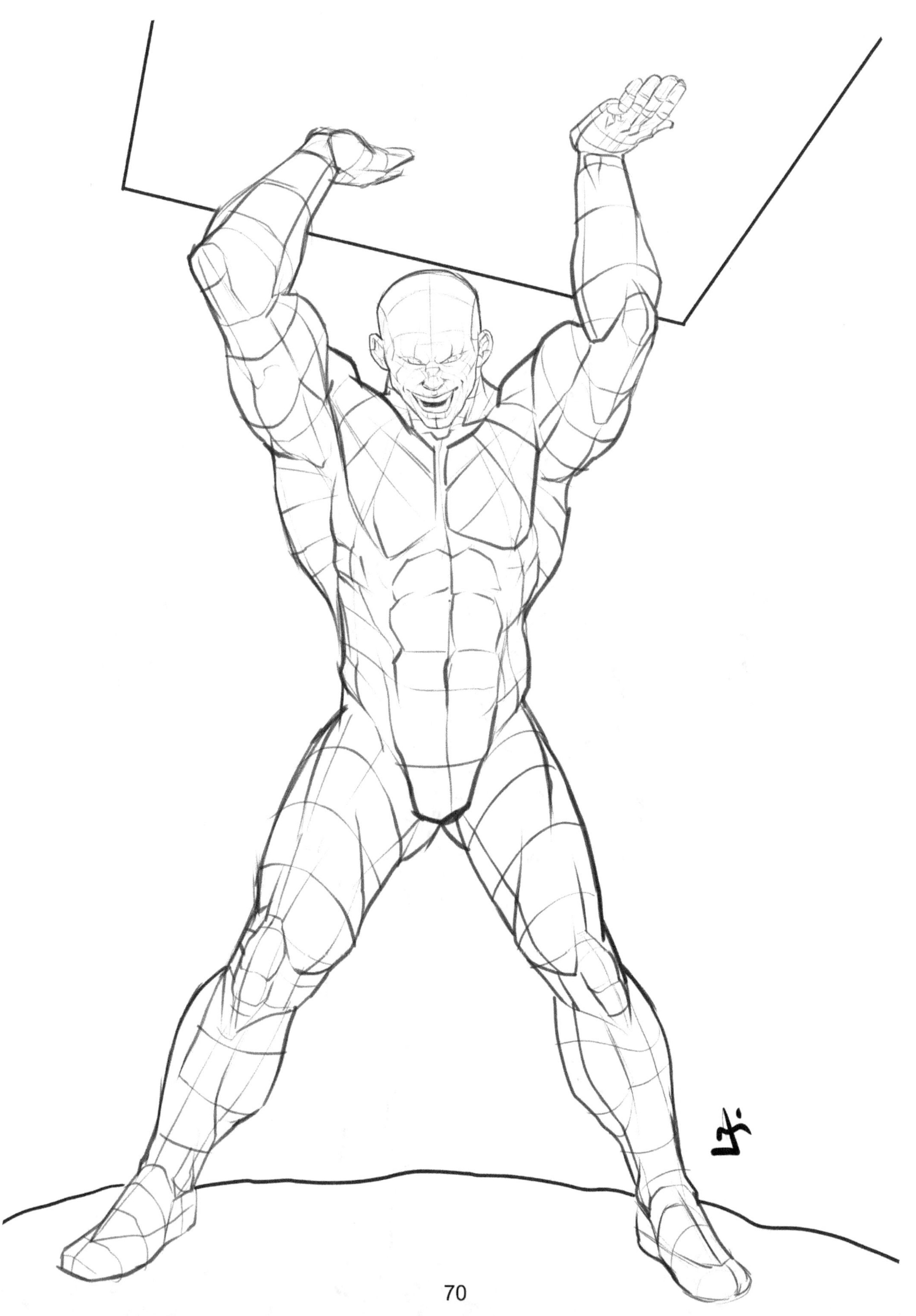

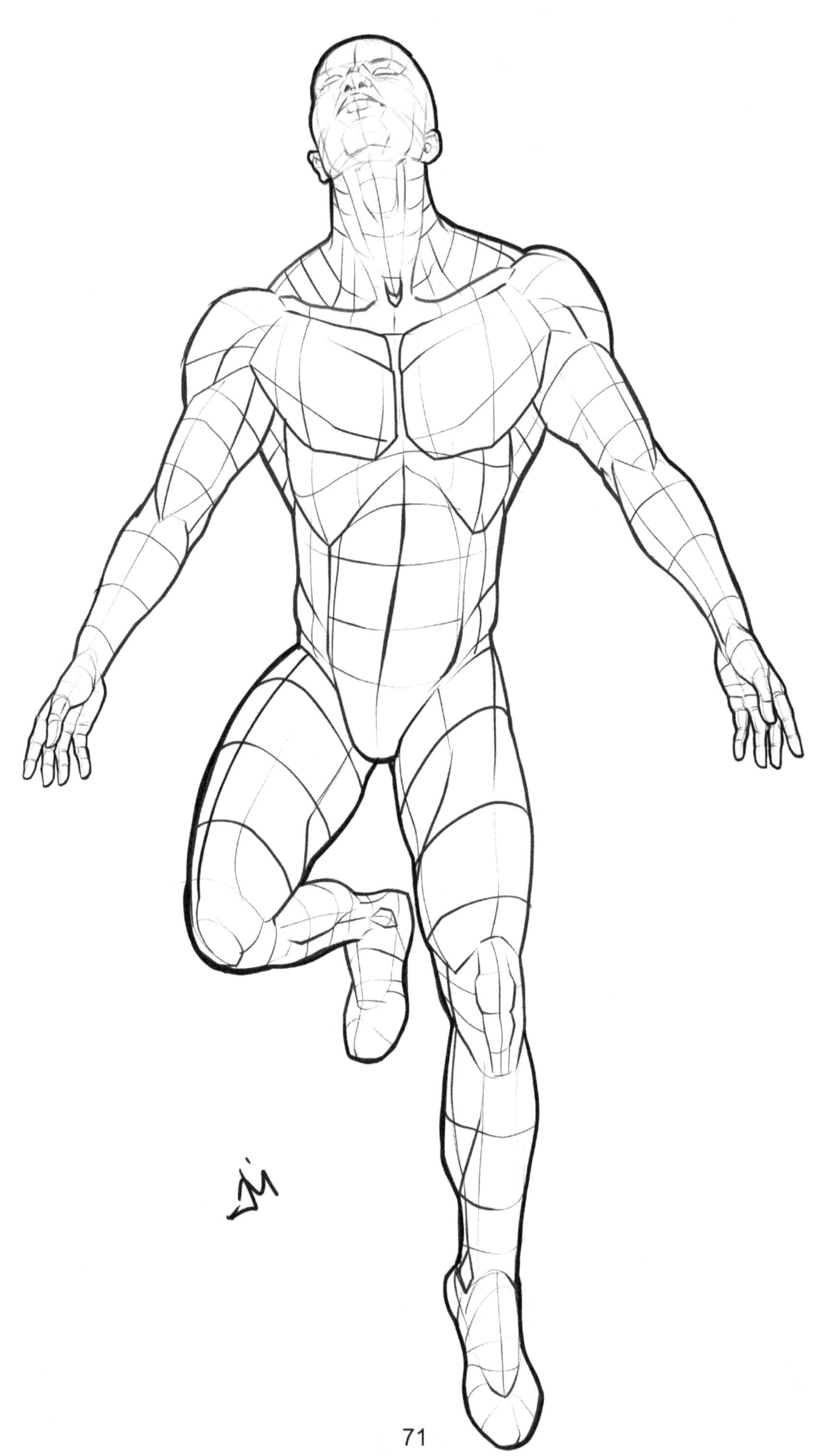

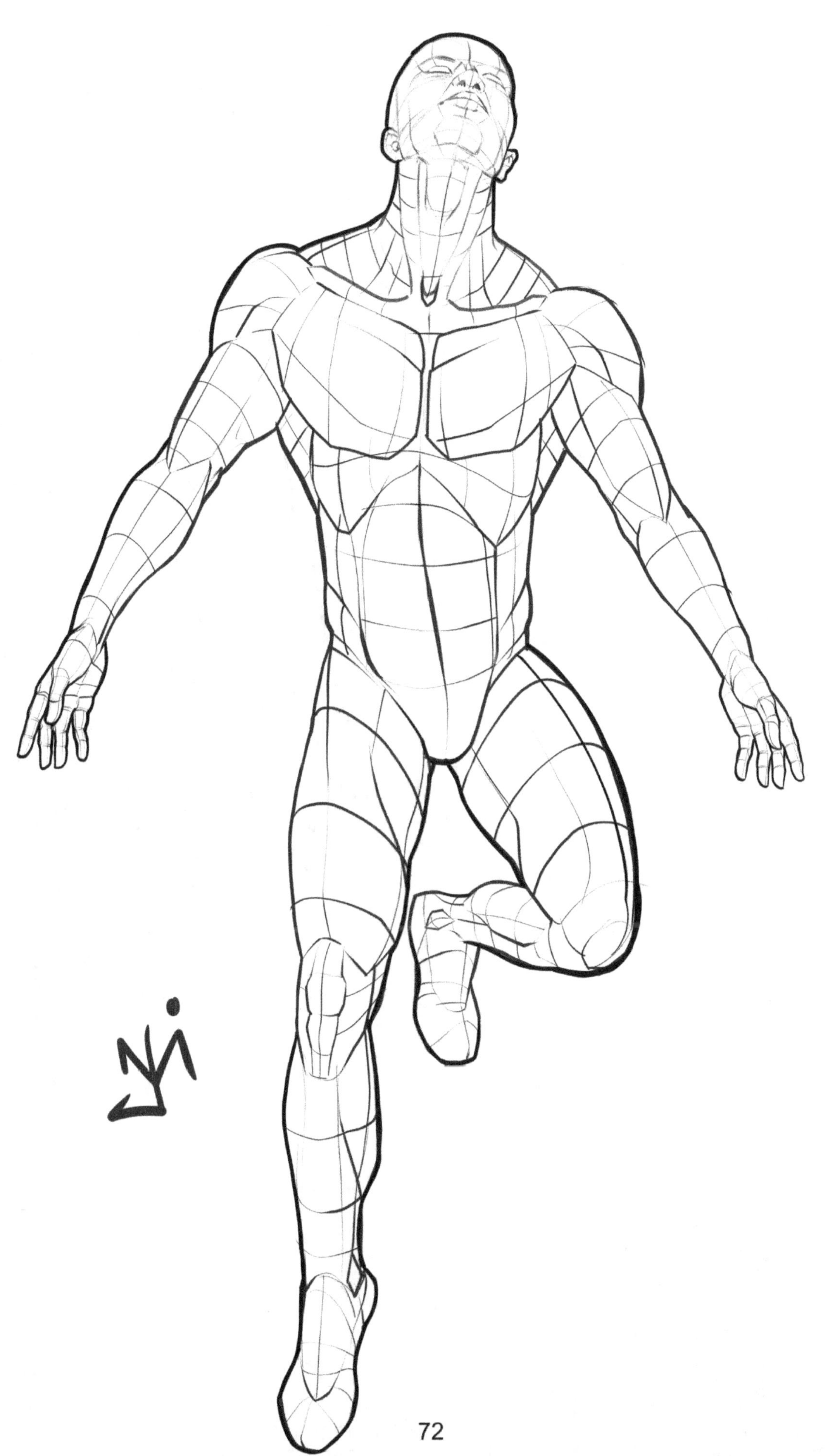

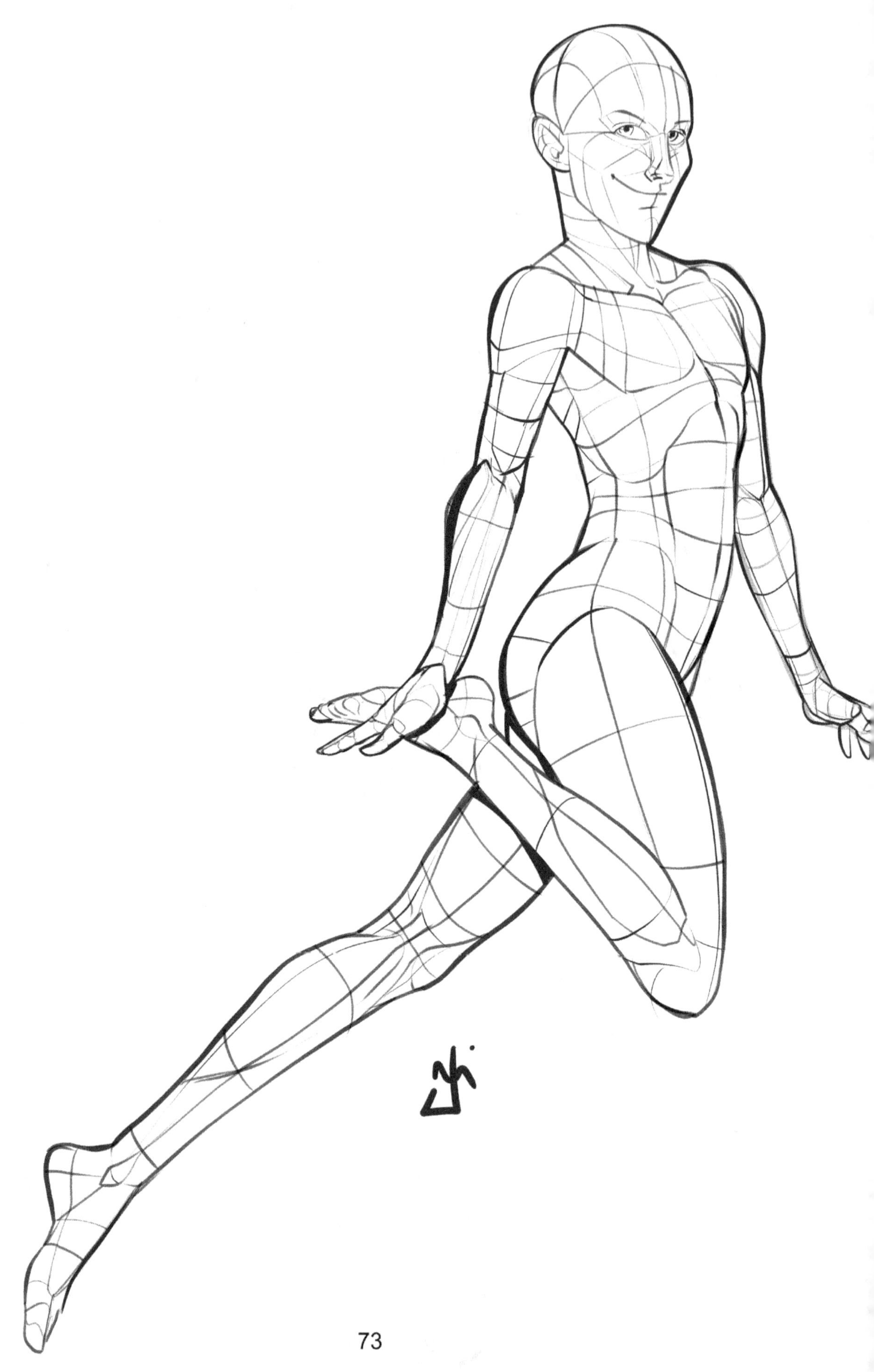

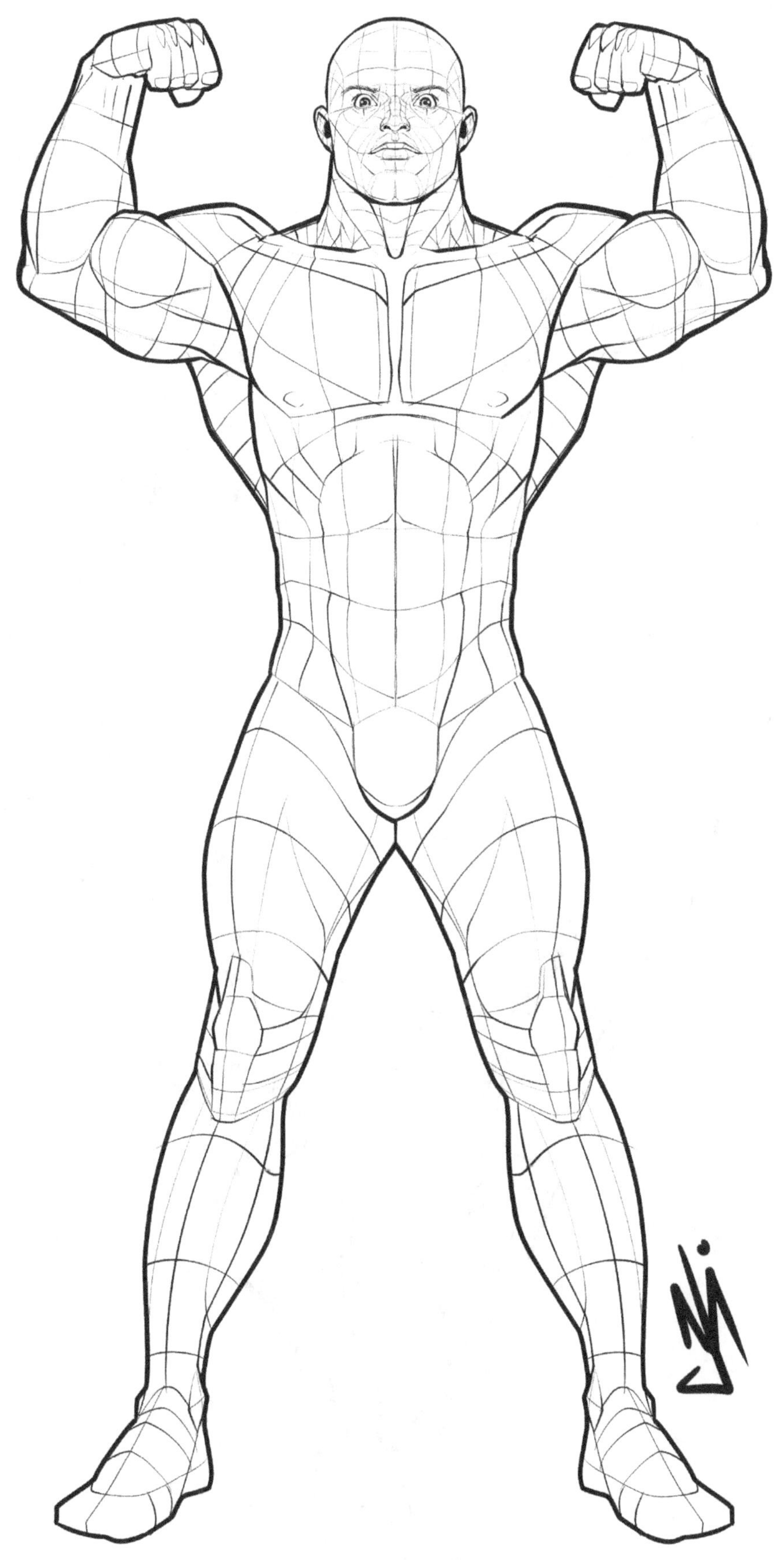

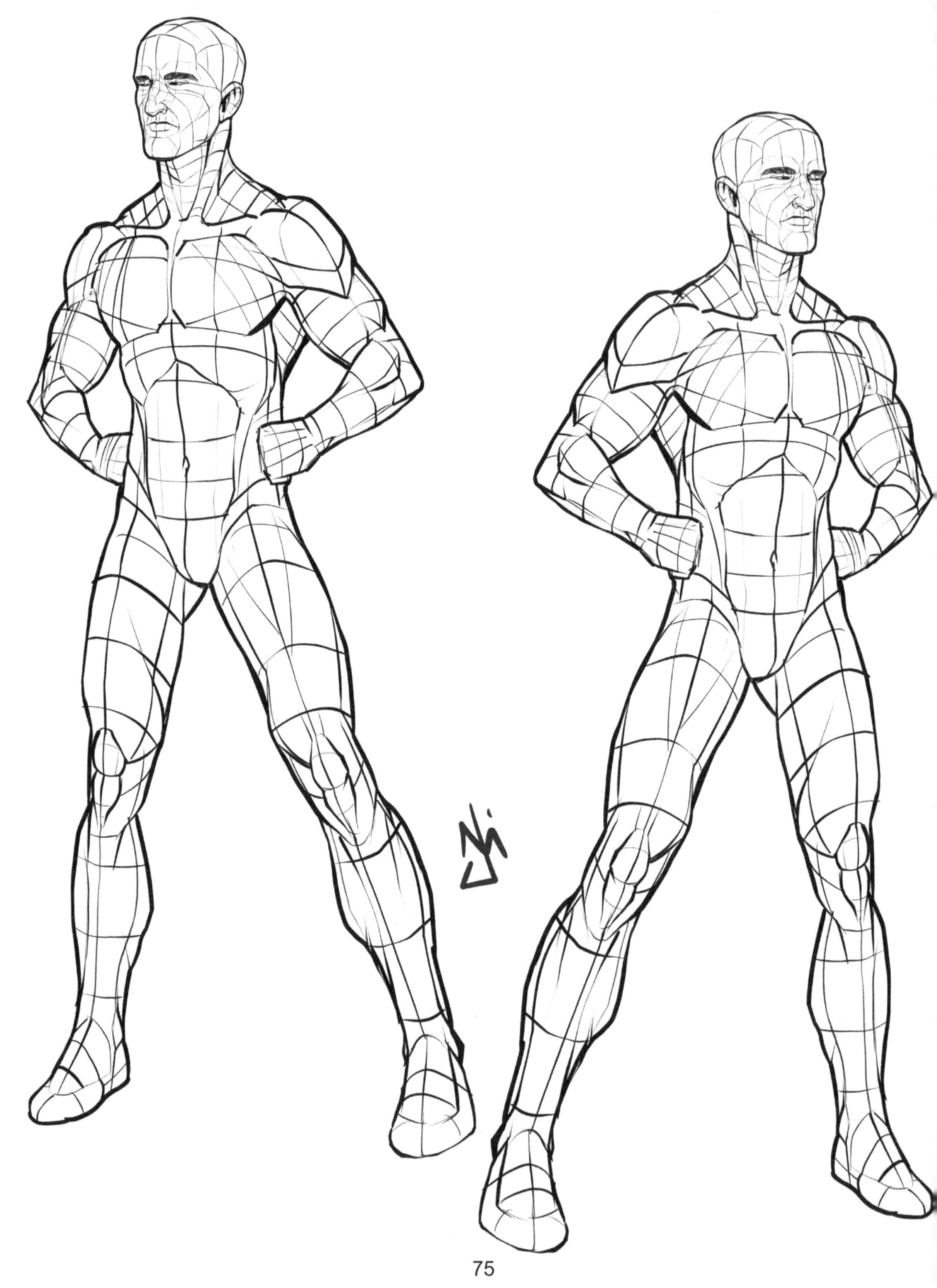

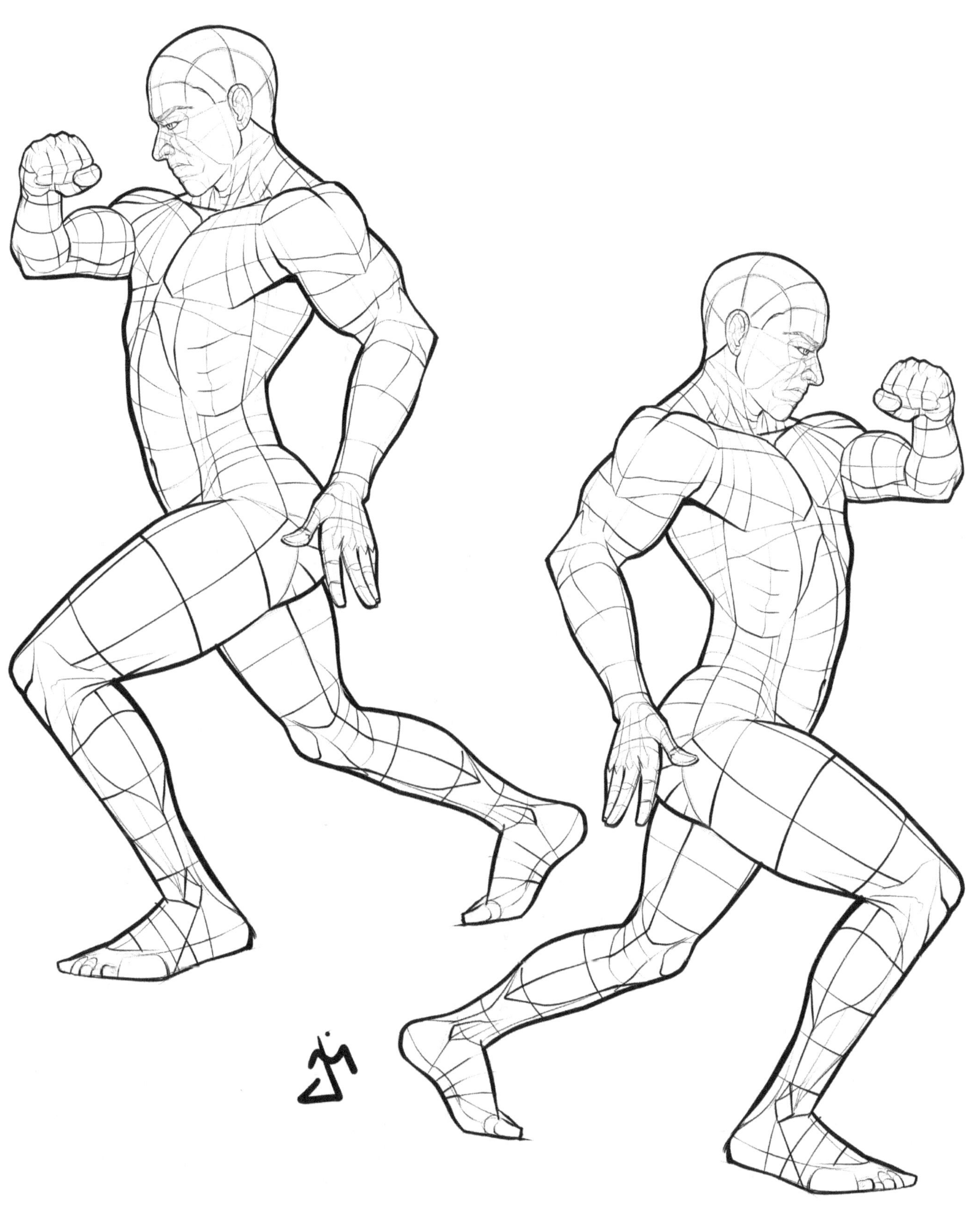

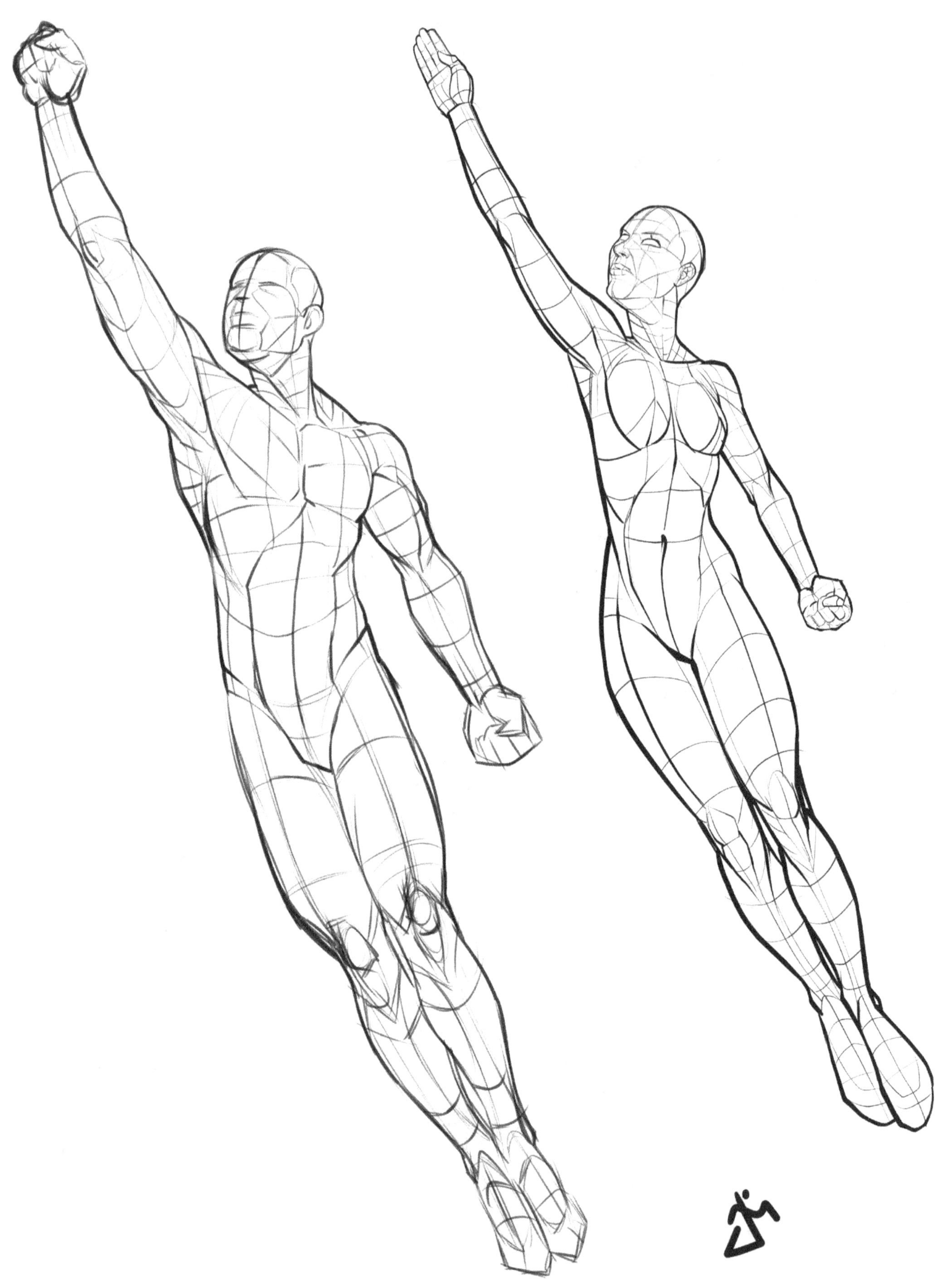

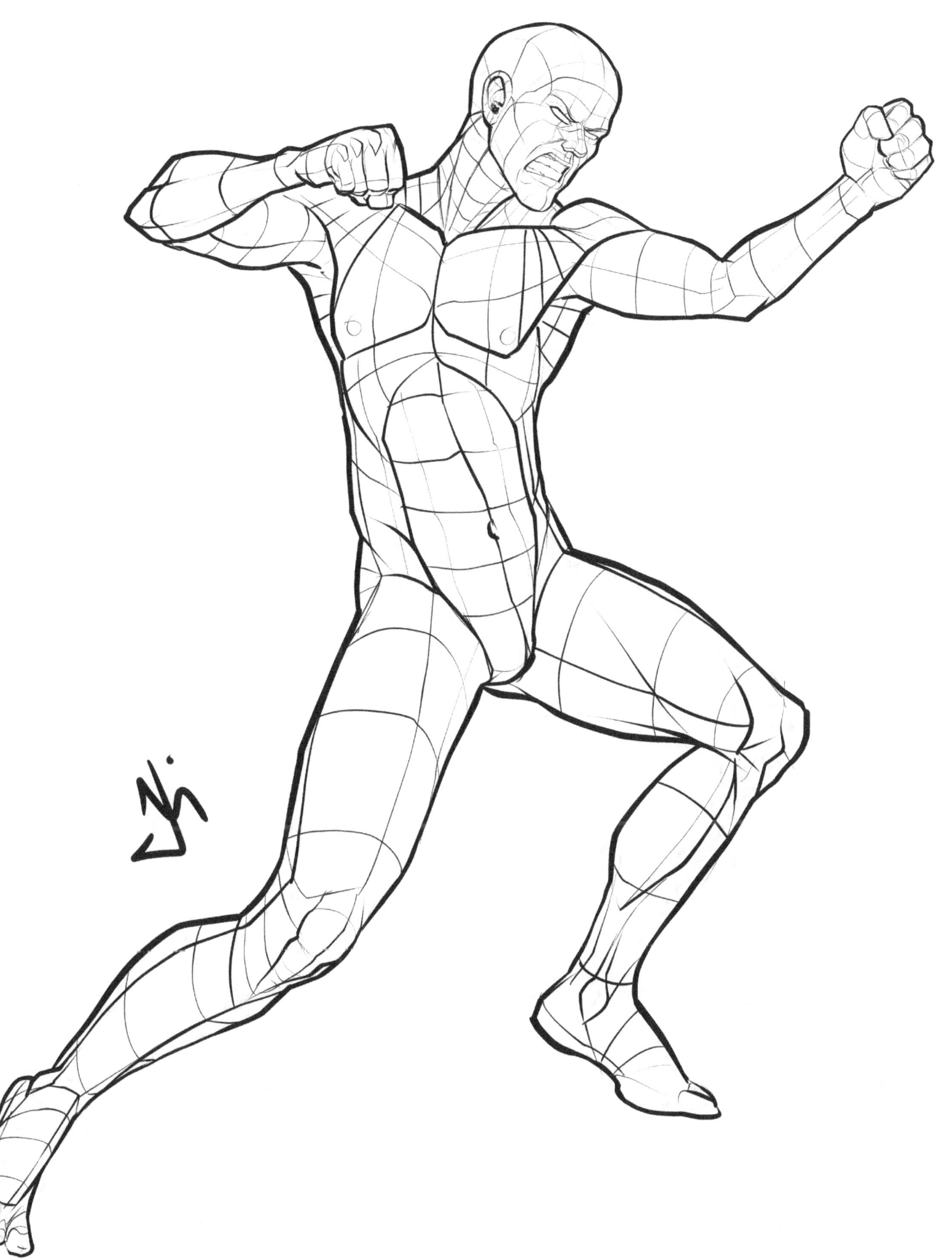

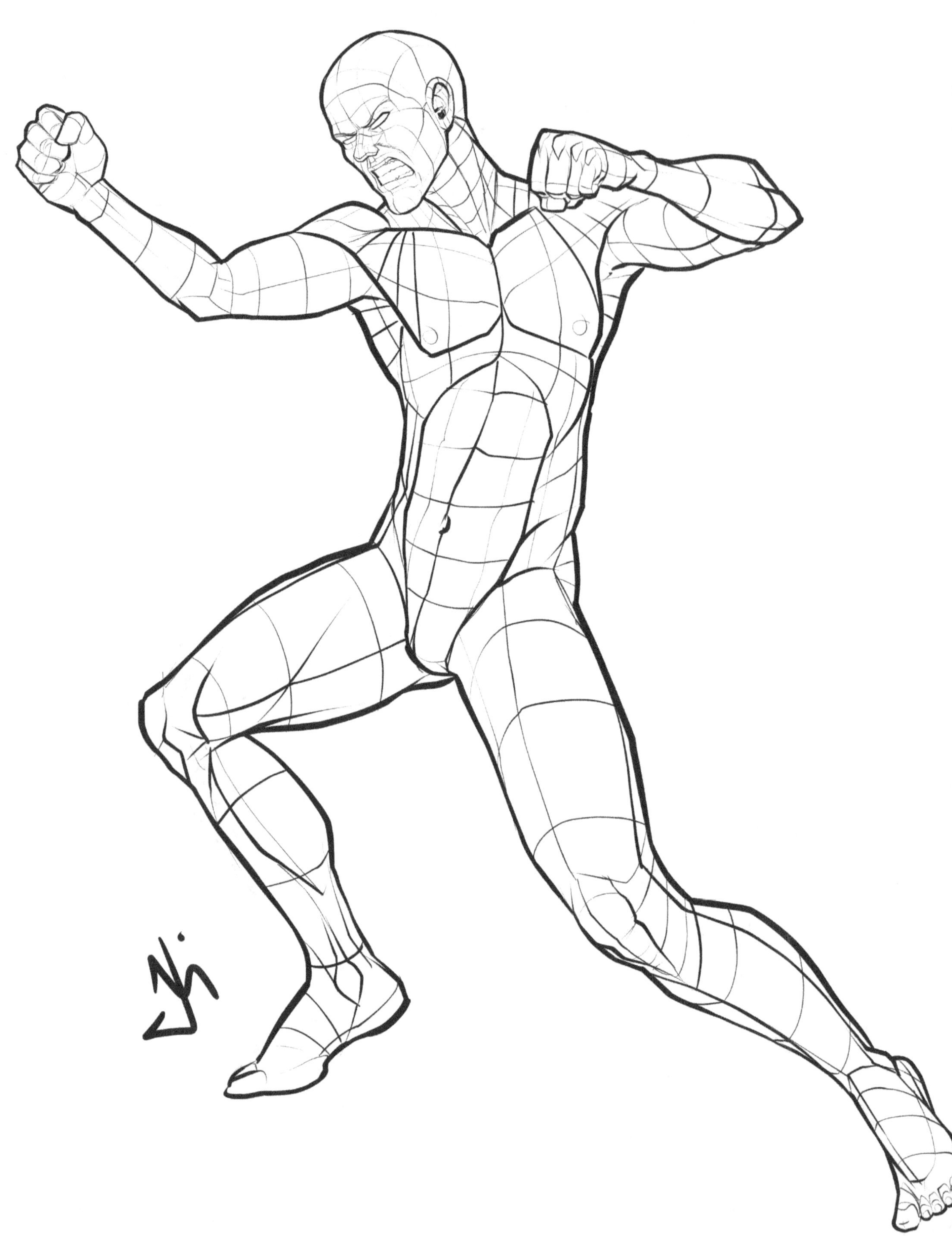

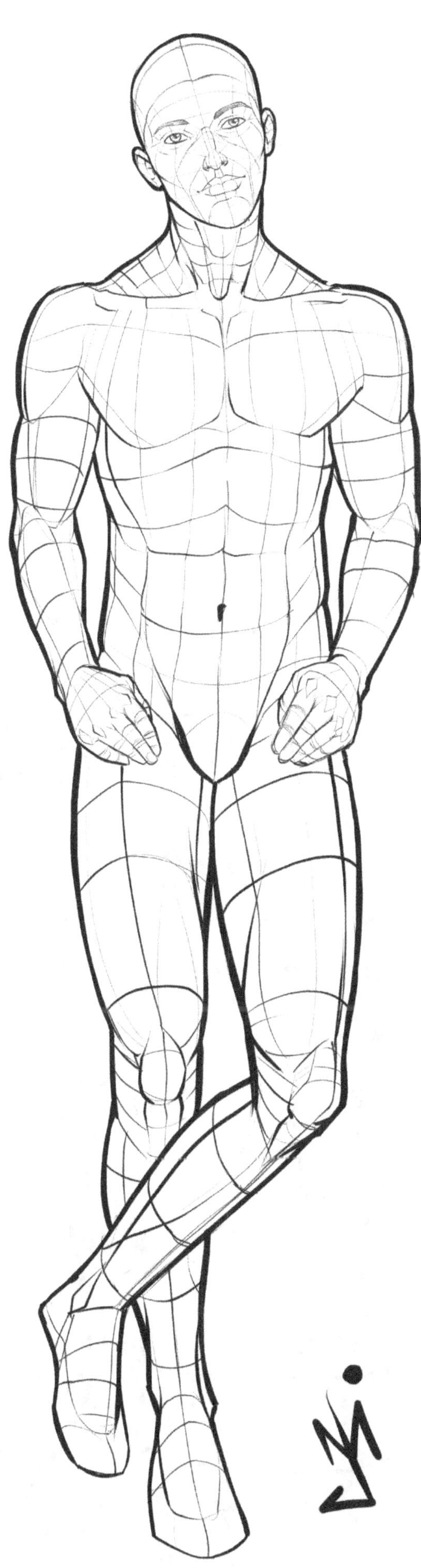
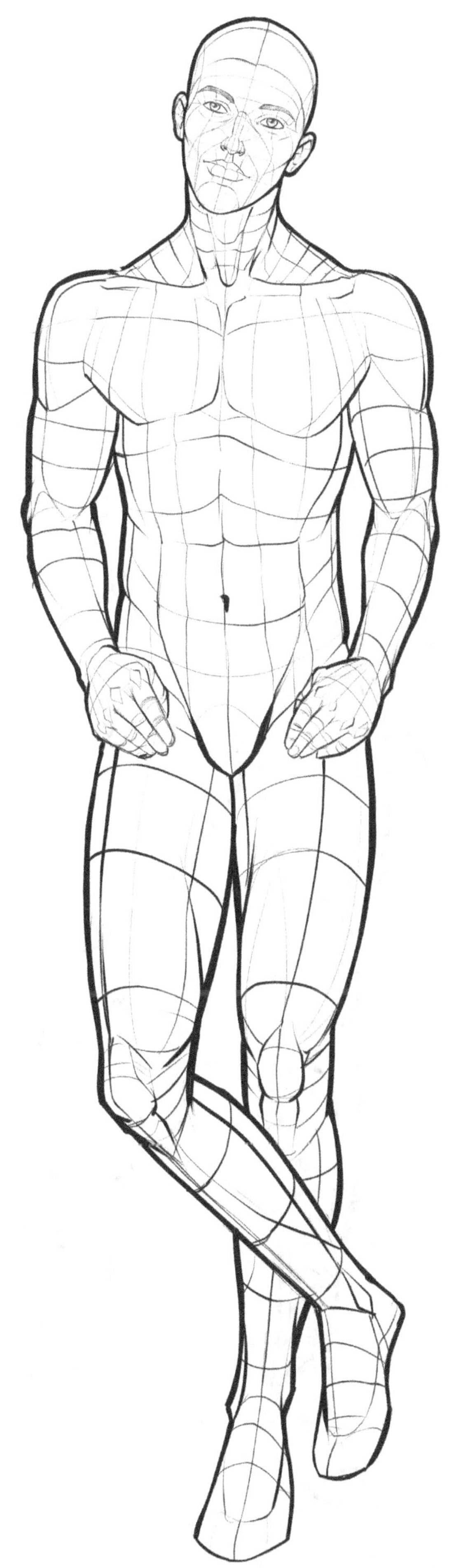

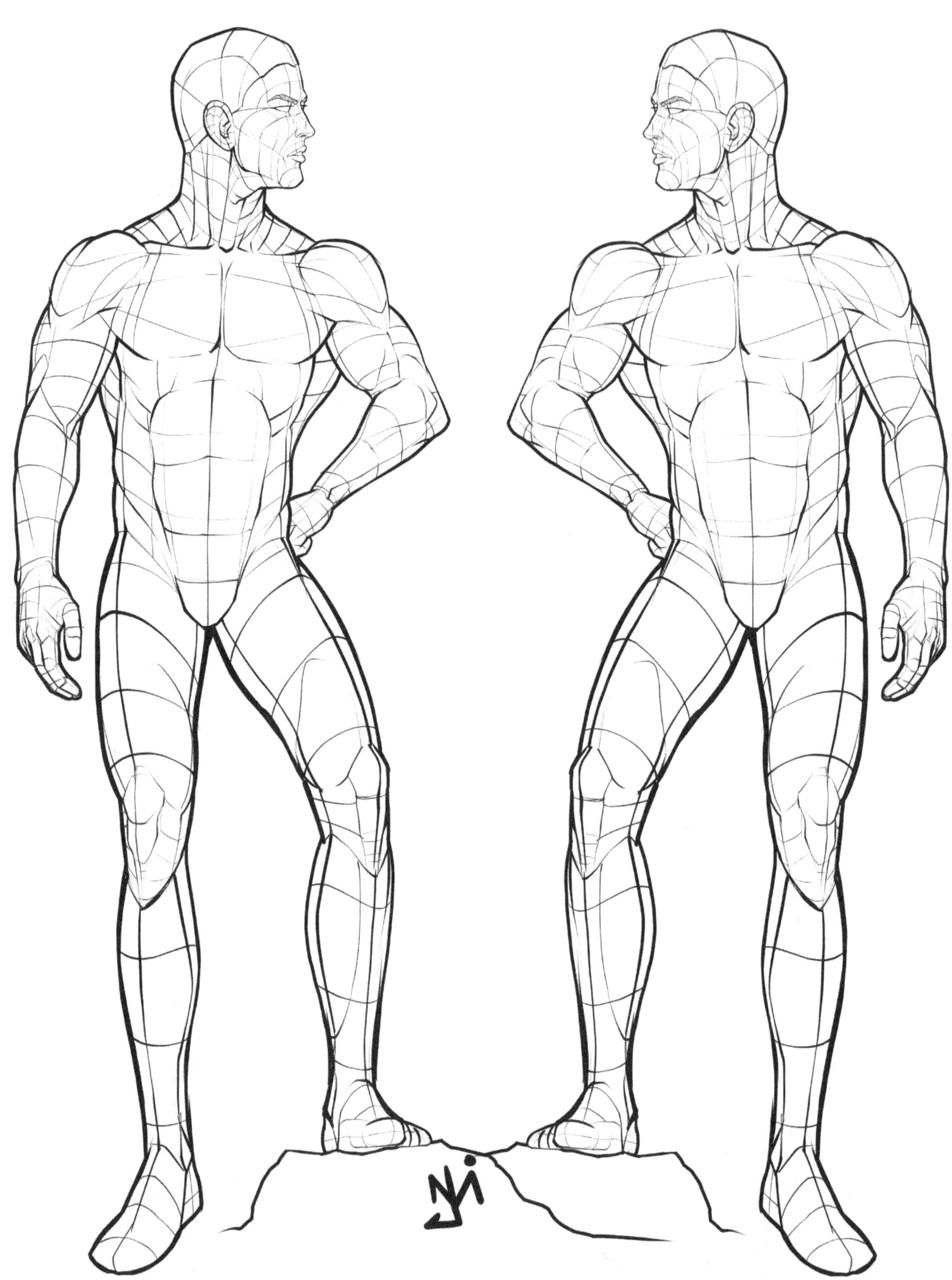

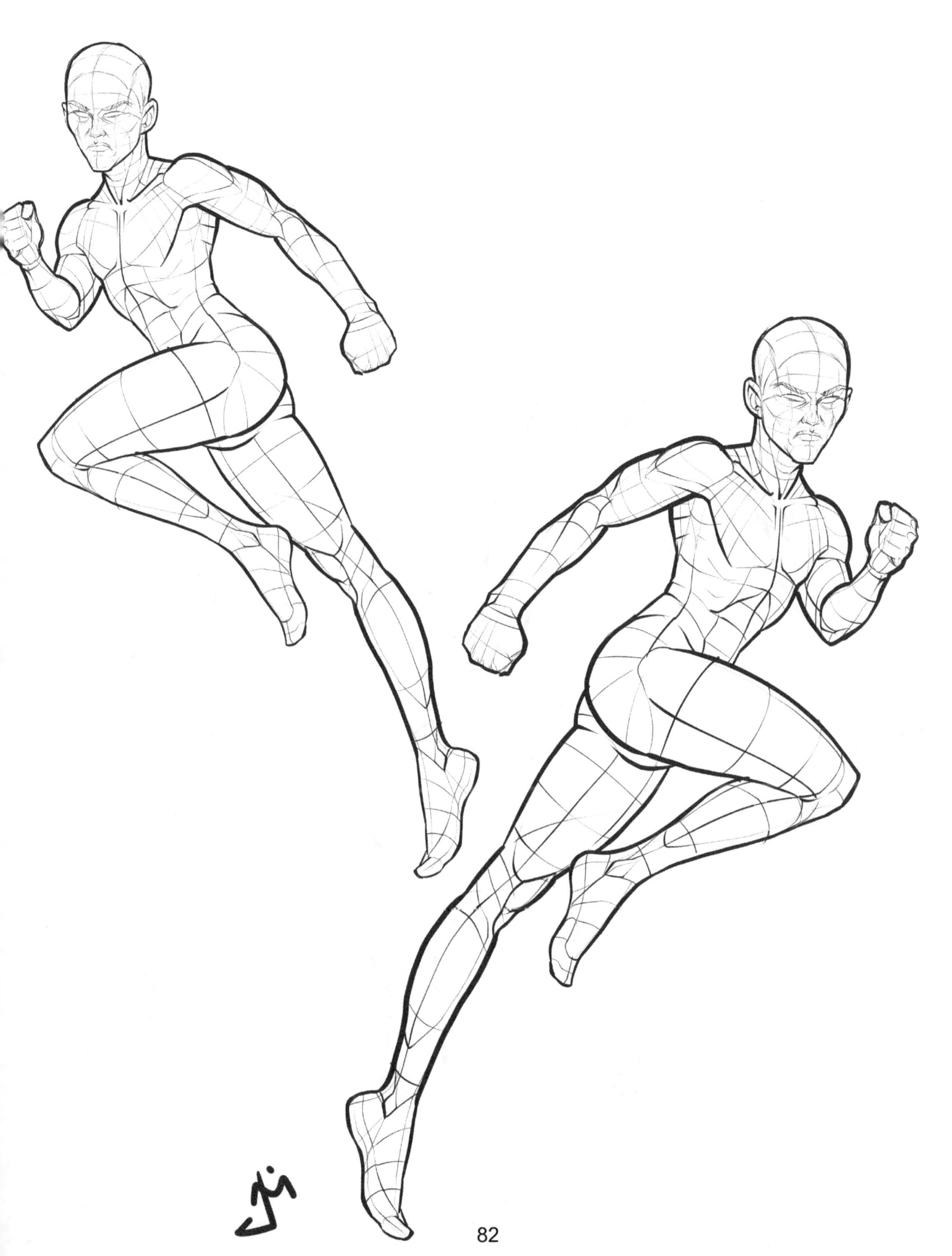

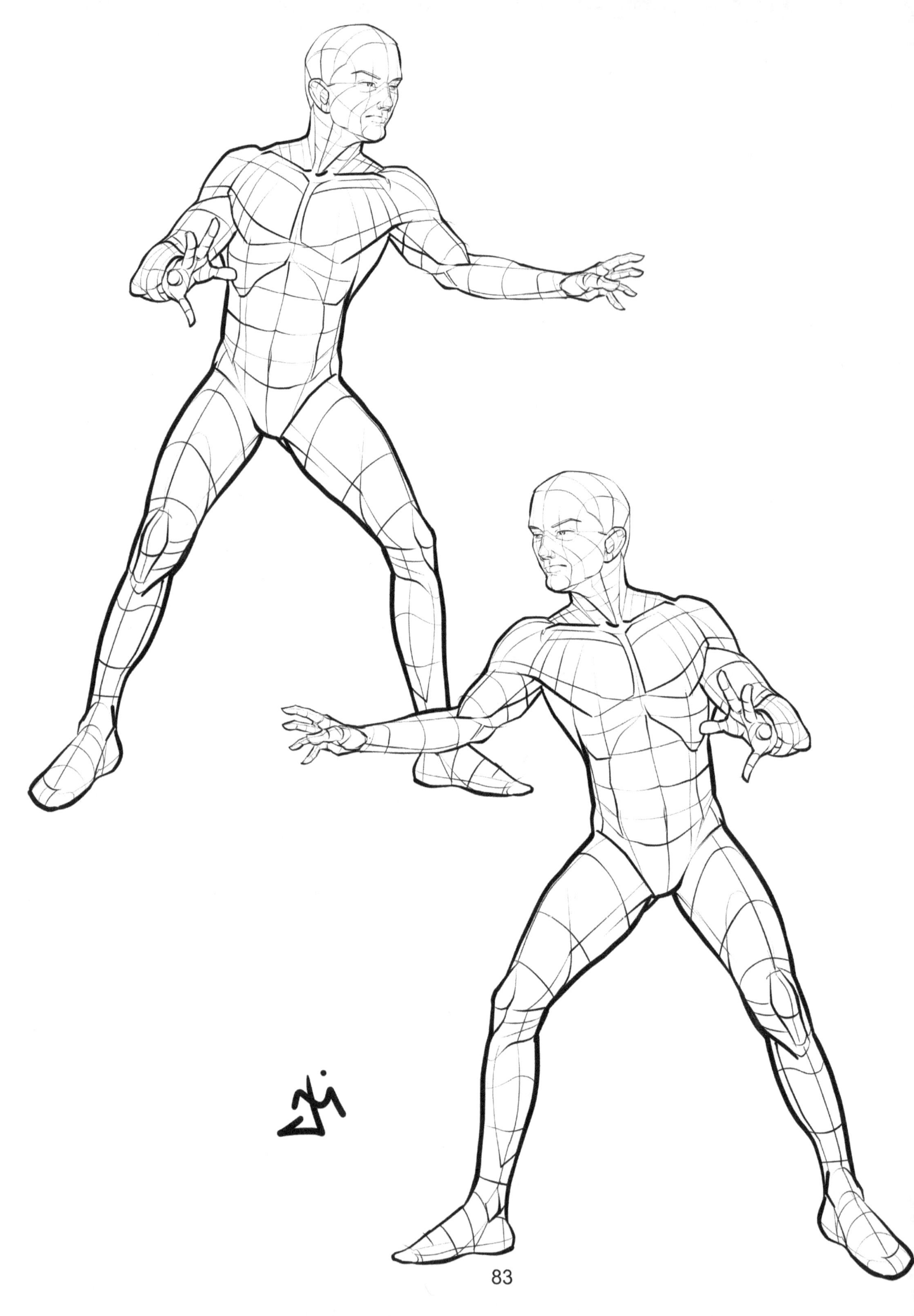

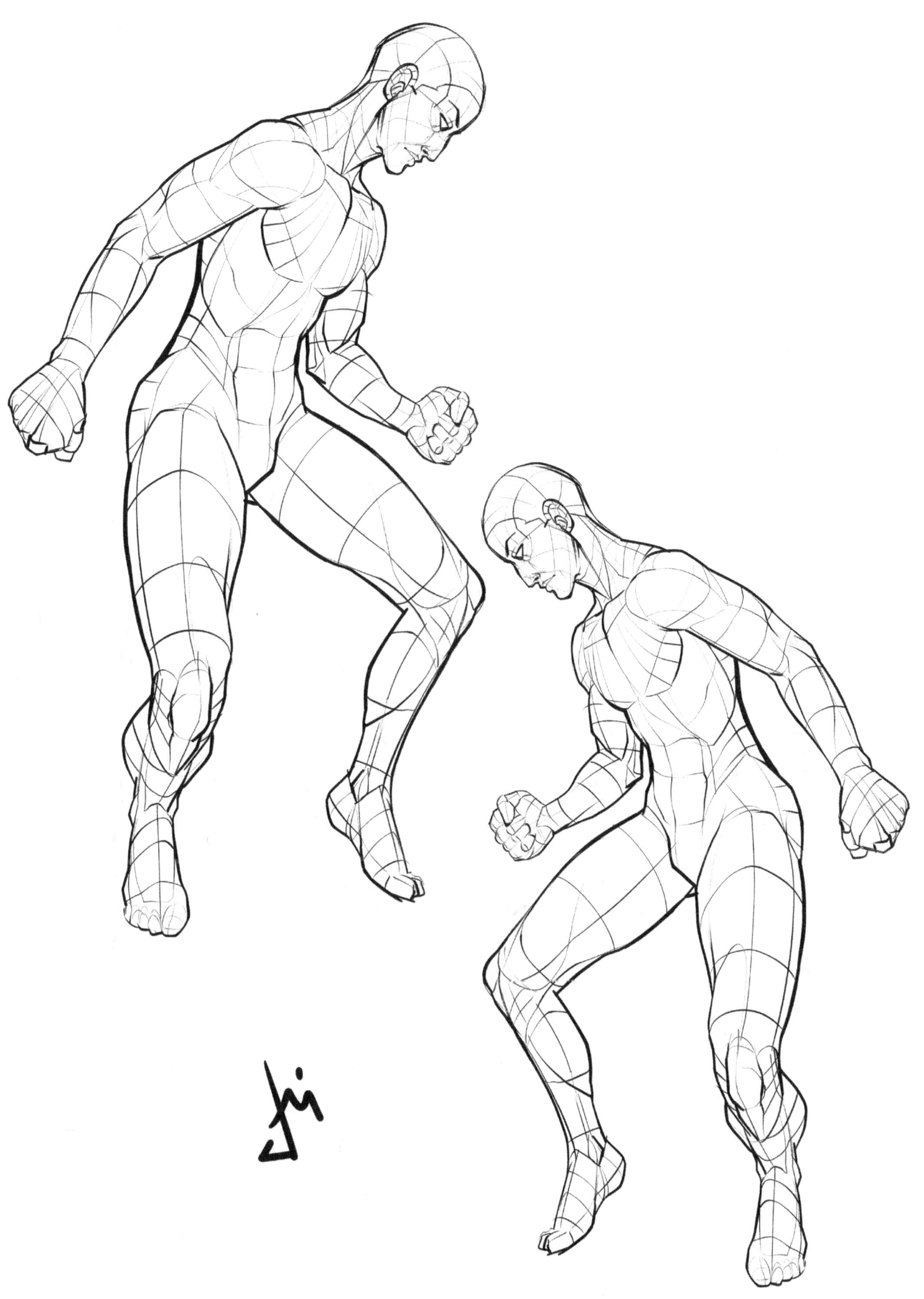

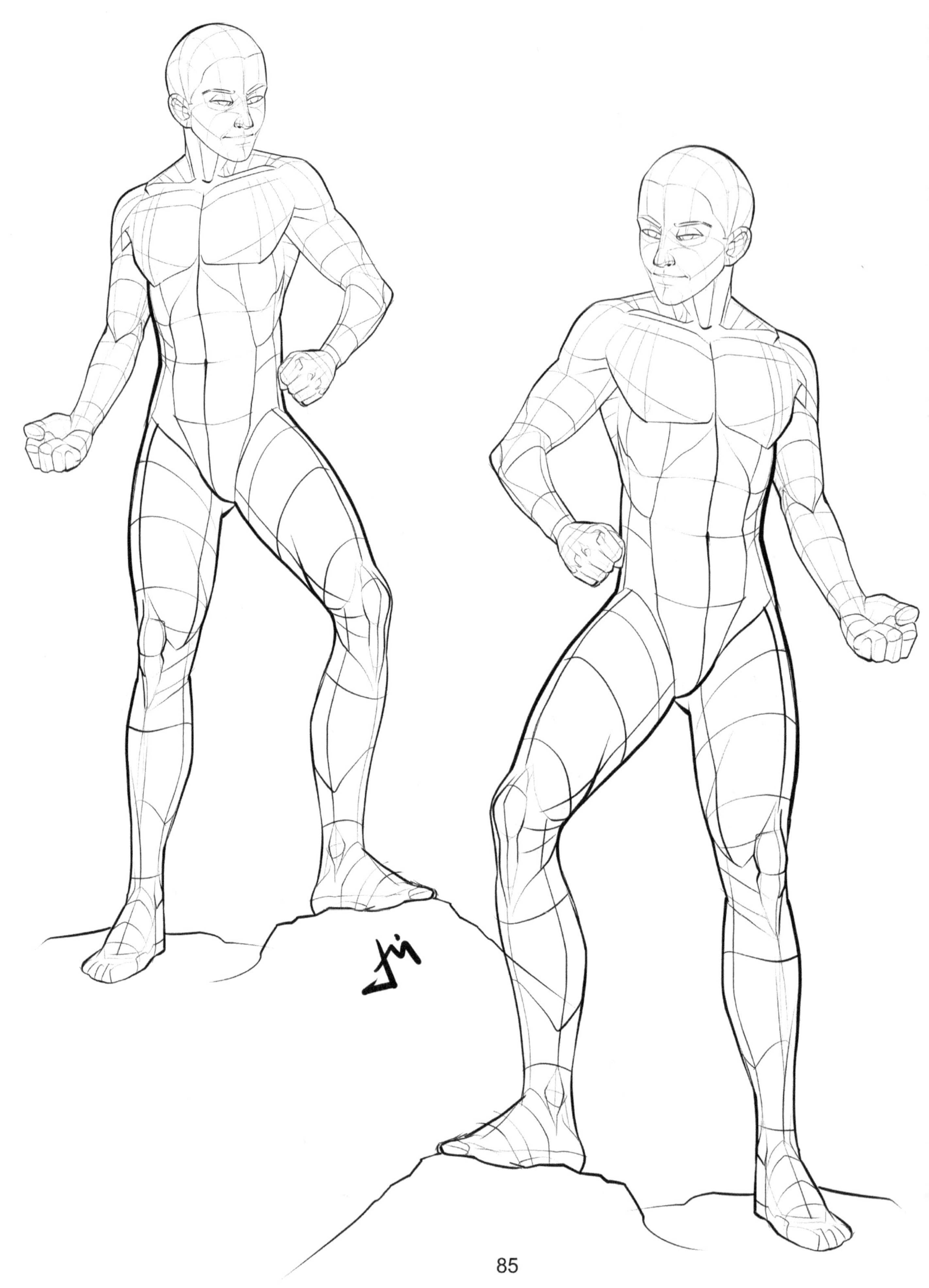

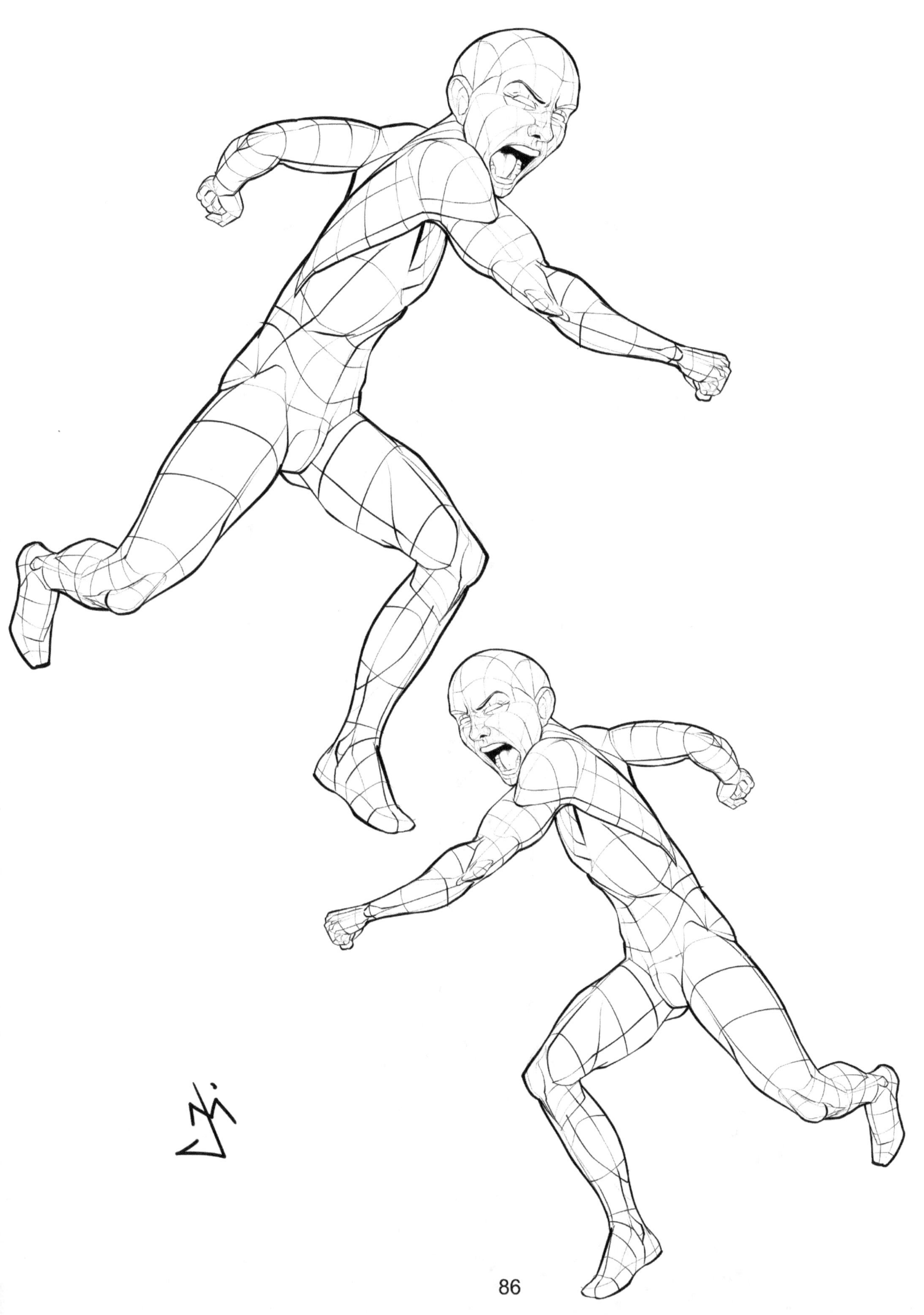

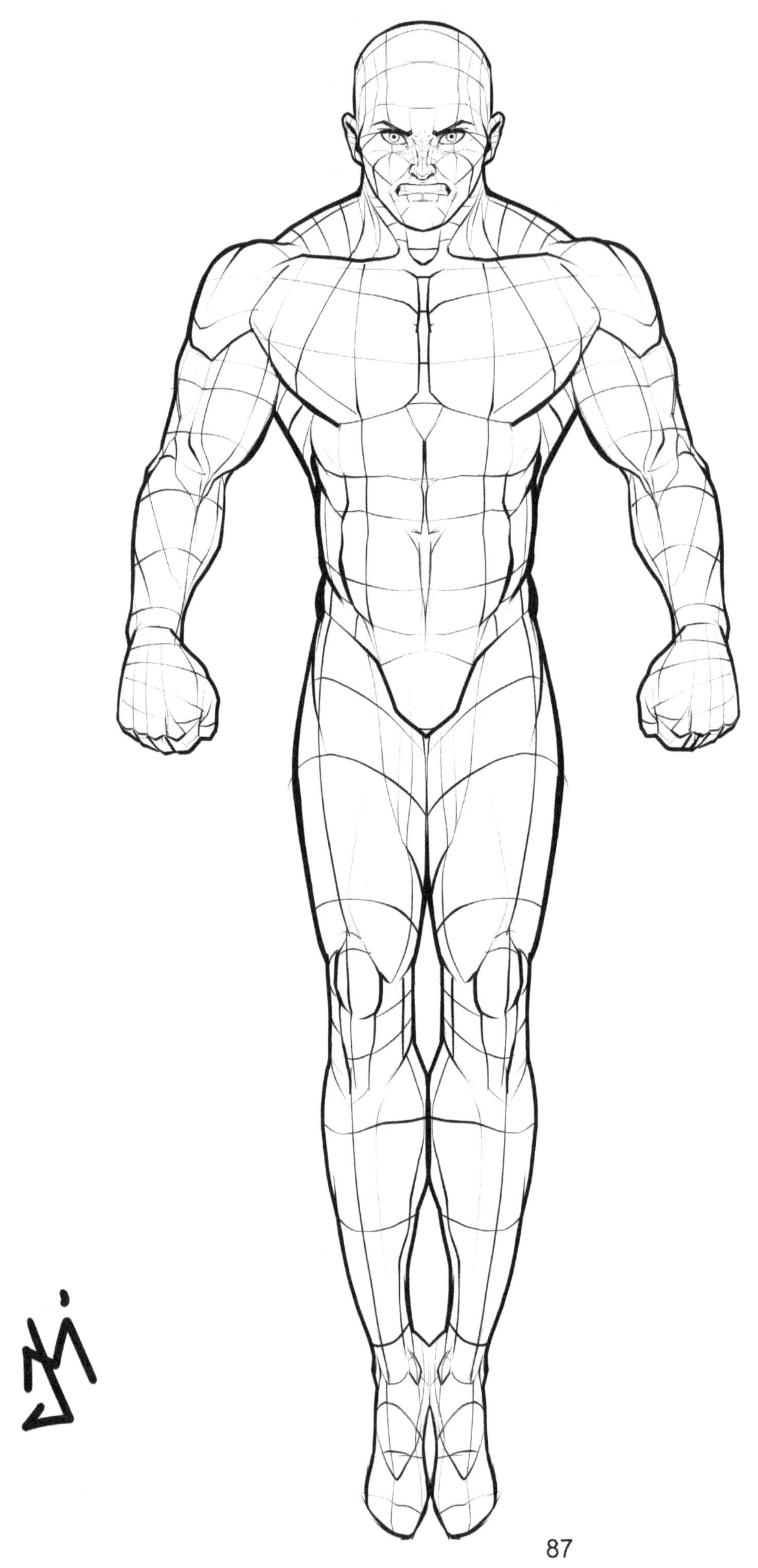

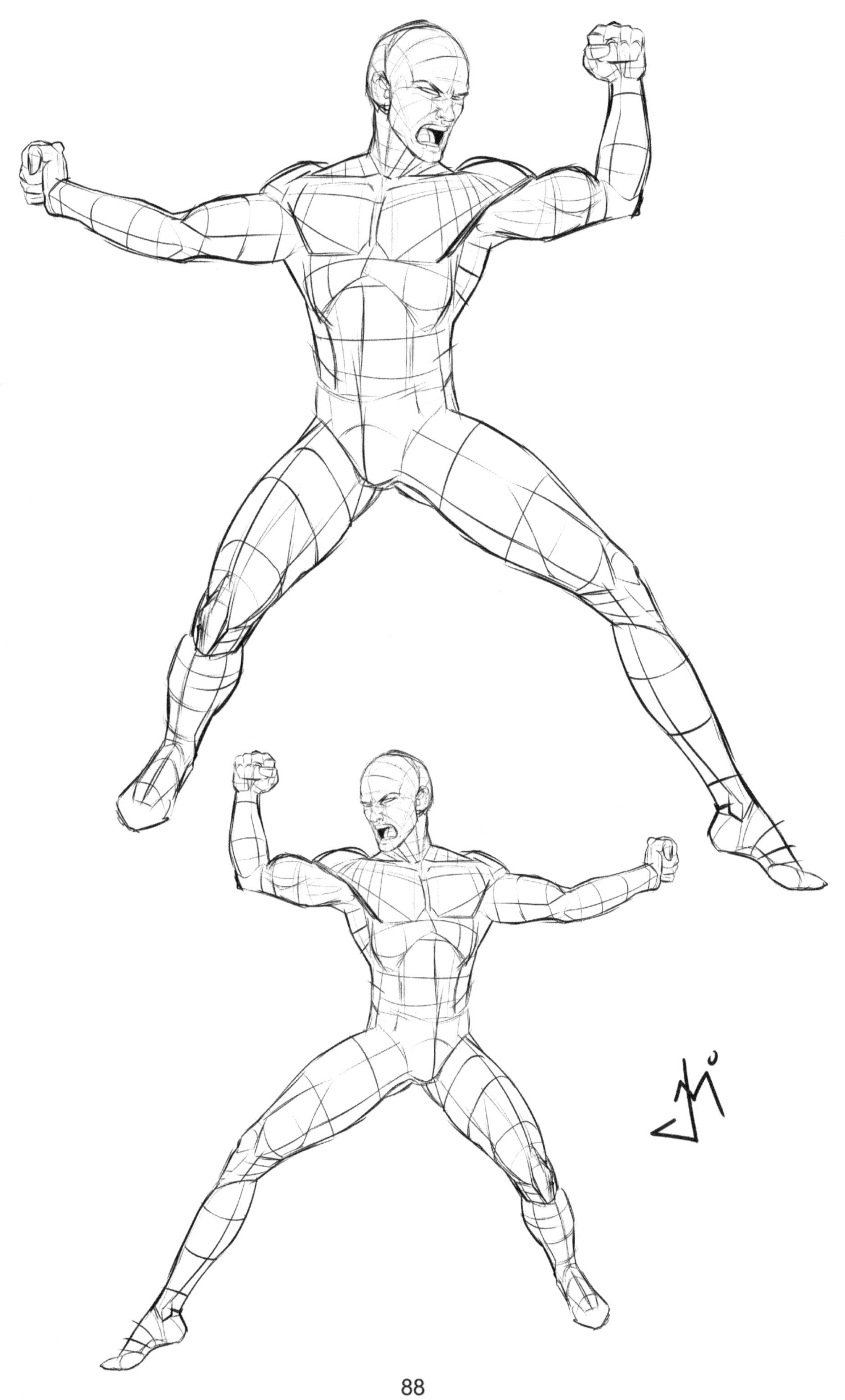

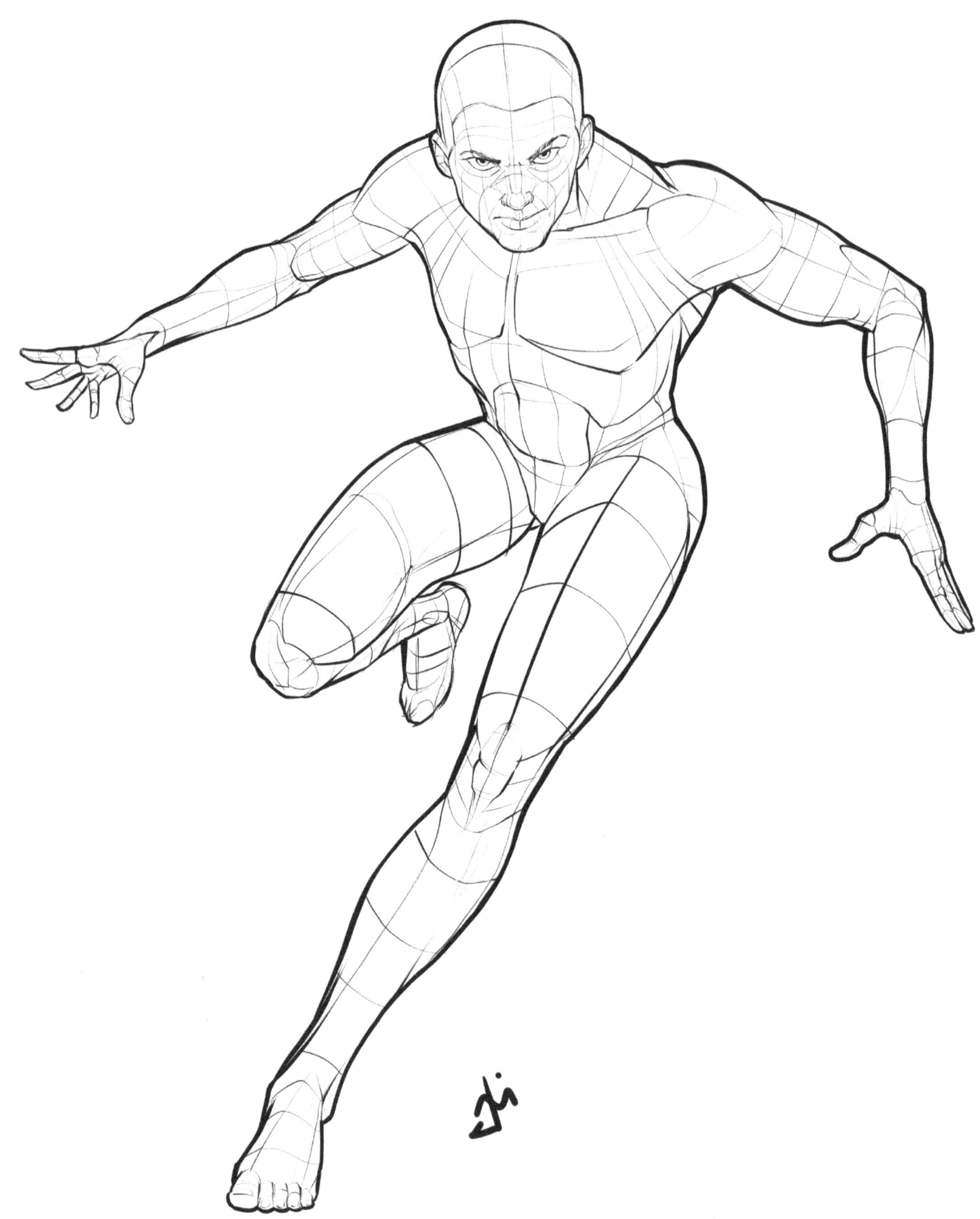

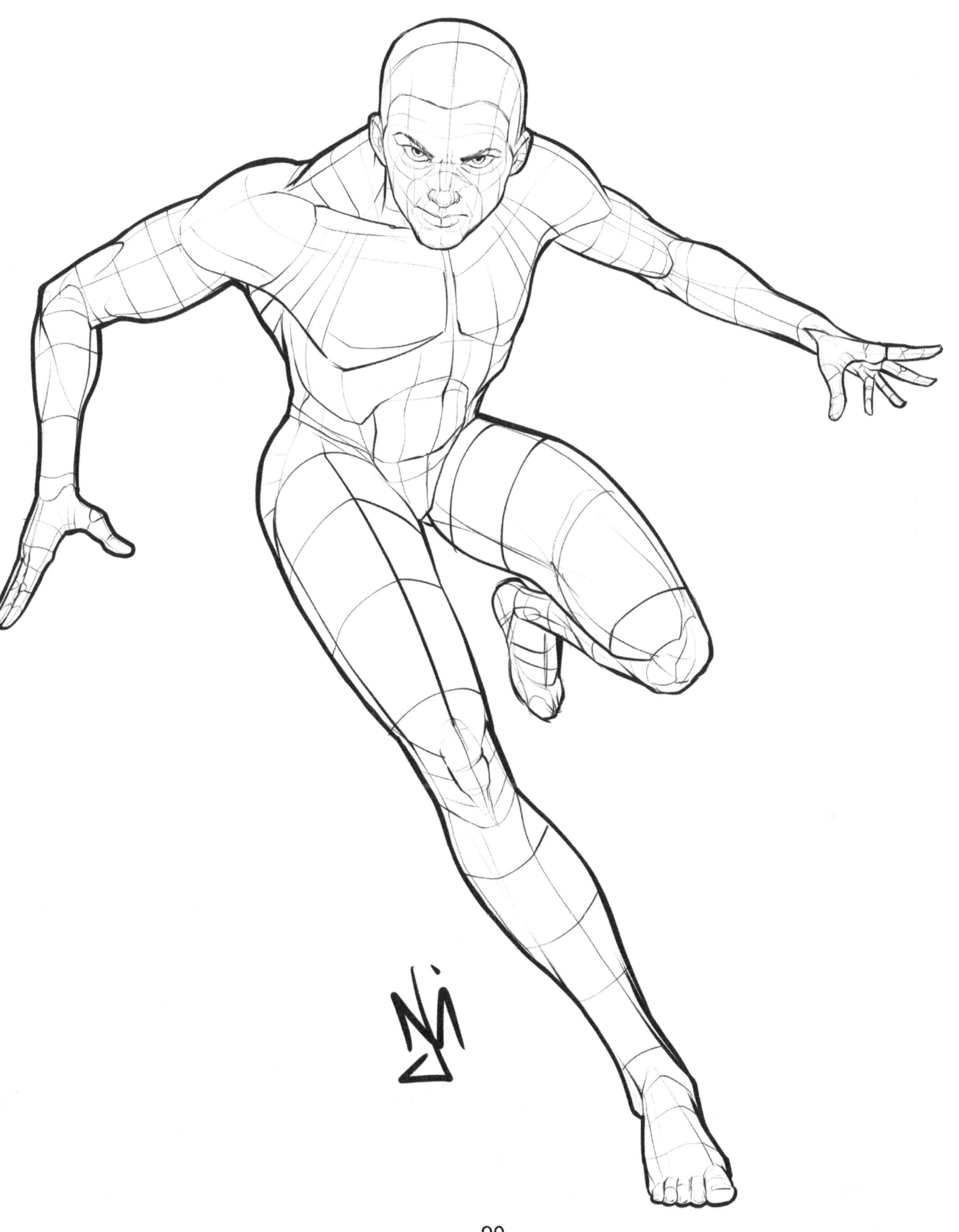

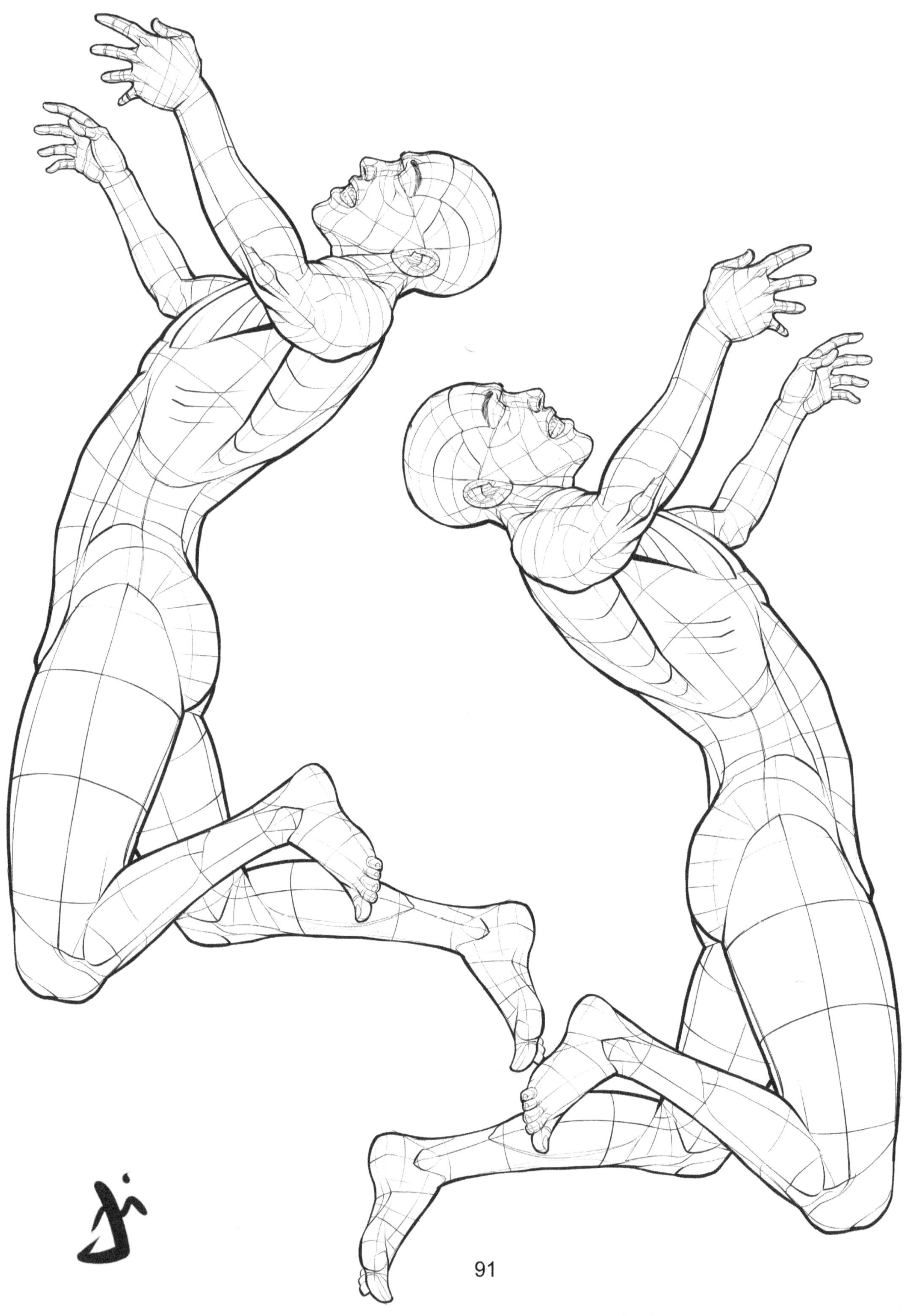

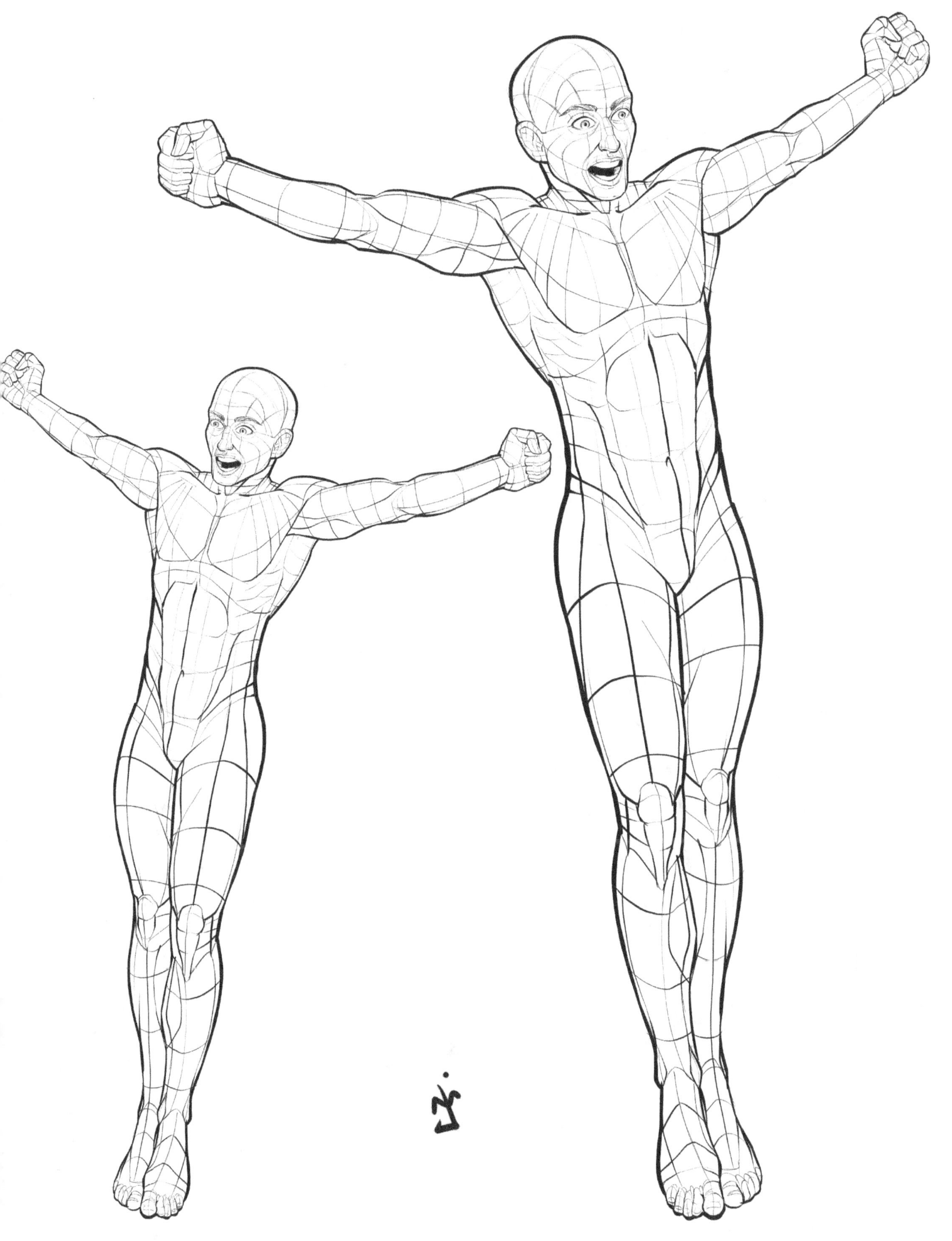

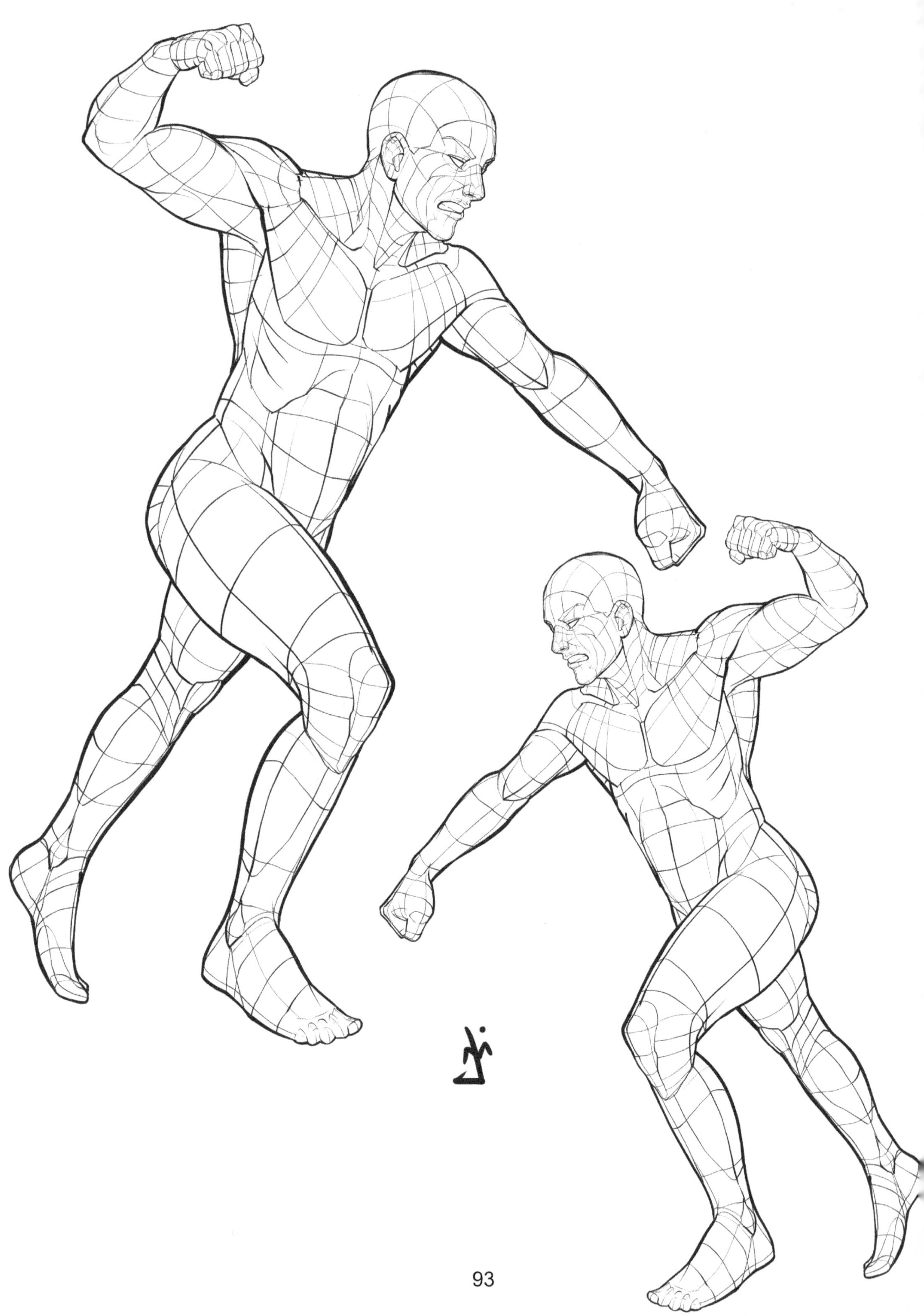

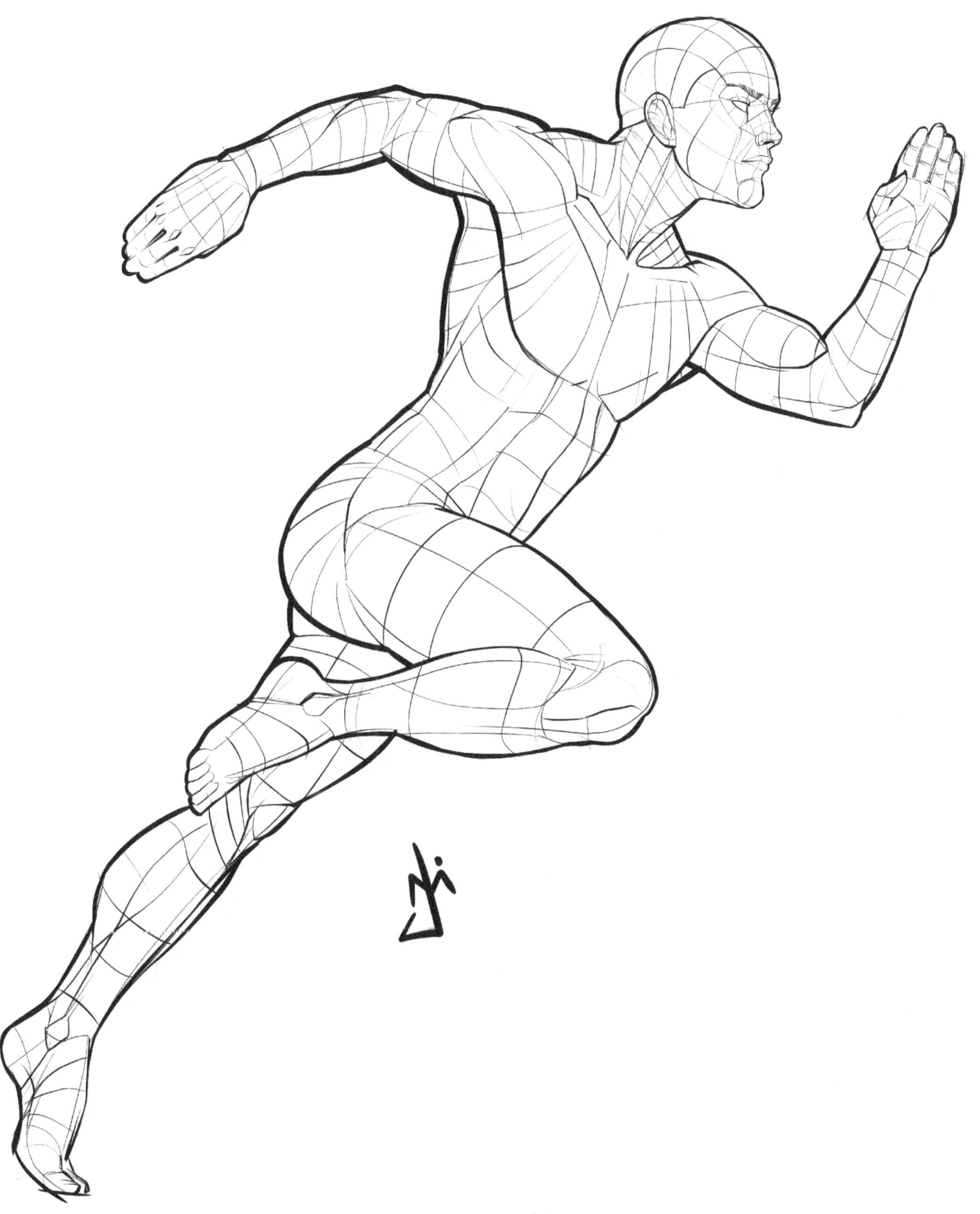

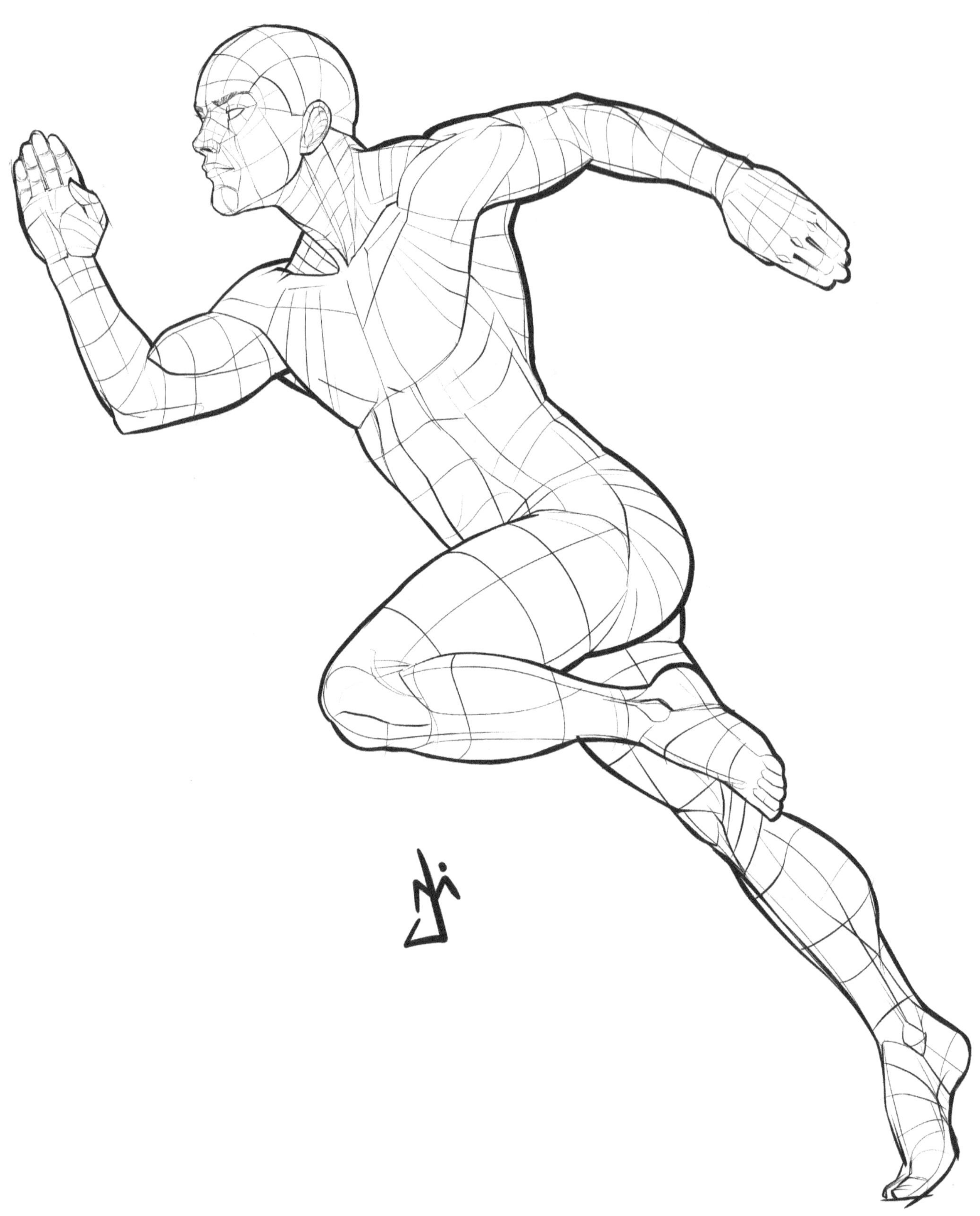

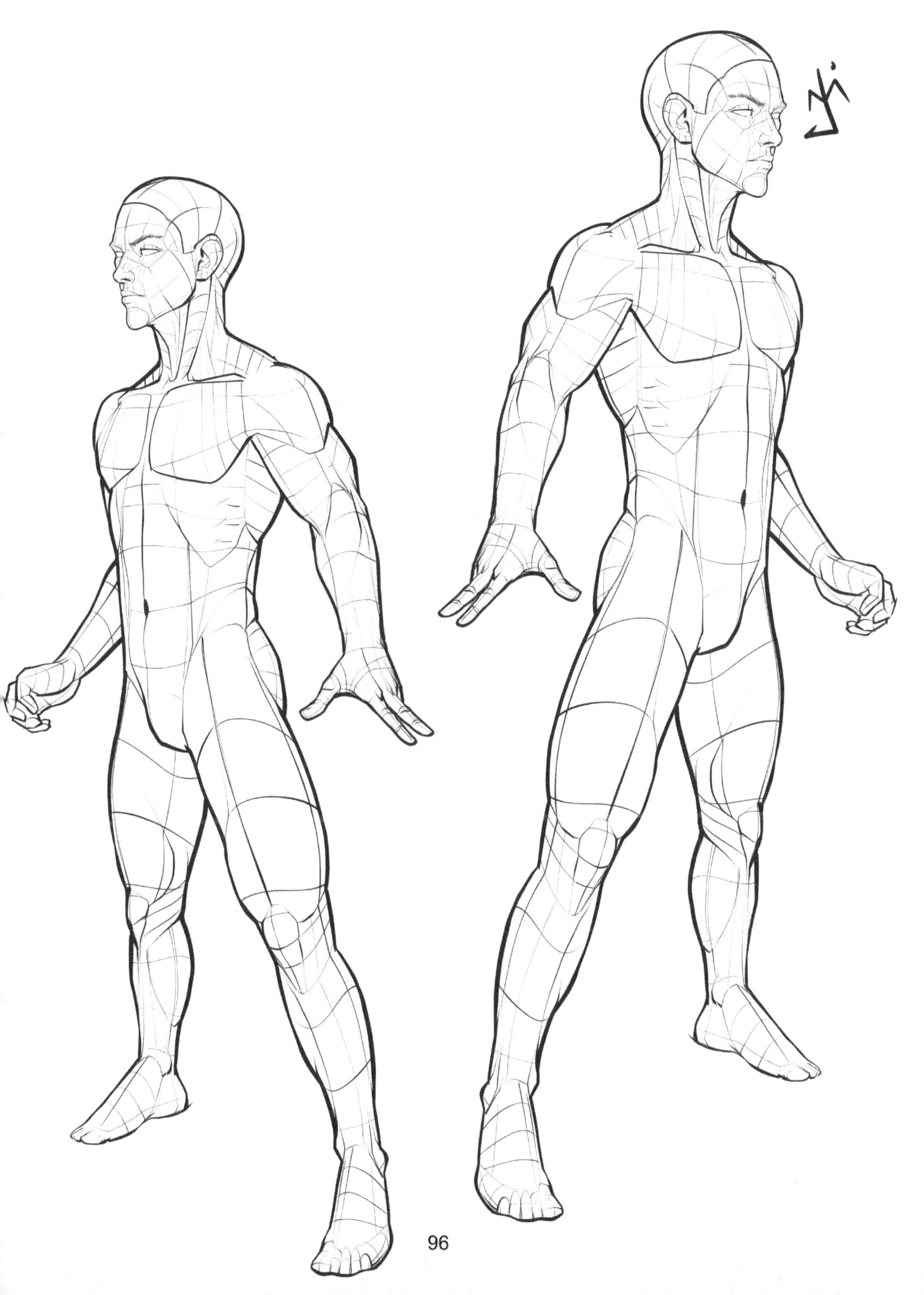

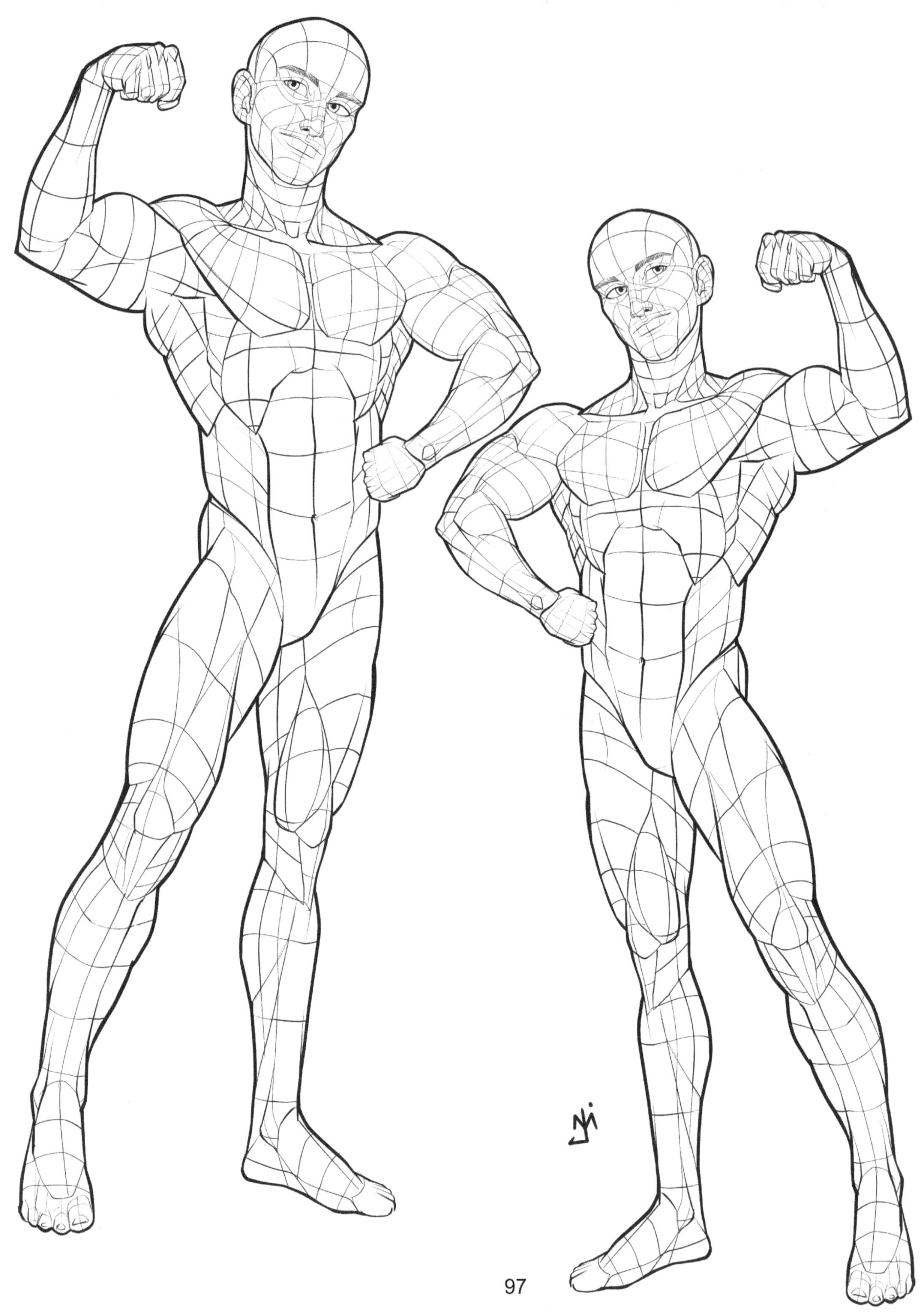

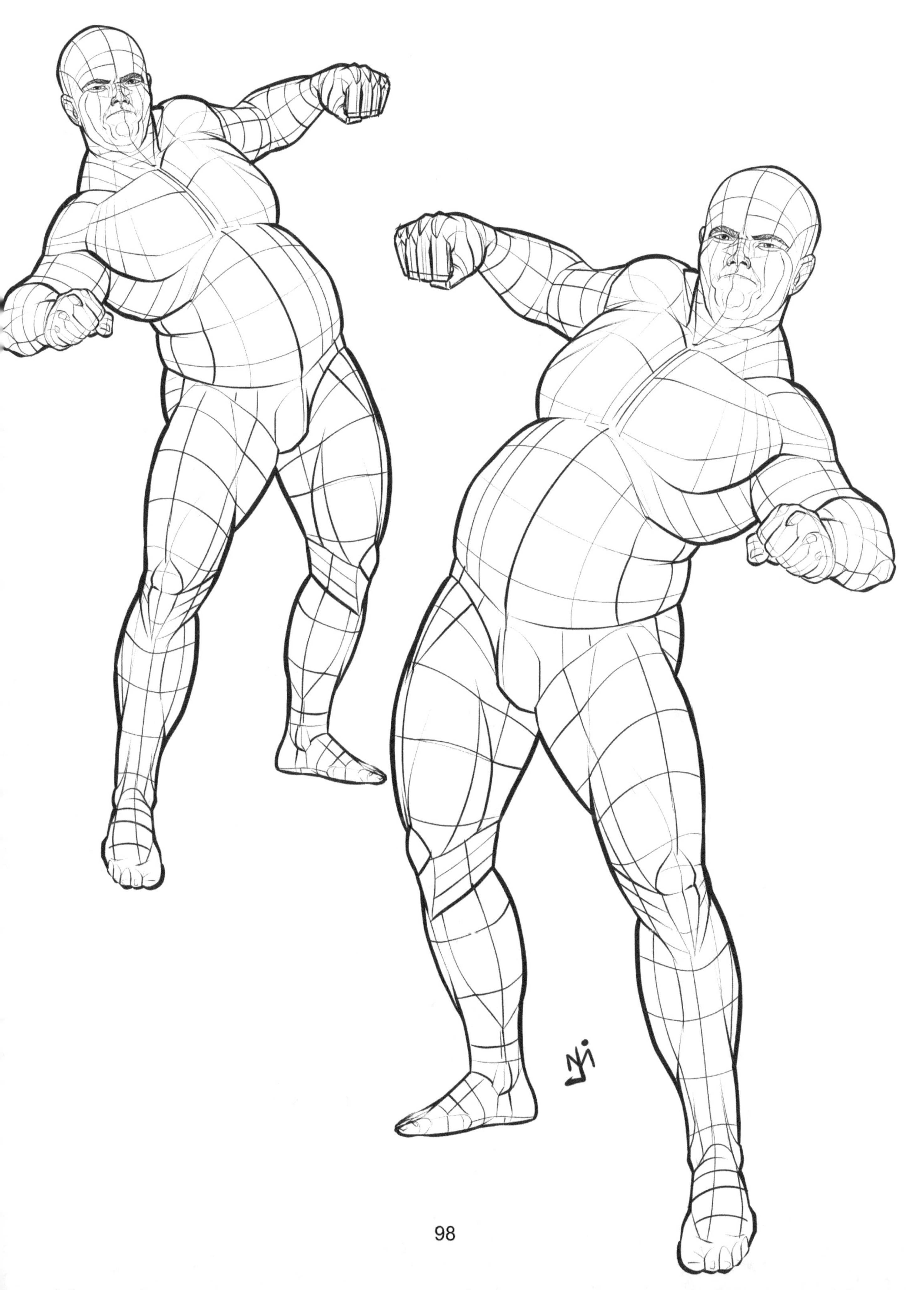

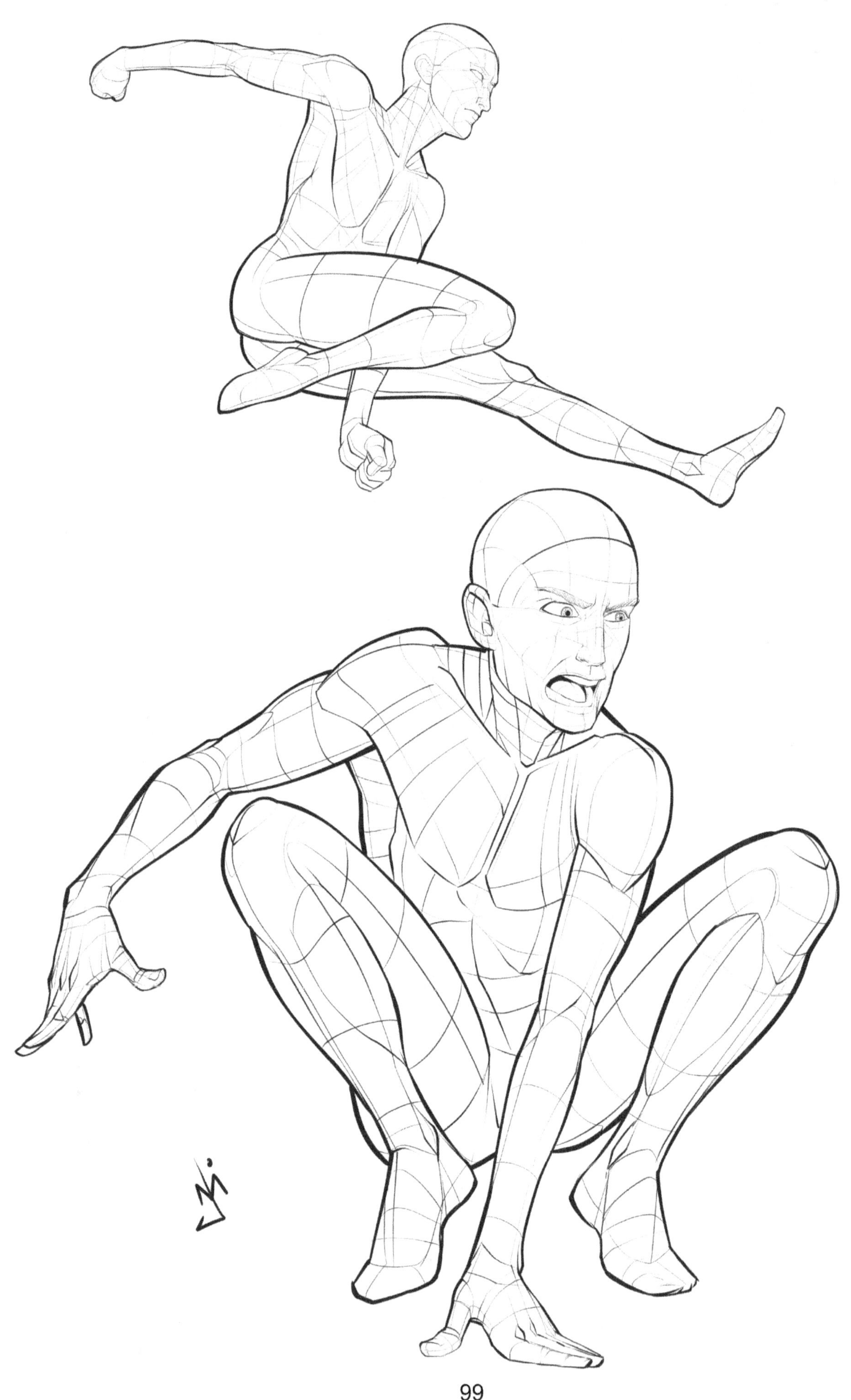

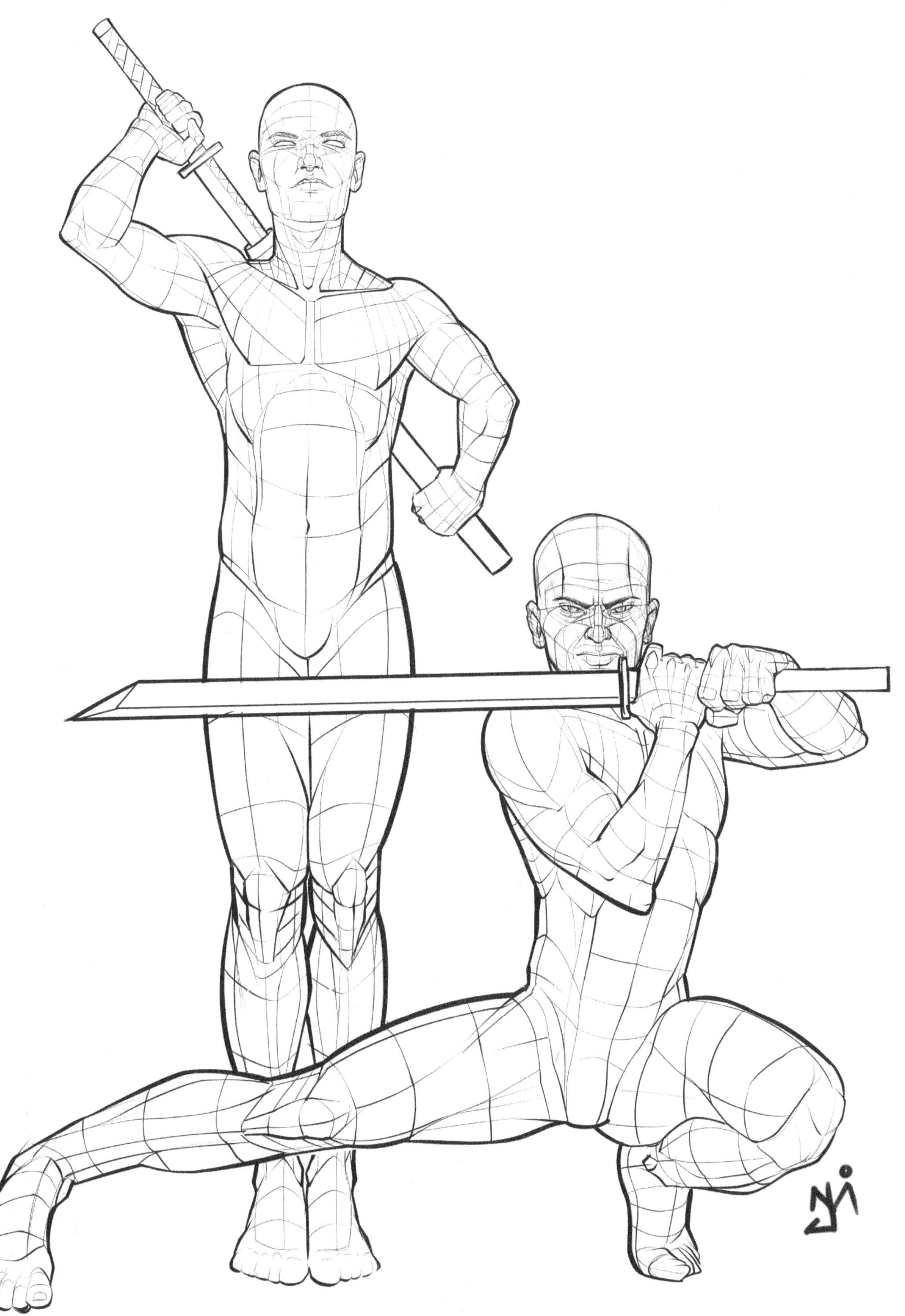

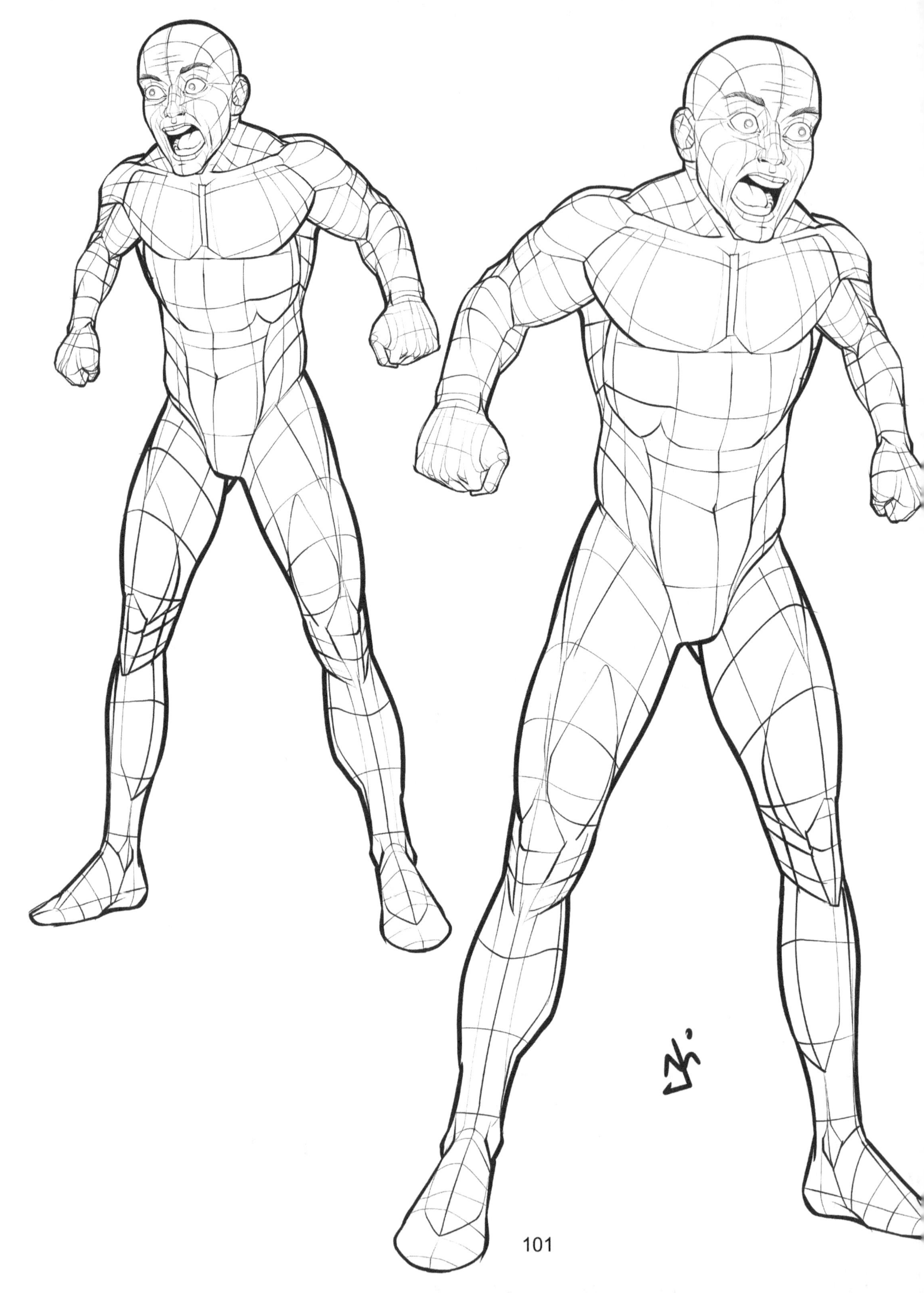

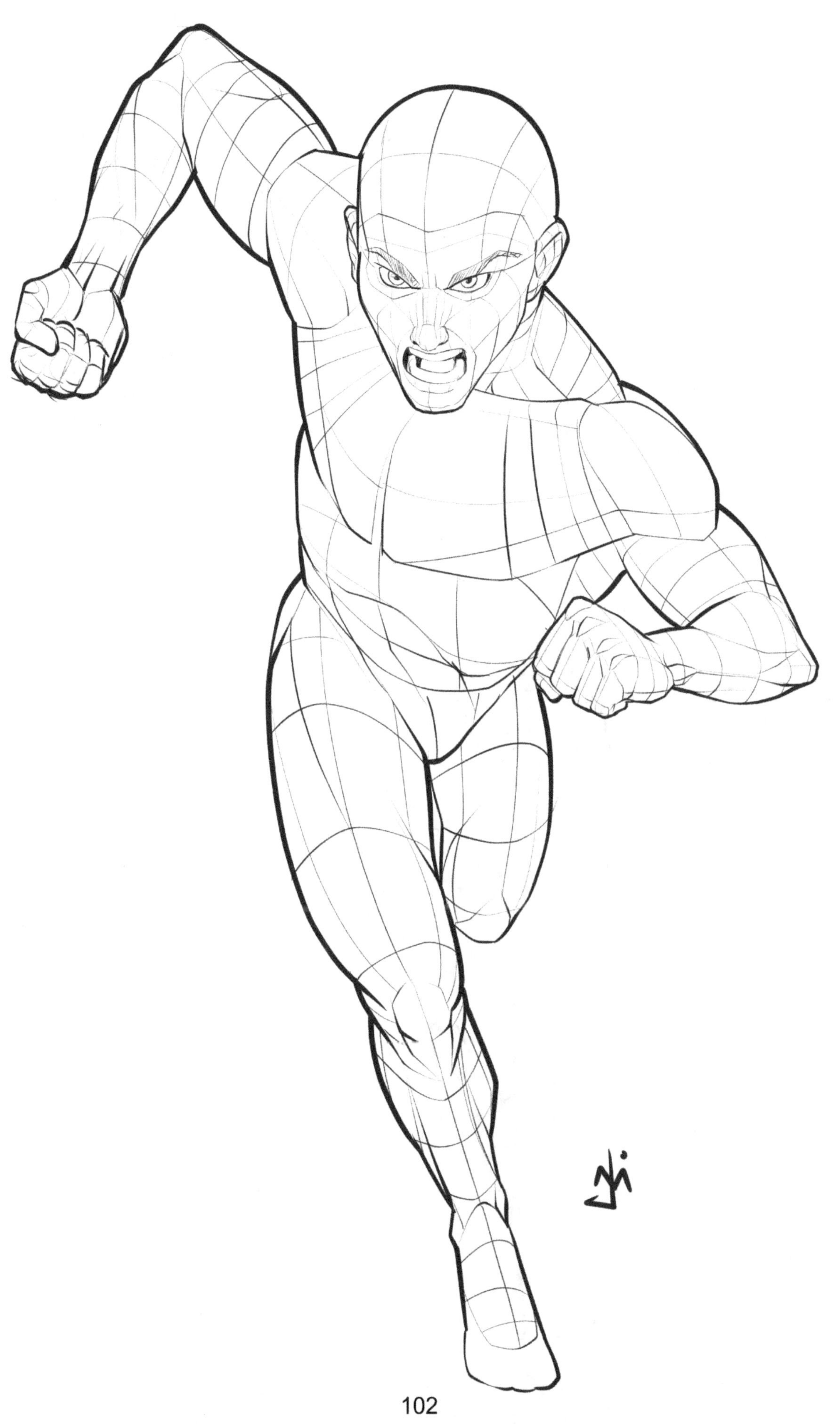

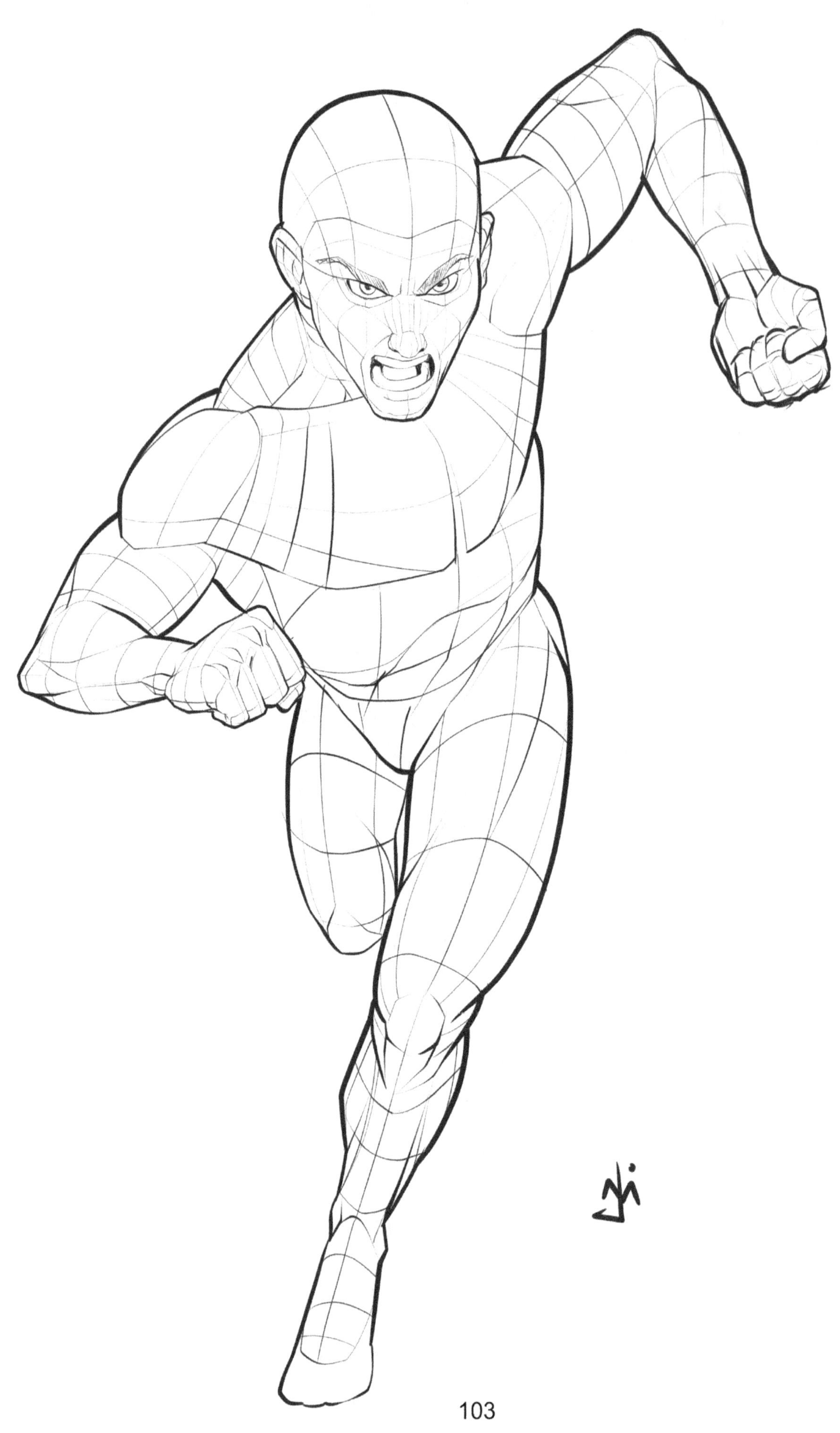

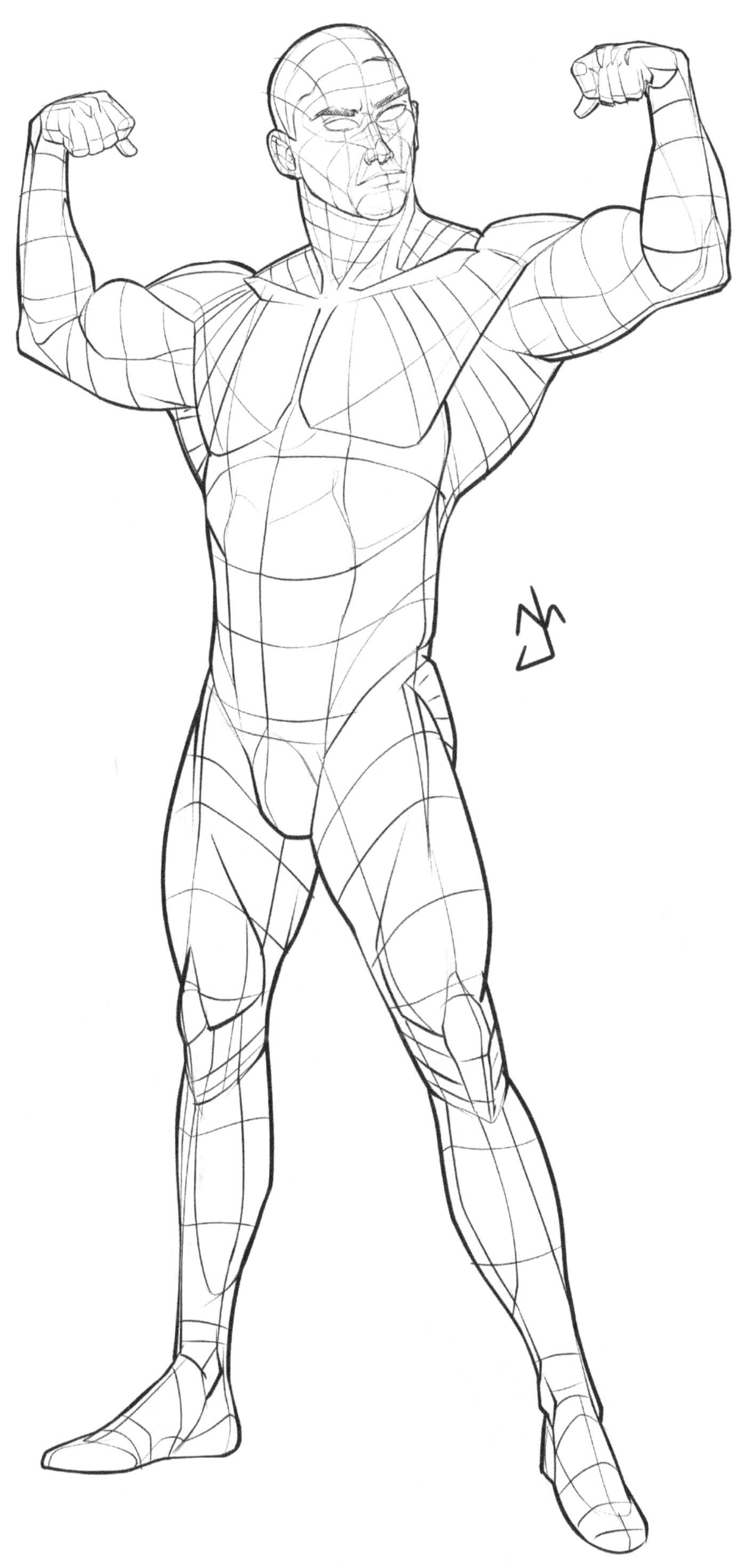

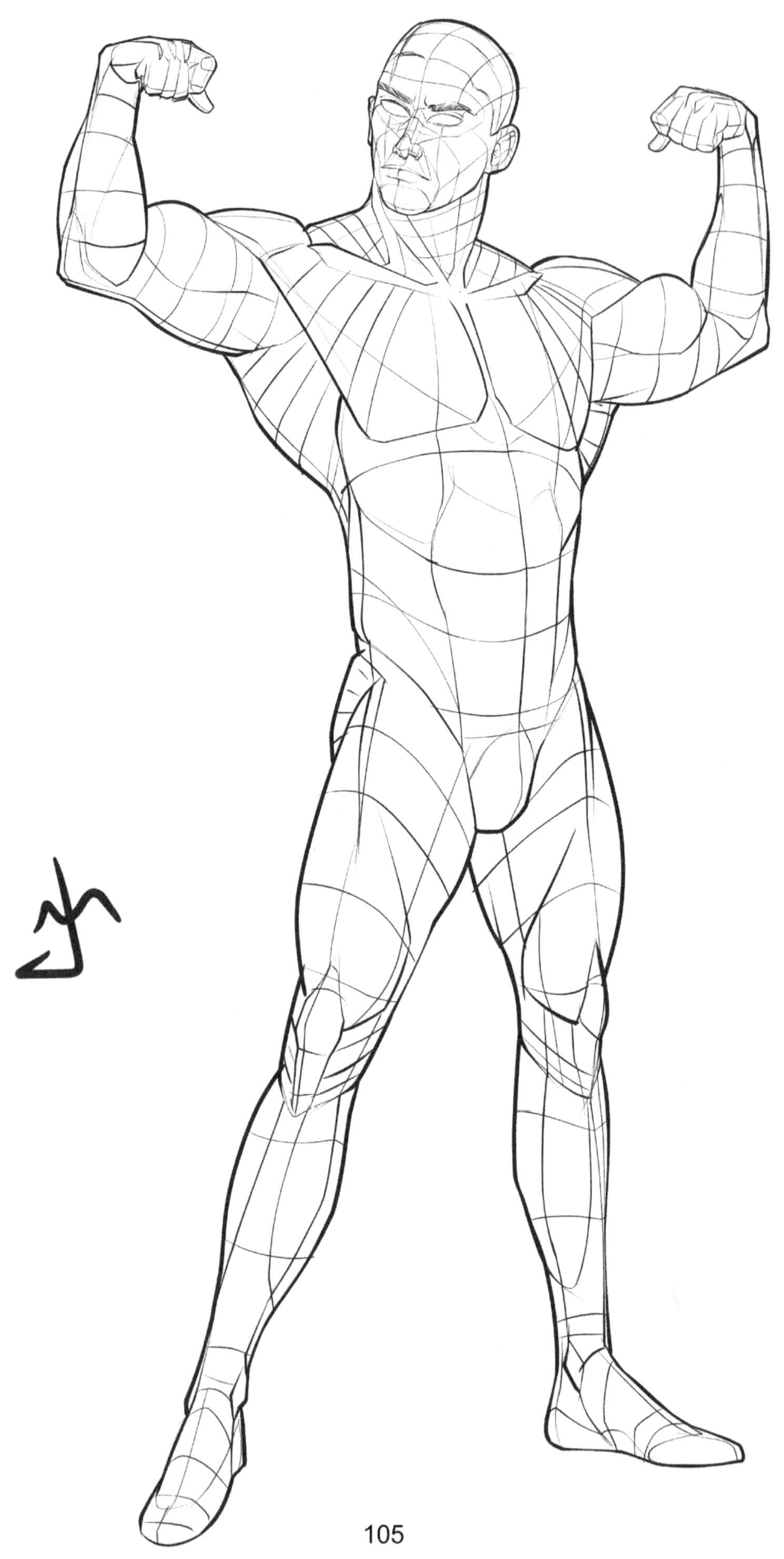

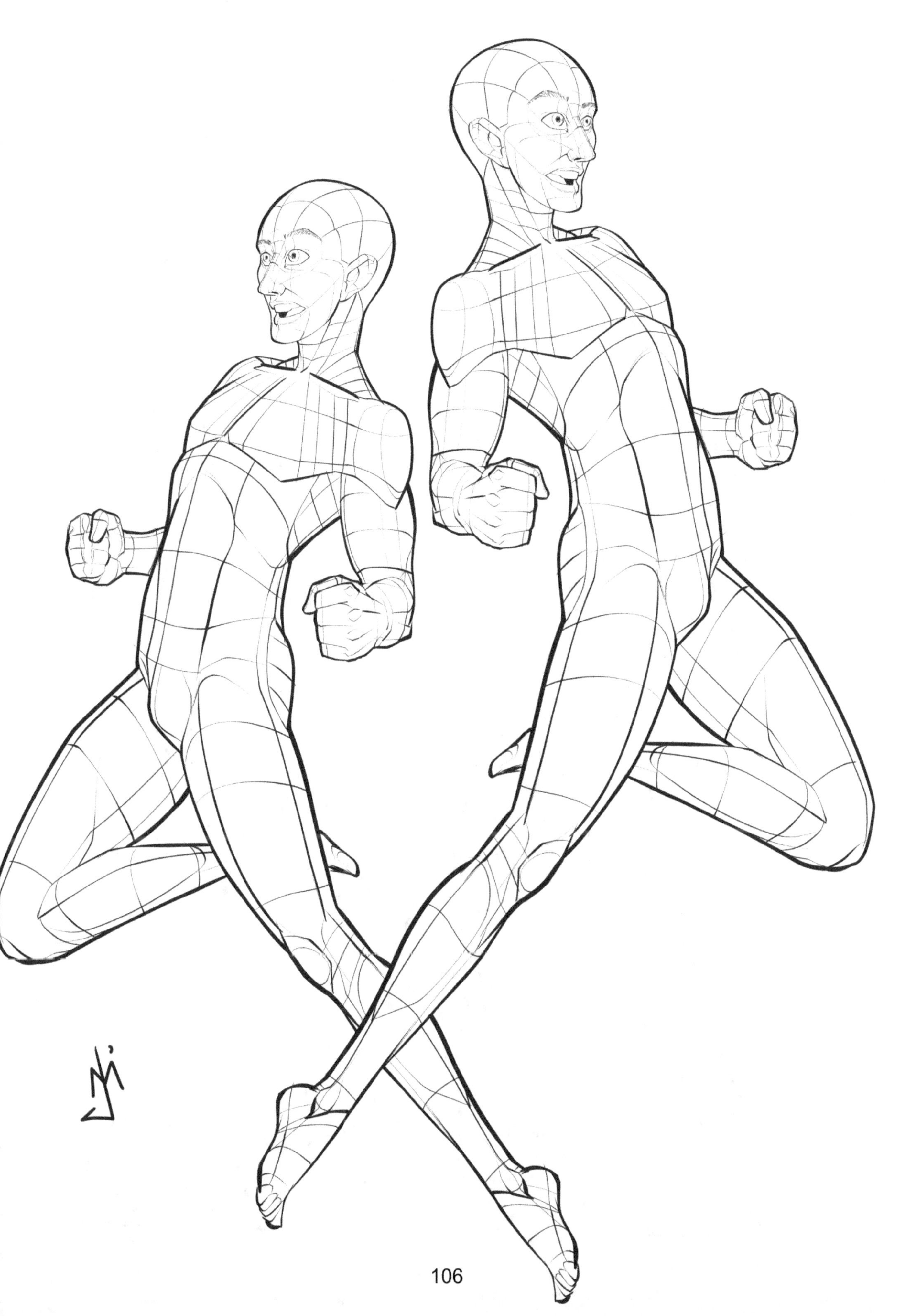

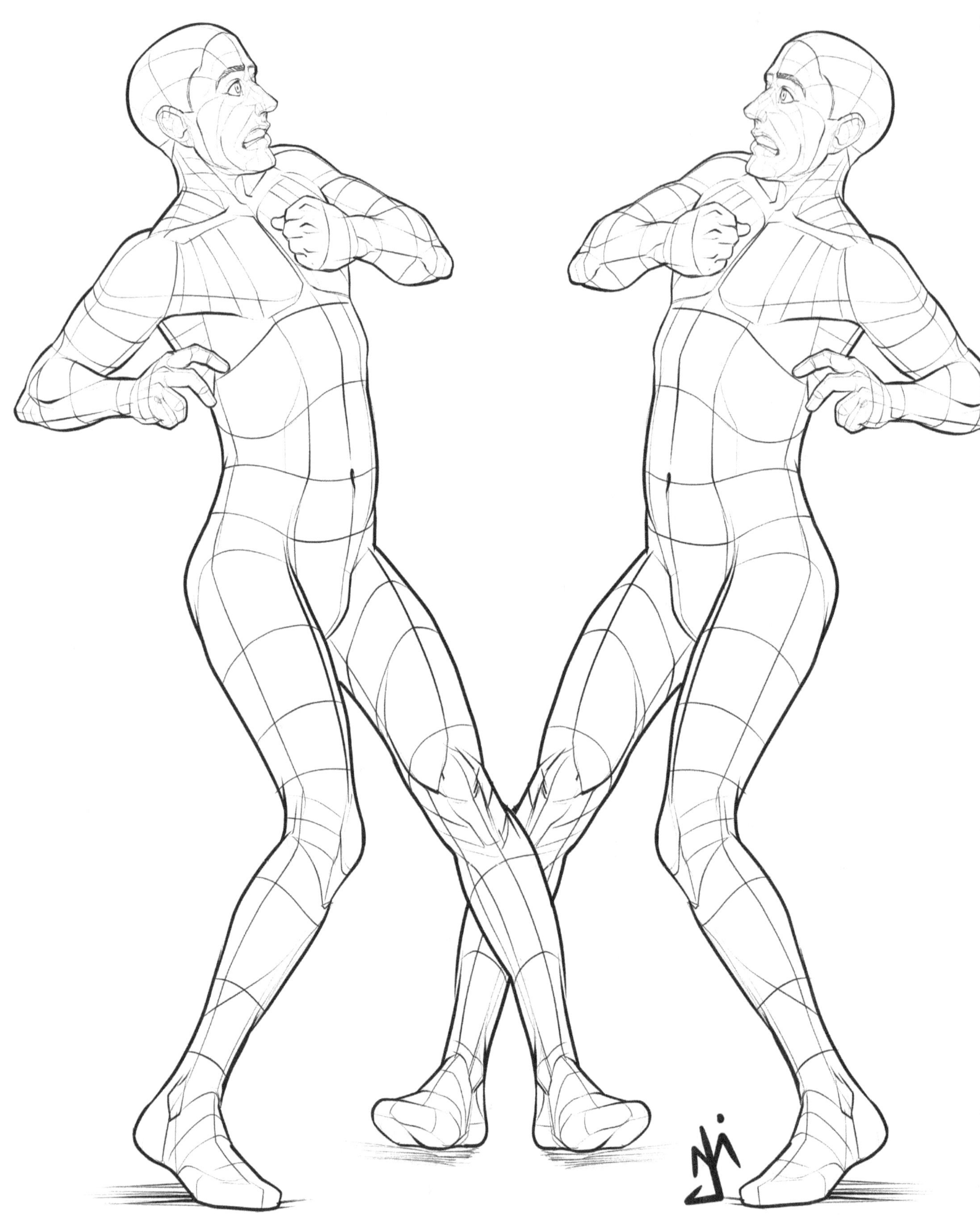

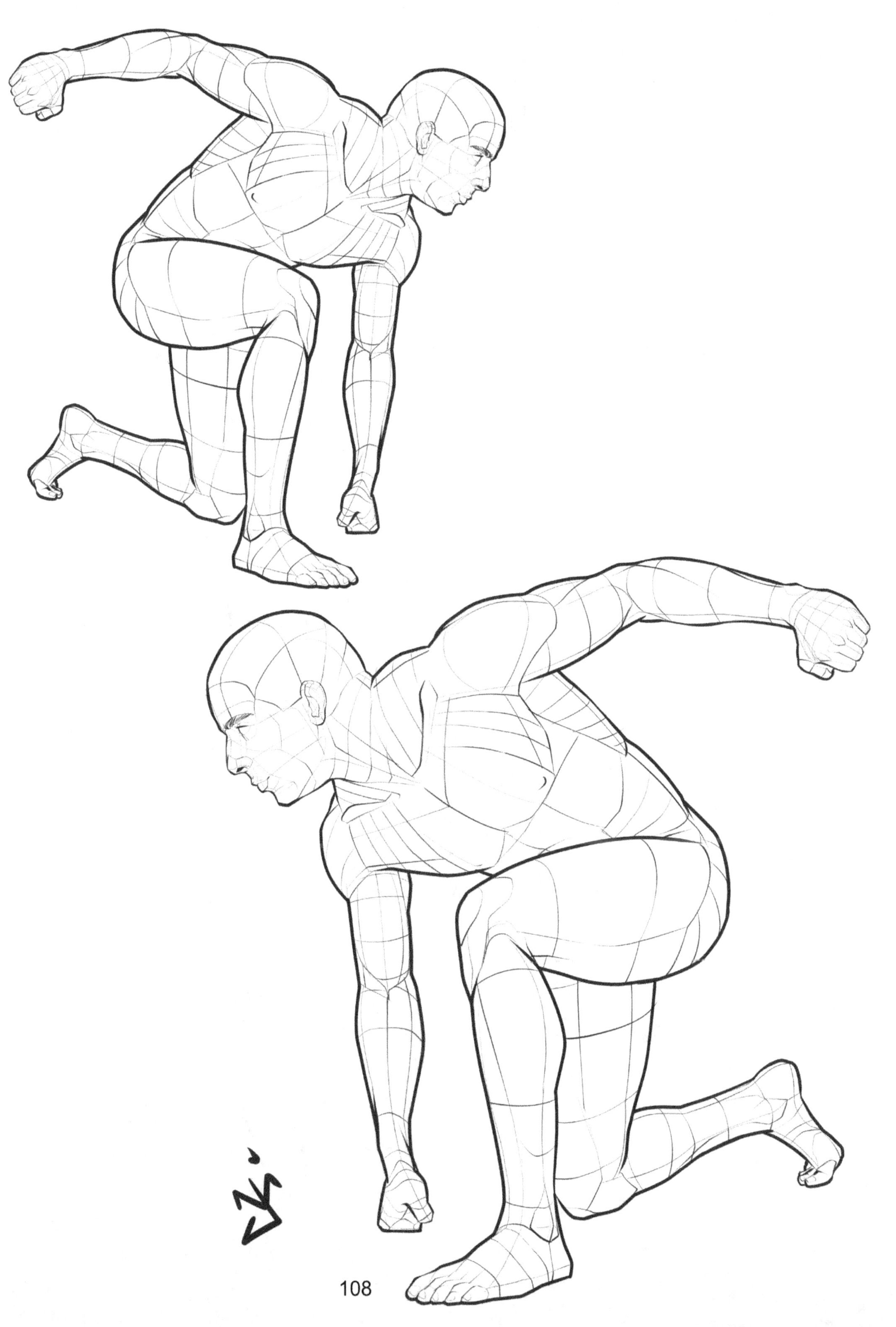

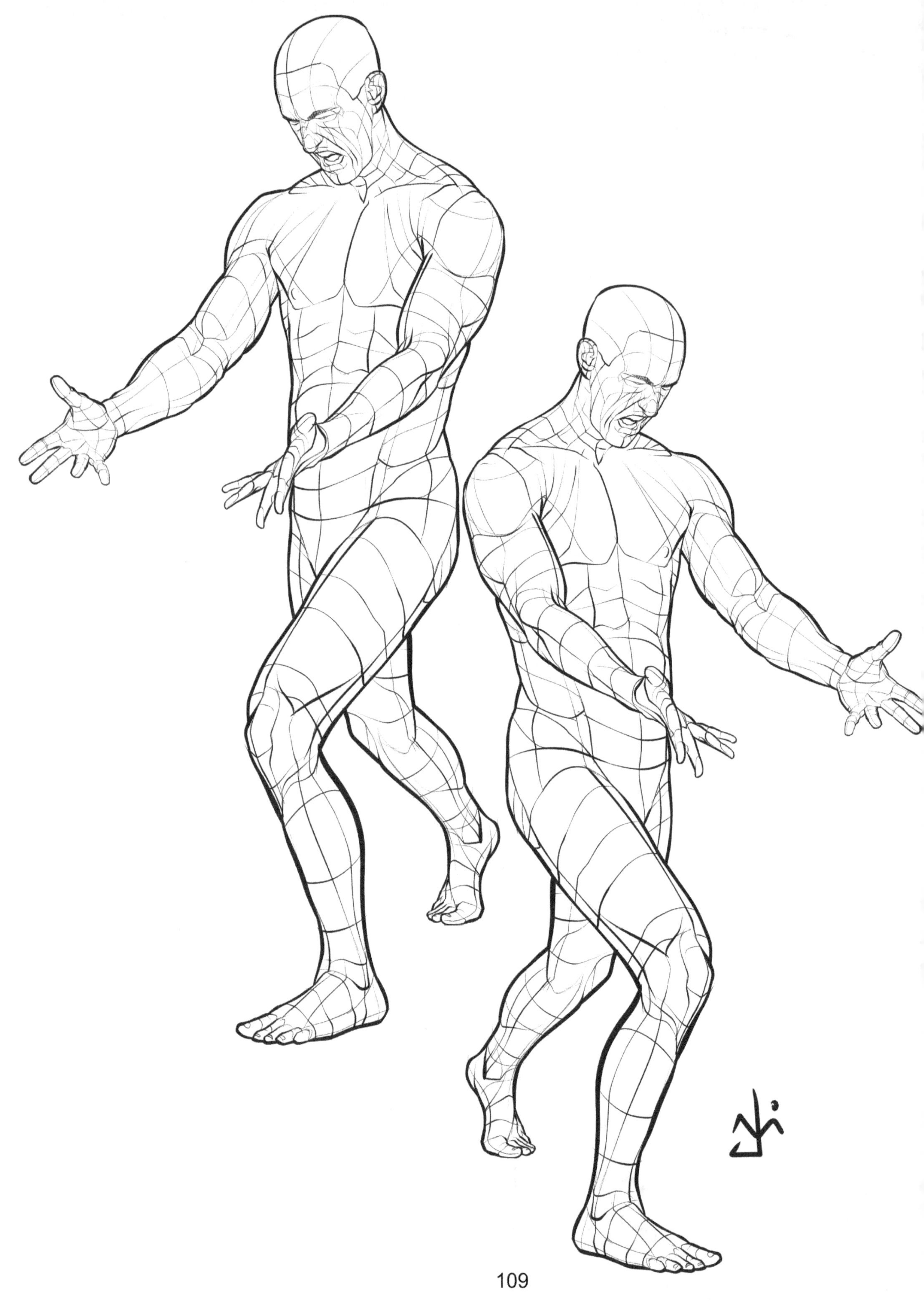

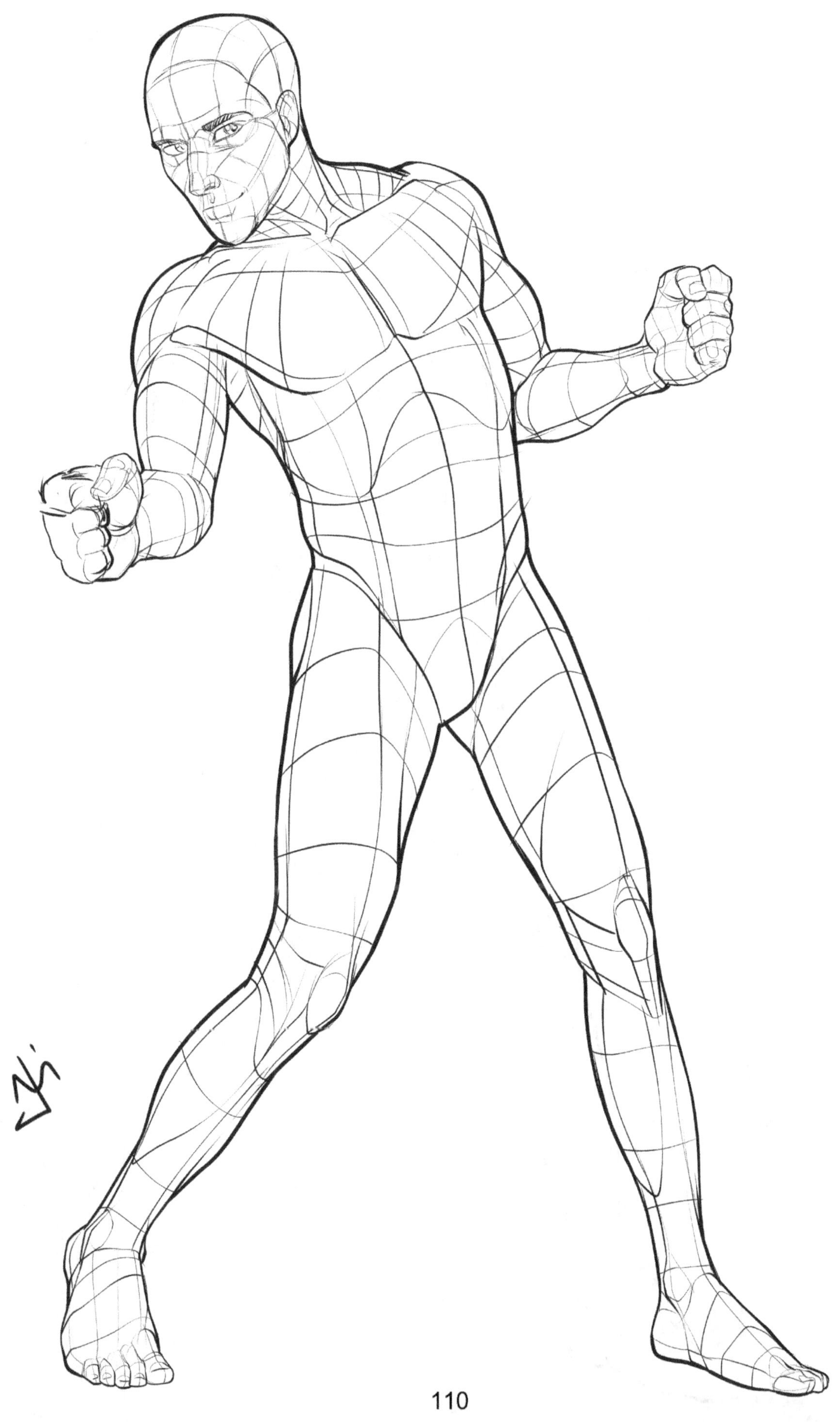

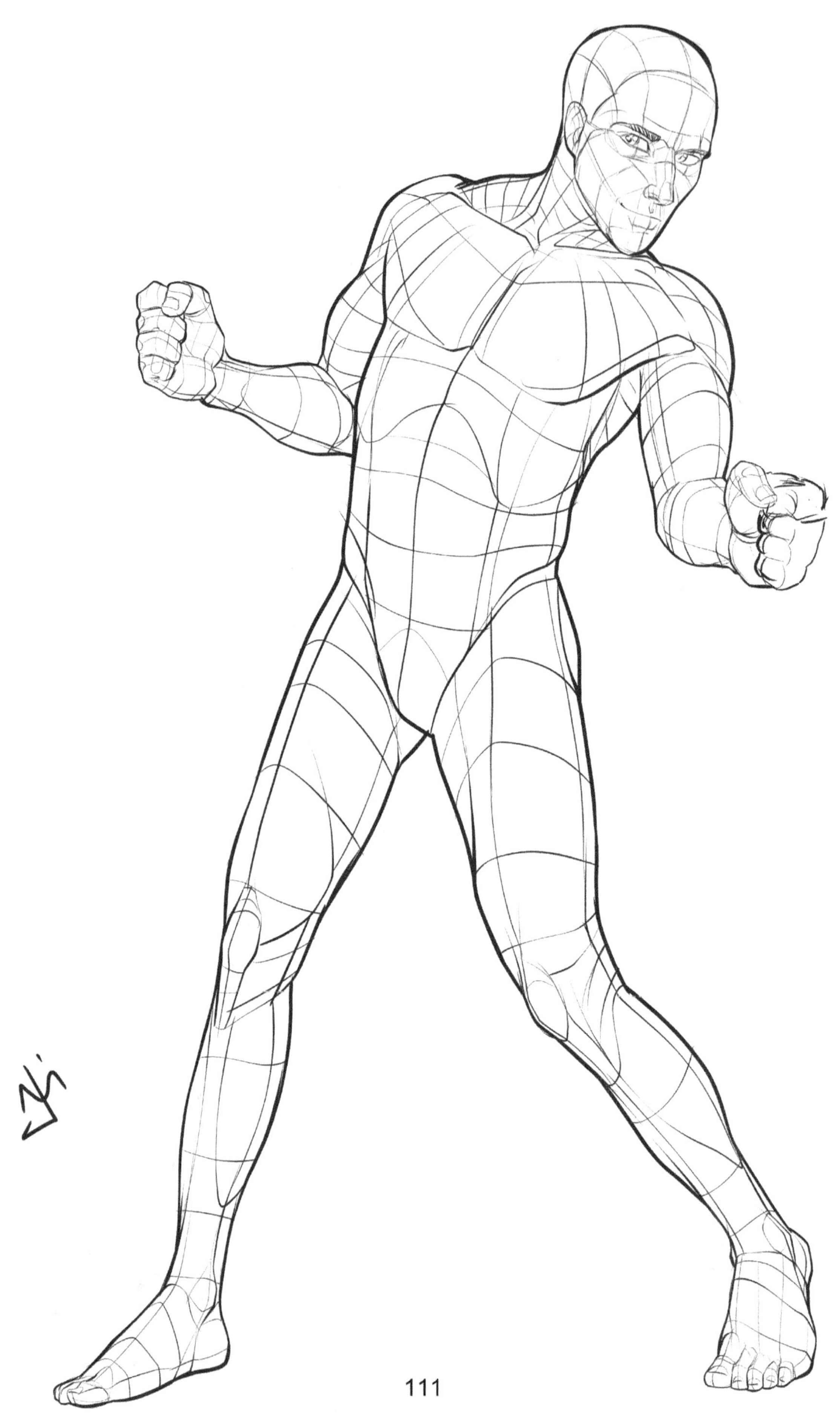

www.ingramcontent.com/pod-product-compliance
Lightning Source LLC
Chambersburg PA
CBHW081619250726
48657CB00009B/2636